People Under Three

Play, work and learning in a childcare setting

Third Edition

Sonia Jackson and Ruth Forbes

Routledge
Taylor & Francis Group

LONDON AND NEW YORK

First and second edition published 1994, 2004
This edition published 2015
by Routledge

2 Park Square, Milton Park, Abingdon, Oxon OX14 4RN
and by Routledge
711 Third Avenue, New York, NY 10017

Routledge is an imprint of the Taylor & Francis Group, an informa business

British Library Cataloguing-in-Publication Data

A catalogue record for this book is available from the British Library

Library of Congress Cataloging-in-Publication Data
Jackson, Sonia.
  People under three : play, work and learning in a childcare setting /
  Sonia Jackson. Ruth Forbes.—Third edition.
    pages cm
  1. Day care centers. 2. Day care centers—Great Britain. 3. Infants—Care.
  I. Forbes. Ruth. II. Title.
  HV851.G65 2014
  362.71′2—dc23   2014012142

ISBN: 978-0-415-66520-9 (hbk)
ISBN: 978-0-415-66521-6 (pbk)
ISBN: 978-1-315-81527-5 (ebk)

Typeset in Sabon
by Keystroke, Station Road, Codsall, Wolverhampton

Printed and bound in Great Britain by
TJ International Ltd, Padstow, Cornwall

People Under Three

Services for young children have gone through a period of rapid transformation in recent years, which have been paralleled by great advances in our knowledge of early child development. However, care and education in the first three years of life continues to be a neglected area.

Thoroughly updated to take account of key policy and practice changes in childcare provision, this landmark text translates child development theory and research into everyday practice. All the practical ideas in the book have been developed and tested in nurseries, Family and Children's Centres and include the importance of providing opportunities for adventurous and exploratory play for babies and toddlers, understanding and responding to children's emotional needs and offering personalised and sensitive care. The book also explores different ways of working with parents and the role of early years settings and practitioners in helping to keep children safe. It includes chapters on:

- Childcare policy and services
- Planning spaces for living, learning and playing
- Babies in day care
- Heuristic play with objects
- Mealtimes
- Learning out of doors
- Leading and managing a childcare centre
- Involving and working with parents
- Safeguarding children.

People Under Three is an established practical text for all those training to work with young children or managing day care facilities. Focusing on the care and learning of very young children, it is designed specifically for those who look after them day by day, as well as being a useful resource for social work students and policy makers.

Sonia Jackson is Emeritus Professor of Social Care and Education at the Institute of Education, University of London, UK. Previously, she worked as a clinical psychologist, teacher and social worker and has published extensively on early childhood education and childcare. She has a special interest in the education of children looked after away from home.

Ruth Forbes is a Children's Centre Cluster Manager for Dorset County Council, UK. She has worked in a range of early years settings in the private and voluntary sectors, leading and managing full day care and supporting staff training and development. She is the author of *Beginning to Play* and has also written and lectured on the sector-endorsed Foundation Degree in Early Years.

To our grandchildren and their parents

He who would do good to another must do it in Minute Particulars

William Blake

We are guilty of many errors and many faults, but our worst crime is abandoning the children, neglecting the fountain of life. Many of the things we need can wait. The child cannot. Right now is the time his bones are being formed, his blood is being made and his senses are being developed. To him we cannot answer 'Tomorrow'. His name is 'Today'.

Gabriela Mistral

Contents

Figures

Preface to the third edition

The ten years since the second edition of this book was published have been a time of unprecedented change in services for young children. Local authority day nurseries, the target readership for the first edition, have virtually disappeared and most of the early childhood practitioners to whom this book is addressed are likely to be leading or working in privately run childcare centres or be independent childminders. At the same time there have been great advances in research on early brain development and growing awareness that the very first weeks and months of life are the period when the foundations of learning, communication and relationships are established. Early childhood education begins at birth, not three years old. Indeed we are now beginning to understand the significance, for health and development, of what happens long before the baby makes his or her first appearance.

Elinor Goldschmied, on whose innovative ideas and creative practice this book is based, died in 2009 after a long illness. She is now recognised as one of the most important pioneers of early childhood education, along with such famous names as Froebel, Pestalozzi and Malaguzzi. I had the great privilege of working closely with her over many years, both in the UK and Italy – and in preparing this new edition, which in some ways has had to be a new book, we have tried to preserve her distinctive voice wherever possible. The final chapter now provides an account of her life and work. The Froebel Institute at the University of Roehampton has established an Archive in her name where her many films and videos can be viewed. However her best memorial is the extent to which her most significant innovations, the Treasure Basket, Heuristic Play and the key person approach, have become standard practice in education and care for young children throughout the UK as well as in many other countries.

One of the many things that has changed over the years is terminology. Childcare has replaced 'day care' and is provided in early childhood centres more often than 'nurseries'. Childcare staff are referred to in official documents as early years practitioners rather than nursery nurses, but we have not tried to be consistent since all these different terms continue to be used side by side.

The sexist nature of the English language also presents difficulties to authors. 'He or she' becomes irritating when too often repeated, but 'they' has a depersonalising effect. We wanted to refer to individual children, stressing their individuality. In this book we have used the device of imagining the child to be a girl or boy in different chapters (except where a specific child is described). In principle we should have done the same in referring to staff, but it seemed unnecessary since we know that the vast majority of early years practitioners are women and there is little prospect that this will change in the near future.

In preparing this edition, I have been fortunate to be joined by Ruth Forbes, who knew Elinor well and is the author of a book on the Treasure Basket, *Beginning to Play*. Ruth has many years' experience in a range of early childhood settings and is a Children's Centre Cluster Manager. I am extremely grateful for her knowledge of current policy and practice, although the time of writing is a period of such rapid change that it is almost impossible to be fully up to date.

Acknowledgements to those who contributed to earlier editions can be found at the end of the book. For the third edition we have had the benefit of advice from Gillian Pugh, Bernadette Duffy, Dorothy Selleck, Peter Elfer, Jacqui Cousins, Anita Hughes and Mary Fawcett, and we have drawn on many conversations, discussions and debates with colleagues across the sector, too numerous to mention. Ruth would particularly like to thank Patricia Darley, Louise Dodds, Collete Ford and Sue Rice, and her husband, Ian, for his patience, humour and unfailing support. We are grateful to the many parents and early childhood settings that allowed us to visit, make observations and take photographs, in particular the Eastwood Centre in Roehampton, the Coram Early Years Centre and Shaftesbury Children's Centre Nursery. Special thanks also to Kornelia Cepok, curator of the Froebel Archive, for her interest and assistance with illustrations, to Olivia Tadman who compiled the list of useful organisations, websites and DVDs, and to my grandson, Benjamin Abrams, for help with formatting the text.

Sonia Jackson
January 2014

Introduction

Elinor Goldschmied believed that a society can be judged by its attitude to its youngest children, 'not only in what is said about them but how this attitude is expressed in what is offered to them as they grow up'. On that criterion we have made considerable progress in Britain over the past fifteen years, more than in the whole of the previous thirty (Jackson 1993, 2014). The landscape of early childhood services now looks very different, but the trees are still quite sparse and most of them are only saplings, vulnerable to the winds of economic downturn or the whims of politicians.

Despite great advances in our knowledge of how an infant develops from before birth to maturity, we are still far from giving serious recognition in this country to the importance of the first three years. The absence until the very end of the twentieth century of any coherent policy for early childhood care and education placed almost the entire burden of bringing up the next generation upon the shoulders of young parents, in social conditions that created high levels of stress, both economic and psychological. As we show in Chapter 1, the low value set on this vital task continues to be reflected in the status, salaries, working conditions and lack of career opportunities and training for those who share the daily care of children in a variety of services and institutions (Nutbrown 2012b).

At the time that this book was originally written, day care for children under three was still largely provided in council-run day nurseries and by private childminders who received a minimum level of support from local authorities. There were a few family centres and combined nursery centres that provided day care and nursery education on the same site, but education was not seen as part of a nursery worker's job – that was for teachers. Although increasing numbers of mothers were working outside the home, there was still a widespread view that this was undesirable, and if both parents chose to work it was up to them to make whatever arrangements they could for the care of their children.

All this changed with the election of a Labour government in 1997. The reality of women's work and the great importance of the earliest months and years of children's lives for future learning and development were officially recognised for the first time. The key events, discussed in more detail in Chapter 1, were the announcement of a National Childcare Strategy in 1998 and the transfer of responsibility for early years from the social services system under the Department of Health into the education department. This was a very important step towards ending the split between care and education that had blighted early childhood services for so long. It was followed by the 2006 Childcare Act, the first ever piece of legislation to be exclusively concerned with early years and childcare, and by the investment of billions of pounds in the Sure Start Programme, a national initiative, for the first time aimed specifically at the birth-to-three age group (Eisenstadt 2011).

It is increasingly common in all European countries for young children to spend at least part of the day away from their own homes, but this is usually in a publicly funded childcare centre with well-qualified staff. In Britain, day care away from home may mean a private childcare centre, neighbourhood nursery or Children's Centre, a family centre, workplace crèche, playgroup, the home of a childminder, a community, voluntary or commercial childcare setting, or any combination of these.

Provision for the early years in Britain still falls far behind Nordic and most other European countries, but from being a marginal activity, affecting only a small proportion of children and families, childcare for children under three has become part of the mainstream. Increasingly professional women are postponing childbirth until their thirties and returning to work when their maternity leave runs out. It has become far more acceptable, and indeed expected, for mothers of young children to work outside the home. This does not mean that they do so without anxiety. There is, rightly, a growing concern with the quality of the child's experience and no longer simply with availability.

In 1994, when this book was first published, most children under three in group day care came from families with severe social or health problems, very often with only one parent at home. We pointed out then how harmful this clustering of the most needy children was, both to the children and to the staff caring for them. Fortunately this is now less likely to happen. Most children attending childcare centres part-time are not in social need and the majority of babies and toddlers in full-time day care have parents working in relatively well paid professional jobs.

However in this country, unlike most others, children may spend long hours in childcare settings from an early age when their mothers return to work, since our provision for maternity and parental leave is very inadequate by European standards. Some private nurseries advertise care for babies as young as six weeks old. And although families with two working parents may not be poor, they can still be financially stretched to pay high childcare fees and also be under stress from trying to juggle work, social and domestic obligations. So it is as important as ever for childcare staff to work closely with parents and to be sensitive to the pressures on them.

As predicted in the first edition of *People Under Three*, an enormous growth has taken place in the number of private day nurseries and crèches, both in the form of individual businesses and chains of childcare centres run by commercial companies. In response to increased demand and the declining number of childminders, new centres are being set up every day. Day nurseries are the fastest growing small business sector and there are now over 11,500 in the UK. It is estimated that almost two million children are looked after for part of the time in some form of private childcare centre.

This book focuses on under-threes in day care because so little has been written about them by comparison with the extensive literature on pre-school education for three- and four-year-olds. It is intended to be of practical use to people at a variety of levels: to those who look after other people's children day by day in centres or in their own homes, and to managers and organisers of childcare services. It will also be relevant to those whose job is to establish and maintain standards, and to administrators, community workers and the wide range of specialists involved with young children and their families. We believe that it is essential for this second group of people, who normally work at one remove from children, to understand how a child's daily experience is affected by managerial and resource decisions beyond the control of those who look after the children day by day.

We hope, too, that it will be read by the next generation of early years educators, students working towards university degrees in Early Childhood Studies, and will give parents some ideas about how to evaluate the care offered to their children. Knowledge alone is not enough. Good care must be not only educational but sensitive and responsive. It needs to be informed by an imaginative understanding of the experiences and emotional states of young children, especially when they are separated from their parents. That is why we emphasise throughout the book the need for caregivers and teachers to observe the children they look after closely and systematically, to reflect on their observations and to share and discuss them with parents and each other. Whenever possible we draw analogies between things that happen to children and those that we commonly experience as adults. As memories before the age of three are mostly lost, this is one of the few ways available to us of attempting to understand the sensations and feelings of a small child.

We describe and explain three particular innovations derived from the principles outlined above, which were developed by Elinor Goldschmied from her many years of practice in European countries, especially Italy, and her extensive consultancy work with English and Scottish local authorities: the 'Key person approach', the 'Treasure Basket' and 'Heuristic play with objects'. All have been successfully introduced in childcare centres in Britain and overseas and are now to be found in operation throughout the UK, though not always in a form of which Elinor would have approved!

How this book is organised

Our first chapter sets the context within which childcare is provided at the time of writing. We think it is very important that early years practitioners understand how their everyday work is shaped by national and local authority policies and that they can take an informed part in debates on how these may affect young children, including joining with others to challenge them when necessary.

The next section of the book focuses on the care and play opportunities provided in childcare settings for children of different ages. For all children, but particularly the youngest, the relationship they form with their special adult in the setting is crucially important, and this is the subject of Chapter 2, The key person. Chapter 3, Planning spaces for living, playing and learning, is concerned with the environment in which the children spend their days. It recognises that not only the children but the early years practitioners who care for them may spend long hours in the childcare setting. This means that a great deal of thought must be given to how the space that they share can be made pleasant and comfortable for adults as well as children. It must also present an attractive and welcoming aspect to parents and visitors. Especially when space is limited, the precise layout and organisation of furniture, play materials and storage can have a considerable impact on the quality of the children's play and learning.

Chapters 4 to 9 are concerned with the everyday care and development of children in childcare settings from babyhood to their third year, and how practical arrangements and the attitudes and behaviour of staff can create the best possible environment for their early learning experiences. Chapter 5 explains the principles underlying the now well-known concept of the Treasure Basket and attempts to dispel some of the misconceptions and misgivings that are sometimes expressed by practitioners. Chapter 7 shows how the same principles can be extended to provide a rich play experience for babies and toddlers once they become mobile.

Chapter 9 centres on the midday meal, a period of the day which is often experienced as stressful by practitioners. With the close attention to detail always advocated by Elinor Goldschmied, it can instead become entirely pleasurable, an important time for conversation, and learning about different kinds of food and about healthy eating. The interval while the meal is being set up and before it is served provides an opportunity for the key person to have a special time with her small group, an 'island of intimacy'.

Government requirements now state that childcare settings must provide opportunities for children to be out of doors every day. Chapter 10 is about some ways to develop and organise outside space to make it a genuine outdoor learning area, for instance to make the most of natural features and planting to create small challenges and interesting enclosures, and introduce first steps in gardening.

Chapters 11 and 12 shift the focus to the roles of leader and staff in the setting, which in the case of a large childcare centre, may involve quite a big group and require high-level management skills. There is much evidence now to show that quality of staff is perhaps the most important factor determining the quality of children's learning and development in childcare settings (Sylva *et al.* 2010). As we show in Chapter 1, there continue to be serious weaknesses in the whole structure of recruitment and training for the early years workforce, so we put a strong emphasis in Chapter 12 on supervision, support and provision for continuing professional development.

Chapter 13 turns to by far the most important element in children's lives, their parents, and how the childcare setting can collaborate harmoniously with them. We have called this chapter 'Bridging the child's two worlds' because that is what needs to happen, and to avoid making any exaggerated claims about 'participation' or 'working with' parents, which may not be possible or appropriate in some settings.

This chapter also discusses the key issues of diversity and inclusion. It is known that the seeds of prejudice and discrimination are sown in infancy (Nutbrown and Clough 2013; Devarakonda 2013). This idea was slow to penetrate early years services, but is now firmly established. It is as relevant to under-threes as to older children and as important in all white areas as in settings where many different cultures mingle.

Throughout the book we emphasise the need to be aware of the messages we convey to children, through our actions as well as words and in the environment we create for them.

Chapter 14 is about the role of early years practitioners in recognising when things are going wrong and what to do about it. Safeguarding, or child protection, might be considered beyond the remit of childcare centres, but we argue that childcare in high-quality settings is the most effective form of prevention and support for families who may be at risk of causing harm to their children. Moreover, nursery workers are especially well placed to recognise early signs of maltreatment or neglect because of their daily contact with children and the close bodily care that they provide. They need to be confident about expressing concerns when necessary and acting quickly and decisively.

Throughout the book we have emphasised the influence of Elinor Goldschmied's principles and ideas on our thinking and practice. Chapter 15 provides a brief account of the life and work of this remarkable woman, now recognised as one of the pioneers of early childhood care and education. As she wrote in the first edition of this book:

> Young children and their parents have the right to expect that the extensive knowledge that we possess today about child development should shape the services that they so greatly need. Attitudes to children are changing. We have moved on from the view that simply because people are very young their thoughts and feelings do not matter, but we still often feel frustrated and mystified in our efforts to understand what little children are trying to say to us. In the same way, many of the things we adults do and say must seem very puzzling to them. We would like to think that this book may in some small measure help to bridge that gap in our understanding of each other.

Childcare policy and visions of childhood

As we noted in the introduction, the experience of early years practitioners and what they can offer to the children in their care is influenced by many different factors outside the immediate work setting. In order to provide the best possible experience for the children in their care, they need to be able to understand how their particular job fits into the overall framework of services for young children and their families.

Issues in childcare and early childhood education

From being ignored by governments over many years, childcare for young children, including in the first three years, has become a hot political issue. However, the key policy debates have remained remarkably constant over many decades (see, for example, Pugh 1993). Five main issues in early years care and education remain unresolved:

- Early childhood education has never become an integral part of the free, statutory state education system. This makes it vulnerable to local government cuts whenever there is an economic downturn, as at the time of writing.
- Pre-school education and childcare developed along separate lines, with differently qualified staff and different conditions of service which still persist.
- As a result, childcare is mainly staffed by poorly paid women with few qualifications, low levels of education and limited prospects of career progression.
- There is a tension between cost and quality in childcare which results in the children in most need receiving the lowest quality service, and leaves many families with no service at all.
- The early age of school entry compared with other European countries raises questions about the suitability of the curriculum and regime for such young children and exerts backward pressure even on childcare for under-threes.

Everyone concerned probably wants to do their best for children, but there is a clear ideological split between the government's outlook and priorities and the ideas of those who research and write about early childhood and developmental psychology. Much of the thinking that underlies both the present and previous government's early years policy comes from the United States and is basically driven by economic imperatives. Publicly funded or subsidised day care is seen primarily as a means of enabling mothers, especially single mothers, to work and support themselves rather than being dependent on welfare payments. The children's day-to-day experience tends to be a secondary consideration.

The other driving force is the desire to raise the educational level of the population. International comparisons consistently show the UK hovering around the middle of the world ratings, much lower than Nordic or many Asian countries (OECD 2010). Modern economies need better educated workers and there is clear evidence that countries which invest heavily in education and skills benefit from that choice, both economically and socially (Schleicher 2006; Jackson and Cameron 2014). Moreover, educational failure is linked to all kinds of undesirable social outcomes – unemployment, ill-health, teenage pregnancy, mental disorder and, above all, crime (Simon and Owen 2006). American early intervention programmes such as Headstart and High Scope have been shown to help disadvantaged children achieve better educational progress, with effects that persist into adult life (Siraj-Blatchford 2014). However, the understanding that children's earliest experiences profoundly affect their learning and development has been slow to penetrate the thinking of those who control educational policy in this country (Allen 2011).

Brief historical background

Early childhood policy develops within a historical, cultural and ideological framework which changes over time. Baldock *et al.* (2013) provide a useful timeline showing how events in the wider world interact with established welfare regimes, shorter-term political priorities, ideas about child development, high profile media events (such as the deaths of Victoria Climbié or Peter Connelly), knowledge generated by research, and economic conditions. All these elements help to shape the services offered (or not) to children and their families.

During the Second World War the government set up day nurseries to enable women with children to take the place of men away in the forces and to work in munitions factories. After the war ended in 1945 these closed quite rapidly, partly so that men could take back the jobs that the women had been doing but also because the prevailing view was that young children should be at home with their mothers. This was justified by reference to the research of John Bowlby (1953) although this was about longer separations, not day care. It was, however, very influential in the thinking of the committee chaired by Lady (Bridget) Plowden, which was set up to consider, among other things, the availability of nursery education.

The present shape of early years provision in England was set nearly fifty years ago by the report of that committee, *Children and their Primary Schools* (CAC 1967). This aimed to achieve a rapid expansion of pre-school education, especially in what were then called 'deprived' areas, by making it all part-time. That was partly to save cost but was also deliberately designed to discourage mothers of young children from working outside the home. The pattern of offering Early Childhood Education and Care (ECEC) on a sessional basis, bearing no relation to normal adult working hours, has persisted right down to the present, so that working parents on average incomes are usually obliged to patch together all kinds of different forms of provision in order to cover the hours of care needed, and during their earliest years children may experience a variety of settings and caregivers over the course of a week.

Despite energetic lobbying over many years by pressure groups and voluntary organisations such as the National Children's Bureau, BAECE and the National Childminding Association (now renamed PACEY), the official view – that government should have no role in the provision of care and education away from home for children under three – was very entrenched, and there was little change in early years services until the election of a Labour government in 1997, after which it often seemed to people in the early childhood field that there was a new initiative every week (Jackson and Fawcett 2009). This resulted in improved access to early education over the next few years, often in infant schools where a fall in the child population had created empty places, filled by admitting four-year-olds to reception classes. In fact four, rather than the statutory age of five, has become the normal age of starting school in most areas (Jackson and Cameron 2014; Brooker 2002). However, the emphasis on childcare as a remedial service focused on families in difficulties or those thought to be providing unsatisfactory care for their children, which also dates back to Plowden, can be clearly seen in current government policy statements and guidance.

Different views of childhood

In other parts of Europe an alternative view of childhood prevails. In most countries children are seen as an asset to the community and this is reflected in the allocation of resources for their care. So when we hear that childcare cannot be afforded, it is very important to understand that this is a political statement, depending on the value we give to supporting family life and children's development as opposed to, say, rescuing insolvent banks or funding military expeditions.

Britons visiting other parts of Europe are often struck by how common it is to see young children having meals in restaurants with their families, and by the way ordinary childish behaviour is met with amused tolerance instead of disapproval. Another everyday example is the ubiquity of children in Scandinavian television dramas, and their invisibility in English and American ones. Tax and welfare systems in France are designed to encourage people to have children and to provide resources to families. In Nordic countries, childcare is regarded as a matter of equal opportunities for women and a citizen right (Miller and Cameron 2014). In this country, by contrast, there has always been a fear of over-population and of giving an incentive for people to have children they cannot afford to support. It is no accident that one of the first actions of the Conservative-led government elected in 2010 was to breach the principle established in 1945 of universal family allowances (child benefit), designed to redistribute income from those without children to those bearing the cost of bringing up the next generation (Holman 2013).

Childcare policy 2007–2010

The election of a Labour government in 1997 also illustrates the impact of political change on childhood services. Almost immediately, the government took the bold step of moving responsibility for all early years services from the welfare (social services) to the education sector. The greatest significance of this move was the implicit recognition that education begins at birth and not simply at the age of entry into formal schooling.

For the first time the state recognised a responsibility for the education and care of its youngest citizens. The next few years saw many other important legislative and policy developments (Baldock *et al.* 2013). The regulation of day care and childminding passed to Ofsted in 2000 (which also made those services potentially eligible for public funding). In 2004 the government published a 'Ten Year Strategy for Childcare', given legal backing by the Children Act 2004. Two years later the Childcare Act 2006 was passed, the first law to be exclusively concerned with early years and childcare.

The intention of this Act was to bring early years within the mainstream of local authority provision, but its provisions fell far short of the universal full-time early childhood education (with extended hours of subsidised childcare if needed) available to all children aged three to six years in Nordic countries and in many other parts of Europe. Because it failed to embed pre-school education as a free universal service on the same basis as school-age education, the important reforms introduced over this period remain highly susceptible to political changes.

At present the government funds part-time pre-school/nursery places for all three- and four-year-olds in England whose parents want them (15 hours a week for 38 weeks) and this was extended to 'vulnerable' two-year-olds in September 2013, though only under stringent conditions. There is considerable pressure on parents to send four-year-olds to full-time school as otherwise they risk not getting a place in the primary school of their choice.

Sure Start

The largest new component of the 2004 Childcare Strategy was Sure Start, the first government programme ever to be targeted at the 0 to 3 age group. The ideas underpinning it were partly derived from the American Headstart programme, which showed very positive long-term outcomes from high-quality early childhood provision, but it was based on sound research and practice knowledge embodied in the 'Birth to Three Matters' framework (Abbott and Langston 2004). Sure Start was an area-based programme providing funds for a variety of different early education, childcare and family support services for children under four in the most disadvantaged areas. Every Sure Start Centre set up under the scheme had to include day care.

Sure Start is generally regarded as one of the major successes of the 2004 Childcare Strategy. Evaluation was built in from the beginning and showed small but significant improvements in outcomes for children – enhanced language development, for instance. More importantly, the Centres were greatly appreciated by the parents who used them and the communities in which they were located. In England, Sure Start projects were largely subsumed into the government's later vision of integrated children's services – with Children's Centres providing early education, childcare, health services, family support and employment advice. This was such an obviously sensible idea that the Treasury allocated substantial funding for the purpose (Eisenstadt 2011). Children's Centres spread like wildfire and might even have become universal but for the change of government in 2010. It is interesting to note that the idea of local centres of this kind available to all parents 'within pram-pushing distance' was first proposed forty years ago by Jack Tizard, the founder of the Thomas Coram Research Unit, in the book *All Our Children* (Tizard *et al.* 1976).

At their height there were 3,500 Children's Centres. Cuts in public services and local authority funding since then have put the process into reverse, with over 400 Children's Centres closing in the first two years of the coalition government and many more since. Even among those that remain open, only 500 continue to offer childcare, although Children's Centres are encouraged to build links with high-quality early education/childcare providers. The original vision of a Children's Centre in every community providing the basis of a universal (as opposed to targeted) childcare service on the European model, seems to have been definitively abandoned. A House of Commons Select Committee in December 2013, while appearing to endorse the idea of Children's Centres, commented on the confusion about their purpose and function and called for them to be reviewed and reshaped (House of Commons Education Committee 2013).

Childcare for working parents

A major weakness of all UK government policy statements on ECEC has always been the failure to differentiate between short-term sessional provision and full day care adapted to standard working hours. Both are described as childcare, although the practical implications for families are very different.

Day care

The Childcare Act 2006 obliges local authorities in England and Wales to ensure that there are sufficient childcare places to meet the needs of working parents. However, publicly provided childcare in England has almost disappeared. Care for children of working parents is found mostly in the private sector, provided either by childminders or in childcare settings run for profit, and increasingly by large commercial chains. Private childcare centres largely serve families where both parents have well-paid jobs and the fees that they charge usually put them out of reach of families on average incomes, despite the government meeting part of the cost through the childcare element of Working Tax Credit (Daycare Trust 2013). Mothers with fewer educational qualifications are much more likely to work part-time and turn to relatives, especially grandmothers, for childcare. Although grandparents, often working themselves, are increasingly unable to provide full-time day care on a regular basis, informal care by relatives is still extensively used to fill gaps in provision (Rutter and Evans 2011).

The Daycare Trust's 2013 report on childcare costs notes that prices are rising above inflation. The cost of a nursery place for a child aged two or under is 77 per cent more than it was in 2003 while wages have remained stagnant. Low-income households spend 20 per cent of their income on childcare compared with 8 per cent on average spent by better-off families. Even that is far more than the proportion spent by families in other countries (Miller and Cameron 2014). Cost is the major restraint on expansion of childcare services.

Childminding

For children under three the most common form of out-of-home care, apart from play-groups and private day centres, is still childminding. Childminding has a long history and has always been extensively used by low-paid working mothers, but its existence was not formally recognised in the UK until 1948 with the passing of the Nurseries and Childminders Regulation Act (amended in 1968). The Act made provision for registration of childminders and inspection of premises but was almost entirely concerned with physical safety (Jackson and Jackson 1979).

There have been many attempts to rename childminding because the term suggests a passive role for the carer, rather than the active promotion of children's learning and development, but they have never succeeded. In other countries care for children provided in private homes is usually called family day care. The National Childminding Association, which has played an important part in training and support since its foundation in 1976, is now known as PACEY (Professional Association for Childcare and Early Years) but still uses 'childminding' on its website (www.pacey. org.uk).

Other countries have better systems for linking family day care workers to provide professional and mutual support and training. For example, in France day nurseries (*crèches collectives*) often have an attached group of home-based childcare workers (*crèches familiales*). They have access to the facilities of the centre and their own coordinator, sometimes the deputy head of the nursery. The government has now proposed a new system of childminder agencies, but these are intended to address the business side of childminding and will operate on a commercial rather than a cooperative model. They will not address the issue of isolation as the earlier model of childminding networks was designed to do.

An important landmark for childminding was the belated recognition by the government that childminders are educators as well as carers. All registered childminders must now offer the Early Years Foundation Stage curriculum and if they receive government funding are inspected by Ofsted. There continues to be a conflict, however, between standards and costs. Childminding is no longer a cheap service for poor parents, and the fees asked by registered childminders are only marginally lower than those charged by private day nurseries. The average cost for 25 hours of childcare from a childminder at the time of writing was £98.15 a week (Daycare Trust 2013). The result is that a high proportion of mothers are obliged to give up work when they have a second or third child (Abrams 2001). In addition, many childminders feel unable to cope with the paperwork required or to meet the requirements of EYFS, with the result that numbers have been declining for several years.

As we said earlier, the government's main interest in childcare is to reduce the cost of welfare payments by enabling mothers, especially those without partners, to return to work earlier. In January 2013 they issued a report entitled, with no sense of irony, *More Great Childcare* (DfE 2013). The most controversial proposal was to 'relax' the regulations about the number of children in proportion to adults in early childhood settings, meaning that one adult could look after six children under five. It was met by a storm of protest, with many commentators pointing out that it would inevitably lead to children receiving less adult attention while it was unlikely to produce any significant reduction in costs for parents (Daycare Trust 2013). In practice, the impact is likely to be greatest on children who already receive the lowest quality care. *More Great Childcare* notes that 'childminders will be free to carry on using existing ratios and parents will be able to choose childminders who care for fewer children if they wish'. But the intention of this measure is to enable childminders and childcare settings to take more children in order to reduce their fees, which they will be under strong economic pressure to do in areas where most parents work for low wages. There is already a marked discrepancy between the Ofsted ratings of nurseries and childminders in more prosperous areas compared with others. In the most disadvantaged areas 39 per cent of childminders failed to achieve a 'good' or 'outstanding' rating from Ofsted as compared with only 23 per cent in richer areas (Ofsted 2012).

Establishing national standards: a curriculum for Early Childhood Education and Care

Until the late 1990s the idea of any kind of structured programme for childcare did not exist. People who looked after young children did their best to keep them occupied and happy but were basically left to get on with it without much direction from above.

The Laming report (2003) following on the death of Victoria Climbié, together with findings from the EPPE project (Sylva *et al.* 2004), initiated a new policy framework called *Every Child Matters*, designed by a civil servant, John Rowlands. Rather contrary to expectations, this proved extremely helpful to schools as well as early childhood settings. The goals were not just to protect children from harm but to stress their entitlement to five positive outcomes:

1. Being healthy – enjoying good physical and mental health and having a healthy lifestyle;
2. Staying safe – being protected from harm and neglect;
3. Enjoying and achieving – getting the most out of life and developing the skills for adulthood;
4. Making a positive contribution – being involved with the community and society and not engaging in antisocial or offending behaviour;

5. Economic well-being – not being prevented by economic disadvantage from achieving their full potential in life, and by implication being equipped by education to access satisfying employment and earn a good income.

What was new about this was looking at children and young people holistically and in terms of desired outcomes instead of services. For young children it underpinned the ten-year strategy *Choice for Parents, the Best Start for Children*. It led to a series of legislative and policy initiatives. These included the development of integrated education, health and social care services, extended school hours, and services more purposefully targeted at children in need. *Every Child Matters* has not been formally rescinded but has been quietly allowed to fall into abeyance. It no longer appears on the official government website.

Improving quality

The ten-year childcare strategy was designed to rationalise and redesign the existing early years initiatives so that they fitted within the *Every Child Matters* framework and would become a coherent approach to improving the quality of services. Since the government had brought under one legislative umbrella all kinds of early years provision and was investing large sums of public money, it needed to find a way of showing that this was of benefit to the nation. This was the rationale for Ofsted to inspect all services and for all children to be assessed through the Early Years Foundation Stage Profile, effectively setting a national curriculum for children aged 0–5.

Early Years Foundation Stage (EYFS)

EYFS became a statutory requirement from September 2008 for every type of early childhood service, including childminding, to be enforced through inspection by Ofsted on a four-year cycle. A review commissioned by the Labour government from Dame Claire Tickell two years after the EYFS was introduced concluded that it had raised standards but endorsed the widespread view that it was far too complicated and burdensome for practitioners (Tickell 2010). She recommended that it should be considerably simplified. From a policy point of view, perhaps the most important part of the review was the section on the workforce, which noted that the majority of those attracted to work in the sector were young girls with poor academic qualifications or none. The report went on to state 'the need to create a strong, resilient and experienced workforce has been a compelling message to this review' (p. 42) and urged the government to 'maintain the ambition' for a graduate-led sector.

EYFS was one aspect of the childcare strategy which survived the change of government in 2010, although following the Tickell review, the revised version which became mandatory in September 2012 was considerably less prescriptive and took account of criticisms of the earlier version. It sets out four themes and principles:

- every child is a **unique child**;
- children learn to be strong and independent through **positive relationships**;
- children learn and develop well in **enabling environments**;
- children develop and learn **in different ways and at different rates**.

Within learning and development there are three 'prime' areas – communication and language; physical development; and personal, social and emotional development – and four 'specific' areas:

1. Literacy
2. Mathematics
3. Understanding the world
4. Expressive arts and design.

The new framework is generally regarded as an improvement on earlier policy guidance in that it largely endorses a play-based, developmentally appropriate approach to childcare and education for children from birth to five. However there is still concern that there is an over-emphasis on preparation for school, exerting backward pressure on early years settings to introduce formal skills too early. Early Education (formerly British Association for Early Childhood Education, BAECE) and other groups have argued that this is damaging to children's current well-being and their future motivation, and many commentators have pointed out that the UK already requires children to start compulsory schooling a year, or in some cases two years, earlier than other European countries. Although government documents pay lip-service to the value of play, it is rather obvious that a much more important aim from their point of view is 'school readiness'.

Ideas about learning

The content of an ECEC programme is influenced by theories of how children learn, which in older textbooks are often identified with Rousseau on the one hand and Locke on the other (Jackson 2014). Do children learn best by experience and exploration or by instruction – being taught? This dichotomy is obviously much too simple, but the persistence of two distinct schools of thought can still be seen. Charles Dickens' novel *Hard Times* caricatures the school of education that discounts imagination, exploration, fantasy and the natural world in favour of attempting to stuff children's heads with information that is divorced from their everyday experience and therefore meaningless to them. The book opens in a schoolroom where Mr Gradgrind is expounding his theories to the schoolmaster and the government inspector:

> Now what I want is, Facts. Teach these boys and girls nothing but Facts. Facts alone are wanted in life. Plant nothing else and root out everything else.
>
> (Dickens 1854)

This approach was firmly rejected by the pioneers of nursery education in Britain (Nutbrown *et al.* 2012). However, it is always hovering in the wings, ready to re-emerge in response to every wave of panic about 'falling standards'. The current prescriptive emphasis on literacy and numeracy and 'school readiness' might be seen to belong to the same tradition.

Another way of looking at these two perceptions of children was proposed by Gunilla Hallden (1991). They are 'the child as project' and 'the child as being'. In the first view the child is seen in terms of the future, someone to be moulded by adults. In this view the success of a pre-school programme would be measured by such indicators as early literacy, ability to follow instructions and conformity to adult expectations – in other words, being prepared socially for formal schooling. The 'child as being' implies that the child develops autonomously as an individual with his or her own driving force to learn and grow, needing adults as supporters not instructors. Children's early experience is valued for its own sake, not simply for what it might contribute to their future development. Nevertheless, although it may not be made explicit, the kinds of people we want children to be and become influences the nature of early years and childcare provision and the beliefs and behaviours of parents, professionals and policy makers.

This book in some ways occupies an intermediate position. We feel strongly that an essential aspect of the work of an adult caring for a small child is to see that for as much of the time as possible he or she is happy. Life holds quite enough pain and frustration without deliberately adding to it by unnecessary restriction of any kind. On the other hand, we don't think that unlimited freedom is likely to lead either to happiness or optimal development. Therefore, although we may appear to take a typically non-interventionist position in urging that whenever possible the adult acts as facilitator for these very young children rather than as director of the child's activities, we do so in the context of a carefully planned and organised environment (see Chapter 3). This is referred to by Siraj-Blatchford (2014) as the 'open learning approach' and is strongly supported by research.

Decision-making and negotiation

Adults play an important part in shaping children's behaviour, but they can choose to do it in authoritarian or cooperative ways. There is good evidence that the second way is by far the more effective, as well as leading to less conflict and distress. That is one reason why we put so much emphasis both on caregivers negotiating with children rather than coercing them, and also on the need for adults to help children to negotiate with each other. This is not just a matter of expediency, but of children's right to be respected as individuals, to be listened to and taken seriously, so that as they grow older they can take greater responsibility for exercising their own rights. There is continuing resistance to the idea of a rights-based approach to children in this country, where there is a strong cultural tradition that they are 'owned' by their parents (Lansdown and Lancaster 2001). If we wish them to grow up as active and participating citizens, however, we need to accept that even the youngest children should be given the opportunity to express their opinions as soon as they are competent to do so. When a baby at the Treasure Basket (see Chapter 5), without adult interference, chooses to pick one object rather than another, that is the very first step in independent decision-making (Forbes 2004).

The importance of play

The contribution of play to children's development is a subject which well illustrates the pendulum effect. The attitudes parodied by Dickens in *Hard Times*, which characterised play as a frivolous activity of no value compared with the learning of useful information, persisted in a modified form well into the second half of the twentieth century. Play was what children did when not under the immediate control of adults, at best time-filling and always in potential conflict with 'sitting still and being good' or with more useful kinds of activity. Although the opposing view that 'play is children's work' has enjoyed a long period of dominance in psychological and educational theory (Moyles 2010; Wood and Attfield 2005), early years experts have had to fight very hard to keep it at the centre of the EYFS.

One problem for nursery and infant teachers and playgroup leaders has always been to convince parents that their child is learning through their play experiences. It may be that parents in disadvantaged circumstances have some reason to resist the prevailing orthodoxy because there is good evidence that learning to read early, for example, enables children from low-income families to do better at school than would be expected. In many cultures play is given little importance; no attempt is made to provide children with specially designed playthings, and although one can see that children do play spontaneously, their activities are not accorded any particular adult attention. Yet the children appear to develop normally and may achieve well educationally. It does seem that, at least for academic and occupational success, other qualities of the environment may be equally important.

This illustrates two points: first, that play does not depend on provision of special children's places or giving children objects called 'toys', and secondly that it is only one element in promoting child development. Nevertheless, we do consider the quality of play to be of the greatest importance in any childcare setting. There are good pragmatic reasons for this. The better the quality and richness of the play opportunities offered to them, the more pleasurable the experience, both for adults and children.

What we are learning to do is to discriminate better between different types of play, to encourage complex, concentrated play in preference to flitting from one thing to another (Siraj-Blatchford *et al.* 2002, 2003). To do this without introducing constraint and coercion is a highly skilled task, requiring detailed personal knowledge of each individual child and, above all, an adequate number of adults in proportion to children.

The quality of play we have observed in some childcare settings is notably inferior to that seen in nursery schools. Where the children are under three there is not such a long-established body of knowledge to call on, and this is one reason why we have devoted a major part of this book to the provision and organisation of play opportunities for these very young children. In this book the discussion of play is set in the context of the childcare setting as a total environment in which every aspect of organisation and every activity offered makes a contribution to the child's development and learning.

Care and education

The educational content of care for children living in disadvantaged areas requires particular emphasis, and we think the staff group should always include people with higher-level educational qualifications. All early years practitioners need to understand the educational importance of their work so that the experiences of the young children they look after are not only satisfying in themselves but foster the qualities, such as curiosity, creativity, concentration and persistence in the face of difficulties, which will stand them in good stead in later years. As Siraj-Blatchford (2014) points out, high-quality early childhood education can be a strong equaliser for the most disadvantaged children. While all children benefit from education and care in an excellent early years setting, for some it will have an important effect in compensating for shortcomings in their home environment. This is the rationale for the scheme to provide free childcare for 40 per cent of the 'most deprived' two-year-olds by September 2014, but only for 15 hours and 38 weeks (i.e. school terms). There are serious doubts if the government funding on offer will enable local authorities to deliver early education in good or outstanding settings on this scale (Keohane 2014).

Professional education and development

One of the strongest findings of the EPPE research (Sylva *et al.* 2010) was that the quality of an early childhood setting is strongly related to the education and qualifications of the staff. Having accepted the main recommendations of the Tickell review on the content of the early years curriculum, the coalition government went on to commission a review specifically of the early years workforce from Professor Cathy Nutbrown. Nutbrown's interim report drew attention to the way that early childhood courses had proliferated, particularly in further education colleges, making it difficult for employers to know which of the literally hundreds of qualifications available were relevant for work with young children or what standard they represented. The final report, *Foundations for Quality*, published in June 2012, was based on very extensive consultation and was widely welcomed. It made 19 recommendations designed to ensure that:

> staff are as good as they can be, and have the skills, knowledge and understanding to make the most of the Government's investment in the early years. Working in the early years sector should be a recognized and fulfilling career that attracts the best men and women.
>
> (Nutbrown 2012b)

The aim should be for every early childhood setting to be led by someone with graduate-level qualifications. This was rather a modest aspiration as in many other countries they would be led, if not staffed, by qualified teachers.

The government claimed that it had accepted most of the recommendations and incorporated them into the policy document *More Great Childcare* (DfE 2013), but Nutbrown herself published an angry response accusing the government of 'shaking the foundations of quality'. She pointed out that the overall thrust of her report had been brushed aside and most of her recommendations had, in effect, been rejected (Nutbrown 2013). Most importantly, the opportunity to rationalise the education and career structure of early years work was lost. Nutbrown was particularly incensed by the proposal to introduce a new title of Early Years Teacher, instead of allowing early years professionals to undertake a Postgraduate Certificate of Education (PGCE) and be awarded Qualified Teacher Status as she had recommended, once again reinforcing the existence of a two-tier profession, offering those who work with the youngest children or in childcare settings as opposed to schools, lesser status and poorer pay and conditions than those teaching older children. This makes it an unattractive career option for academically able young people, especially boys, perpetuating the gender imbalance in the profession (discussed in Chapter 12). It makes the aspiration for every setting to be led by a graduate look more remote than ever. The government, in *More Great Childcare*, argued that requiring those proposing to train as early years practitioners to have English and Mathematics GCSEs at Grade C or above would justify allowing them to look after more children. Nutbrown was quite clear that to use the hoped-for improvement in quality of staff as a justification for increasing child–adult ratios 'makes no sense at all'.

> Do I think changing the ratios will make a difference if people are better qualified? The difference will be too few adults with too many little children, too few moments in the day for a toddler to have uninterrupted time with their key person, and too few early years practitioners to talk and work with children . . . Childcare may be cheaper but children will be footing the bill.
>
> (Nutbrown 2013, p. 9)

In fact there were serious doubts if reducing the ratio of adults to children would have any effect on costs, and particular concern about the potential effect on outdoor play. There was such an outcry of protest at the proposal that the government was forced to backpedal and eventually to scrap the idea. After all, as Polly Toynbee pointed out in an article in the *Guardian*, 'How do you fit six children into a buggy?' (Toynbee 2013).

Summary

Early years educators at every level need to understand the policy context within which they carry out their work. This chapter has outlined some of the influences that have shaped early childhood services in the UK and the problems that continue to exist. There have been important advances. Under the Labour government of 1997–2010 attention finally turned to the developmental and educational needs of the youngest children, who had not previously come within the sights of politicians.

However, following a brief period when early childhood care and education rose to the top of the political agenda and attracted substantial investment, public services for pre-school children are once again shrinking back. In contrast to other European countries, nearly all childcare is provided in the private sector, at prices unaffordable by those on average incomes. The present government sees its role as enforcing standards by inspection and regulation and by detailed prescription of the content of the early childhood curriculum through the Early Years Foundation Stage.

At the same time, local authority budgets are under severe pressure, reducing resources available for advice and support to early childhood settings. Children's Centres, the great success story of the last government, no longer seem confident of their purpose, although they continue to provide many useful services. The situation is still very uncertain, creating problems for local authorities, voluntary sector providers, practitioners and leaders and managers of Children's Centres. However, early years professionals are nothing if not resilient and we can only hope that even with reduced funding they will continue to provide multi-agency, multi-professional services for the families who most need them, whilst at the same time ensuring a level of universal services to ensure that Children's Centres are sustained and embedded as part of their local community.

2 | The key person

...remember the time
Before the wax hardened,
When everyone was like a seal.
Each of us bears the imprint
Of a friend met along the way;
(Primo Levi, 1985)

In this chapter we will consider:

- The principles and ethos of the key person approach and how it can be introduced in a group setting;
- Why a key person approach is needed;
- Responding to the young child's emotional needs;
- The value of a key person approach;
- Implementing and organising the system;
- The benefits and challenges of key person working.

The key person approach is one of Elinor Goldschmied's most important legacies to the early childhood field. She developed it over many years as a way of ensuring an individualised approach to young children in day care settings, and it has since inspired many researchers, writers and practitioners in the UK and other countries.

We believe that the value of the key person approach is no longer in doubt; it has been recognised by leading early years experts worldwide and is now a statutory element of the Early Years Foundation Stage. Having an effective key person approach in place strengthens relationships with parents and, alongside effective supervision, enables practitioners to work out their own feelings and emotions in the complex work of caring for other people's children. The key person approach is most effective when the whole organisation focuses on and shares an ethos that enables and supports close attachments between nursery staff and young children, creating 'a triangle of trust and communication' between parents, key person and baby (Goldschmied and Selleck 1996).

Why the key person approach?

In the days when very young children were in residential nurseries and children's homes, visitors would often find that children would come round them, ask their names, want to sit on their knees and touch or even kiss them. Frequently, these children were described as being sociable, friendly or 'very affectionate'. We know now that this is not a normal way for children to react to strangers and that such behaviour indicates that they are seriously deprived in their personal relationships, with little or no experience of truly affectionate contact with anyone.

This different way of interpreting what we see comes from the knowledge we have gained through observation and research about the way that a young child develops his ability to make relationships. Real sociability comes through the experience of the reliable affection of a few close people. Human beings have great resilience and some individuals show an amazing capacity to catch up and recover from damaging early experiences, but many do not.

Unless the key person approach is given primacy in the organisation of the day, the child may have no more contact with his designated practitioner than with any of the other adults. In that case the relationship can have no real meaning for him. Very small children can only recognise a special interest if it is expressed in close personal interaction, day by day.

Most people who work with young children are well aware that satisfactory growth depends on all aspects of their development being seen as a whole. At one time it was thought that if food and warmth, cleanliness, sleep and safety were adequate, this would ensure healthy early development. In the past the instinctive loving feelings of close adults for babies were often disregarded or actively discouraged, while the feelings of babies were hardly taken into account at all. We now know that secure relationships with key persons are very important for young children's cognitive development (Shemmings and Shemmings 2011). The young child's capacity to become an autonomous learner and the development of self-regulation needs to be supported and promoted. In order for our young children to develop self-regulation they need an environment that provides secure attachment and emotional warmth (Whitebread 2011; Bronson 2000). Self-regulated learning is about self-awareness, self-motivation and setting goals; essentially it is about the learner believing that they can learn. We see this fundamentally in babies – they are powerful learners as identified in the 'Birth to Three Matters' framework (2002). Babies are motivated to explore, they practise new skills until they have mastered them. Watch a baby beginning to roll over or starting to push themselves up when on their tummies to get a better view of the world and particularly the special people around them. They don't give up; they believe or know that they will eventually be able to reach out for the shiny ball being temptingly rolled in front of them. Self-regulated learning is discussed again in Chapter 7.

In a full day care setting where the very young child might spend up to 10 hours of their day, a key person or close adult, working with the parent and the family to fulfil these needs, is paramount. Many settings will find themselves working with and supporting families who are unable to provide all the basic needs for their young children. The setting may be a nursery attached to a Children's Centre, the childminder used regularly by Children's Social Care or a nursery where vulnerable families attend and are supported by a social worker or outreach worker from a Children's Centre. With increasing numbers of families living on or below the poverty line, not able to provide nutritious food, a safe home, or a safe neighbourhood to live in, the pressure on the nursery staff team greatly increases. This can put pressure on the relationships between staff and families. Supervision, discussed later, becomes essential for both the practitioner and the leader of the setting.

The importance of close personal relationships

Over the last twenty years our understanding of young children's emotions and emotional well-being has deepened, and evidence from a range of disciplines and professions across the early years field has raised questions about how we support young children's emotional development and well-being. Understanding more, as we now do, about how young children feel, has not made our task in childcare any easier. In fact it has made the work more difficult, more complex and more demanding. There is no excuse for us to repeat the mistakes of the past in the care we provide for young children today. The denial of close personal relationships is a serious flaw in much group childcare, which can partly be overcome by changes in organisation. However, it is essential that everyone concerned understands the reasons for such changes and is committed to making them work. There is an extensive literature on attachment but very little research located in day care settings (Nutbrown and Page 2008).

Brain development and the cortisol effect

Our increasing knowledge of child development has led to a greater understanding of the complexity and rapidity of development in the first three years. We know from brain research that the neural connections are few at birth, but grow at a rapid rate until the child is about six years (Carter 1999). Every day the stimulation and rich experiences offered to the new baby enable the brain to lay down more connections – the day-to-day experiences of being talked to, sung to, everything baby sees, hears, smells and all the kinaesthetic experiences of movement, the sensation of being rocked, jiggled and jogged on laps or in arms. We know that brain development is not only about cognitive development, it is also about social and emotional development, about relationships and the laying down of early memories. Magnetic Resonance Imaging (MRI) scans show that the glutamate system, which is not properly established in the frontal lobe of babies and small children's brains, is responsible for clearly defined thoughts and intentions. Sunderland (2007) tells us that this means that babies and small children cannot be deliberately naughty or manipulative, a small but helpful scientific fact which practitioners can use to help them support parents who may have unrealistic expectations of their baby or toddler's behaviour. Sunderland suggests that parents looking for a nursery or childminder spend some time with the prospective carer and should observe 'laughter, delight, a feeling of warmth in the room between the prospective carer and your child'. She says that practitioners demonstrating this behaviour will be a good source of opioid and dopamine activation, the chemicals essential for a child's social and emotional brain (2007, p. 58). Practitioners who can activate the calm and well-being systems of the young brain, those of care and attachment, the desire to learn and explore and play, will enable the young child to grow up to be warm, empathic and loving learning (Sunderland 2013).

Studies have shown that young children's cortisol levels become raised when exposed to high levels of stress. Research has shown that for young children at home the levels fall in the course of the day but for children starting nursery they are higher than normal, and remain so (Pereira-Gray 2013). One study in a German nursery, by Ahnert and Lamb, showed that during the first few weeks of nursery, the children experienced high levels of stress on separating from their mothers, and five months later their cortisol levels remained higher than normal even though the children appeared to have settled into the nursery (Ward 2005). We should remember this when children have time away from the nursery, or move into another room/age group.

Figure 2.1 The morning greeting

This is why it matters that the key person gently welcomes the child into nursery every time and that the parent actually places the baby or toddler in the practitioner's arms. Babies and toddlers who are repeatedly ignored when they are upset and distressed simply shut down. They stop crying (for example if left to cry themselves to sleep) believing that this is all they can expect from an adult, and this can also lead to them failing to develop empathy. However all practitioners should understand that babies need emotionally warm one-to-one attention throughout the day, not only when they are upset.

What makes a key person special?

In some nurseries the key person is known as the 'special person' (Elfer *et al.* 2003, 2012), and that is their main responsibility – to be a special person for an individual child and parent.

Manning-Morton and Thorp (2001, p. 9) identified some fifteen elements which make up key working, including:

- Settling new key children into the setting gradually;
- Developing secure trusting relationships with your key children and parents;
- Holding key children who are bottle-fed on your lap to feed, maintaining eye contact and conversations;
- Changing and toileting your key children, using sensitive handling and familiar words;
- Interacting with your key children with reciprocal sounds, words, facial expressions and gestures, according to their individual temperament;
- Providing a secure base for your key children by being physically and emotionally available, by sitting at their level and in close proximity to them;
- Having regular opportunities to reflect on the emotional aspects of key working with a skilled, knowledgeable manager or colleague.

Many of these points could be considered as the finer detail of a person specification or elements of a job description when considering new staff for a nursery team (see Chapter 12). Staff teams would find it useful to look at the full list in the Key Times Framework and video and use this as a starting point for discussions. For established teams, revisiting the list as a reminder or affirmation of their ethos and values might help to reinforce why they are working to the key person approach. Some elements of the list could be used during supervision, for the manager or supervisor to do some checking back with staff, especially if the member of staff is new to a key person approach. It is the small details and consistency to the principles that make the approach work.

The emotional impact of the key person approach

When we think about the value of the key person approach we have to consider not only the point of view of the child, but also that of the worker who takes on the emotional responsibility. Thinking of our own relationships as adults may give us some answers. Most of us have, or would like to have, a special relationship with some person on whom we can rely, a relationship which is significant and precious to us. If we are parted from that person we have ways of preserving continuity even through long separations. We use mobiles, email, texts, social networking sites, letters, photographs, recollections, dreams and fantasies to keep alive the comfort that we derive from such human relationships. When we lose them, we experience sadness and often deep feelings of despair. If we look back we may recall important people in our early lives who, though they are not there in person, give continuity and significance to how we conduct our present lives. Often we seek to repeat and to enjoy again the warmth of those relationships in a different form.

The young children with whom we work, and who do not yet have language to express what they are experiencing, need to have these special relationships too, and deeply need to have them in a very immediate and concrete way. It is against this backcloth of what we know from our own experience that we have to consider the meaning of a key person for a young child. We can never remind ourselves too often that a child, particularly a very young and almost totally dependent one, is the only person in the nursery who cannot understand why he is there. He can only explain it as abandonment, and unless he is helped in a positive and affectionate way, this will mean levels of anxiety greater than he can tolerate.

The relationship that the child develops with his key person is in no sense a substitute for the relationship between child and parent. For a start the arrangement can only be for part of the day. Even then the key person will have to be shared with other children. To the parent we can explain it as our attempt in the nursery to offer children a person to whom they can relate in a special way during some of the often long hours which they spend away from home. Staffing ratios for under-twos usually allow for a key person to focus on a subgroup of three or four children for some of the time, though for older children the group may have to be five or six. During the rest of the day the child will be cared for by another or probably two other members of staff, whom, however, he will also know well. The way this can be organised is explained later in the chapter.

Anxieties and barriers to the key person approach

There needs to be positive discussion regarding the potential barriers to implementing the key person approach, otherwise it can become a system that is put in place to 'tick a box', but not properly explored or implemented and therefore not of any benefit to the children, parents or staff.

All kinds of objections may be put forward to the idea that we should offer a young child some form of special relationship with a member of staff. Some are of a practical organisational kind and others concerned with the emotional impact on nursery workers. An undeniable difficulty lies in the apprehension many people feel about taking on a relationship with a child who is not their own. We need to recognise such fears and not try to pretend that they do not exist.

When the idea of a key person approach is first introduced, staff will often say 'Yes, it seems a nice idea, but we couldn't do it here because . . .'. It is important then for nursery managers not to get caught up in the 'Yes but' game but to respond to the anxiety underlying this reaction. First, it may be necessary to help people recognise that there is a problem. It is important that a distinction is made between the role of a key person and a key worker. The former is that of developing a trusting triangular relationship between parent, practitioner and child. Key worker is more often used to describe someone with responsibility for liaising with other professionals without necessarily having a close relationship with the child. We also have to recognise that moving to a key person approach is not necessarily straightforward for nursery staff. Some will already have suffered the pain of parting from a child whom they have grown to love. They may have found that when attachments develop, children become more demanding and possessive.

Observers in group settings have recorded the numbers of different people who carry out the individual and intimate care needs of one child; the results have surprised if not shocked (Marshall 1982; Elfer *et al*. 2012). It might be a useful exercise to do some careful observation in your own setting, to ensure that the principles of the approach are understood and being adhered to by all staff.

Juliet Hopkins, who ran a group for nursery workers designed to help them develop more intimate relationships with children, identified two particular sources of conflict: the ideal of equality and the goal of fostering independence (Hopkins 1988). The workers believed that children should be treated equally and be given equal attention, but in practice this seemed to mean avoiding any significant involvement with individual children for fear that the others might feel ignored or become jealous. In addition, 'The counterpart of the belief that all children should be treated equally was the apparent belief that all nurses should be equal and therefore interchangeable' (Hopkins 1988). More than twenty years later, Dorothy Selleck and Peter Elfer found that in some settings these attitudes still persisted (Elfer *et al*. 2012). There was considerable pressure for children to attain early independence, both physical and emotional, under the apparent misapprehension that this can be equated with 'good' development. In fact, other research suggests that it is more likely to produce a kind of 'pseudo self-reliance' described by Eva Holmes (1977), which prevents children from seeking appropriate support from adults and inhibits their learning processes.

Another aspect of the key person relationship which may be uncomfortable for some practitioners and parents (and managers) concerns the physical element of a close relationship; watch any parent, grandparent, close relative with a familiar child – holding, cuddling, comforting, and hugging – physical contact is happening all the time. However staff might have difficulty in explaining to parents the importance of the physical part of the relationship they make with the young child.

The unplanned activity of touching, holding and cuddling needs to be thought about, discussed and shared with parents. Many staff may have experienced unhelpful discussion and guidance from training sessions, and some settings have even created policies on 'no touching'. This of course is an absolute nonsense and goes against everything we know about babies and 'young children's ordinary but vital needs for sustained and consistent human contact with a particular person who knows the child well' (Elfer *et al.* 2012, p. 7). Not holding, comforting and touching small children would be disrespectful of their needs. Physical and emotional dependency cannot be separated – they intertwine, and young babies and toddlers depend on practitioners who will respond to their physical and emotional need for a celebratory hug or a reassuring cuddle.

Elfer *et al.* do suggest, however, that the baby or young child should be the leader in any physical contact, and that it is 'motivated by the baby's or child's needs, not those of the practitioner' (2012, p. 7).

Overcoming staff absences

One common objection to the key person approach is that staff members are quite often away for various reasons, such as holidays, illness or training days. This is quite true, but the way to reduce or modify a child's sense of loss when his or her key person is not available is to anticipate and plan for such contingencies by having a named alternative person. In the case of holidays or training where the dates are known in advance, the key person should explain to her children, however young and seemingly unable to understand, that she will not be there for a while, and name the nursery worker who will look after them. Parents, too, need to be told. When the child arrives at the nursery on a day when his special person is not there, the alternative worker will take the initiative in making it clear to him that he is expected and welcome.

When a worker is absent through illness, the nursery is usually not informed until the beginning of a working day. Whoever receives the message in the morning should take responsibility for informing the alternative worker and ensuring that the agreed arrangement works properly. No child should feel in doubt about who is standing in for his key person. If there is a parents' noticeboard at the entrance to the group room or main door of the nursery (a whiteboard is best for instant and changing messages) it is helpful to put up a reminder for parents – that 'Helen in the baby room is on a training course today, Sarah is covering her shift and working with her children'. In some nurseries photographs of the key person and second (or 'buddy') person and their key children have been helpful. When the key person is absent the alternative worker can point to the photograph on the wall, saying to the child, 'Shamira is away today; she's staying at home because she isn't well; she'll be back soon'. Long before they can talk, young children are aware of our mood and our concern for them even if they do not understand our words exactly. Think how well we can get on in a foreign country where we only have a rudimentary knowledge of the language.

Relations with parents

Another objection often made by staff is that if children are encouraged to develop a special tie with individual nursery workers, parents may not like this or may not see it as a positive thing for their child. Parents differ in this respect, and it is those whose own relationship with the child is least secure who are most likely to be uneasy about other attachments. The safeguard which we build into the key person approach is that at the same time as developing a relationship with a child, the staff member also deepens her relationship with the child's parent(s).

Some parents may need help to understand that sharing love and affection with another caregiver is not like sharing an apple or a sandwich where the more people the less there is for each. Love is learned by loving, and we know from the work of Rudolf Schaffer (1977) that by the end of their first year, most children have formed attachments to several different people. Their love for their mothers and fathers is in no way diminished by this.

It can be very stressful for a staff member when she is key person to a child whom she feels is neglected or unloved by a parent. The emotions generated are intense. The worker may feel that if only she could replace the parent, all would be well. 'I wish I could take her home with me' is a comment that sounds a warning note. The practitioner's natural sympathy and affection for the child are causing her to confuse her role with that of the parent. In such a situation the nursery worker needs help to look at her relationship with the parent(s) and to recognise that it is nearly always possible to achieve some understanding and compassion for them even if she does not approve of aspects of their behaviour or necessarily 'like' them as people. If the practitioner can see her job as working to improve the relationship between parent and child rather than rescuing the child from a 'bad' parent, she may begin to see things differently.

Of course, these issues do not only arise in connection with the key person approach but they are likely to put a greater strain on the carer because of the closeness between individual staff and children, which is the whole purpose of the approach. It is essential that nursery staff should not be left to deal with this emotionally taxing situation on their own. They need opportunities to talk through their feelings with colleagues and senior staff in a climate of acceptance and understanding through which they can achieve a better perspective. This is where supervision becomes an essential element of not only nursery work, but specifically the key person approach. Safeguarding concerns would of course be raised immediately, and not wait for a supervision session. Key children should be on the agenda for supervision, to identify those where there are some challenges, be it with the parents, settling in, or the worker's own feelings. With a planned agenda, all of the children will be discussed over a period of time, and individual children will also be the focus in other meetings, for example at transition points, or regularly in room meetings. This is further discussed in Chapters 11 and 13.

The key person in practice

Home visits

> Home visiting . . . does need to be approached with sensitivity but the rewards will definitely be worth the effort. It is a powerful opportunity to allow children (and families) to get to know new staff on their own territory.
>
> (Practice guidance for the EYFS 2008, p. 2)

Going to see children in their own homes might be considered quite outside the scope of a childcare setting. If a decision about home visits due to the cost of staff time and cover has to be made, then visiting those families with additional or specific needs may be their priority. If home visiting is new to the early years setting, a Children's Centre would be a good place for support and advice on some essential guidelines for visiting families in their own homes. If a Children's Centre has a nursery on site as part of its 'core offer', one of their outreach workers might do a joint home visit if the family is already known to the Children's Centre.

If possible, two members of staff should visit the home; this would be the key person and perhaps the deputy or a senior childcare worker. Some centres told us that if the child is considered a 'Child in Need' or has any additional needs, the Deputy Head/SENCO who leads on those areas would attend the home visit. One centre told us that 98 per cent of parents take up the offer of a home visit, and parents reported very positively on the home visit – that it was 'great to meet you at home'.

Settling in

Separation

From around the age of eight months most children show distress when a strange person takes the place of their mother or father. If the separation is prolonged, they pass through a series of recognisable phases, beginning with bewilderment, followed by violent protest; later, miserable crying alternates with periods of apathy. Unless there is a substitute for the parent with whom they can make a relationship, they may sink into a depression, not wanting to play or eat. Finally, they emerge from this into a state of apparent indifference which may look to the uninformed observer like a return to normal behaviour. This sequence is remarkably similar to the stages that have been recorded in research on bereavement in adults (Worden 1991). We can understand from this that for the child too young to have a concept of time, a separation short in adult terms may feel the same as losing a loved person for ever.

With this insight, we now try as far as possible to avoid inflicting such severe pain on young children. Practice in hospitals, schools, pre-schools and nurseries has altered dramatically. We allow the child to become thoroughly familiar with new surroundings and the new caregiver before the mother attempts any separation at all. Then the mother leaves, at first for a very brief period, then gradually increasing the time she spends away, until the child is able to tolerate the whole session without her. Ideally we should be able to go at the child's pace and the separation should be accomplished without distress.

In the real world, things are rather different. Some mothers may have little choice, with jobs that they will lose if they do not turn up for work. Nursery staff are sometimes critical of parents who appear to ignore a child's pain, but they may have made the quite legitimate calculation that, with jobs in short supply, the child might suffer more in the long term if they were to become unemployed, with the resulting drop in the family income. For this reason, distressing separations cannot be avoided entirely.

When the time comes for a mother actually to leave her child, it is well for the key person to discuss how this is to be managed and to give support and understanding. It is quite natural that the mother should want to reduce her own stress, but the practitioner has to be confident that the separation is handled in the best possible way for the child, while not denying the pain. Scientific research now informs us what is happening in the brain. Margot Sunderland (2007) tells us that if the child remembers a calm soothing mother, who holds him really close to her before placing him in the arms of the key person, this will activate the happy chemicals, oxytocin and opioids, in his brain and will make him feel calmer and the separation experience will be less trying for all concerned.

Sometimes, on the contrary, parents are advised to wait until the child is engrossed in play and then leave quietly. Elinor Goldschmied suggested that to appreciate how a child must feel if his mother slips away when he is not looking, we should think back to some similar occasion in our own adult lives. For example, someone we love accompanies us to the station when we are going away. We get to the platform and settle ourselves in a carriage, while this person watches from outside the train. We look away, perhaps to get something from our luggage, and on returning to the window find that our close person has disappeared, without a word or a wave. How do we feel? Probably abandoned, hurt and rather cross, almost as if we were not worth saying a proper goodbye to.

Once the mother has left, the key person with the child on her lap may have to cope with a burst of crying which can be very upsetting for others in the group. The practitioner needs to find the confidence to listen to this quite appropriate crying and not try to hush it up or distract the child by waving a toy at him, making supposedly comforting noises or jiggling him up and down in her arms. By holding and soothing him, containing and accepting his grief, we offer positive feelings, and help his cortisol levels to fall as he begins to feel safer (Sunderland 2007). Distress needs to be expressed in a context of quiet acceptance, in the same way that we would try to comfort an adult experiencing loss and grief.

One helpful thing to remember when we have a distraught infant in our arms is that his cries may well have touched off a resonance in our own past experience which makes the situation doubly upsetting. This needs to be discussed in a group room meeting or as part of supervision if it is difficult for the practitioner, so that there is mutual support and understanding between colleagues.

Recurrence of distress

Separation distress is not a problem which only occurs at the beginning of a child's time in the nursery. It can also happen when a child has been coming to the nursery for some time and is regarded as 'settled'. Suddenly, he expresses his feeling of loss with desperate crying. Once again the analogy with bereavement is illuminating. Adults who have lost someone they love often report unexpected bursts of misery long after they thought they had come to terms with their loss. Nursery staff need to realise that this is not a rejection of them and the care that they offer. This is when the support and comfort offered by the key person makes all the difference. The child may have been enjoying his play up to that moment and, once comforted, settle down to it happily again.

Similarly, a child who has been attending nursery cheerfully for some time falls ill with a minor physical upset and stays away for a while. When he comes back, the care and presence of his key person are of great importance in helping him to readjust and again cope with the separation from his parent. To understand this, we only have to think of how we feel even in quite ordinary social situations when we walk into a room full of strange people. How pleased we are to catch sight of someone we know, especially if they seem equally pleased to see us!

A closer relationship with a child needs to go alongside closer relations with his parent(s). The customary brief exchanges at the beginning and end of the day are no longer sufficient. Many settings organise regular meetings of parents and key person, arranged at intervals convenient to all, which provide an opportunity for proper discussion and need not take up a great deal of time. Careful planning is the crucial point, and when a worker's particular group is no more than four or five, it is not too difficult to organise. As one worker said:

> Knowing parents in this way seems to take such a lot of the strain out of the work – it helps to avoid our imagining things about each other. We're more real people to each other and can have much more trust.

The need to build in listening time for the children applies equally to a worker's relation with a family.

Change of key person

Aiming to give continuity of relationship to a child and his parent(s) can sometimes seem difficult to achieve, with the inevitable staff changes and the times when it is necessary for a child to move from one group to another. We have to remind ourselves of the difference between child and adult timescales. Six months, which may seem a short time to us, is a considerable slice of a young child's life, so a special relationship is always valuable even if it can only last for a relatively brief period in our terms.

After a close attachment has formed between a child and his key person, a change will involve pain for both of them and obviously should be avoided if possible. When it is unavoidable, the original key person needs support to acknowledge and work through her feelings, and so does the new key person, who may feel rejected when the child wants to go back and perhaps even cries for his previous carer. It can help everybody if the changeover is made gradually and if the child can still see the first key person from time to time. Sometimes a change of key person occurs because someone moves to another job, but most often it is due to a planned transition from the baby to the toddler room or from toddler to preschool group. In this situation, where childcare centres operate a free-flow system and mobile children are able to visit other rooms on their own initiative, the separation becomes much less painful. Usually the child wants to go and see his former key person quite often for a while, but after a time will become attached to the new worker who takes over his daily care. It must not be forgotten that parents, too, may need help to make the transition. There is much to be said for the Italian practice by which the same two teachers (*insegnatori*) move with the children as a group through their first three years. Childcare arrangements and staff are rarely stable enough in Britain for such an arrangement to be feasible, which makes the key person approach all the more essential. We visited a Children's Centre nursery where they were trying out a system where the key person moved with the babies to the toddler home-base and later one of the two staff members in the group room moved to the pre-school room with her key group.

Working with outside specialists

As the key person approach develops in a nursery, the interest and scope of the work will increase. Recognising the adult's intimate knowledge of her particular children means that she will come into contact with the variety of specialists who may visit the centre in the course of their work. In this way the speech therapist, health visitor, physiotherapist, social worker or community physician may well find that their relationships with the nursery become easier and more effective.

Apart from any special observations that she undertakes in collaboration with these outside specialists, the key person will take responsibility for assessment, monitoring and record-keeping in relation to children in her small group. She also provides the main link between the centre and the child's home. This of course has particular significance when the child has special needs or when there is a possibility of abuse or neglect. It will be the key person (supported by the centre leader) who speaks about a child at a child protection conference. Such occasions may arouse anxiety even in experienced workers, but it will help if the worker quietly reminds herself that, except for the parents, she is the one who probably knows most about a child with whom she spends so many hours of the day.

Practical arrangements

We now turn to the practical organisation which is required for the effective operation of a key person approach. It is usual in nurseries for the maximum number of staff to be present during the middle of the day, from approximately 9.30 a.m. until the early afternoon. In order to put the key person arrangement into practice, this is essential. It is during this part of the day that the key person will focus on her small group, playing with and alongside the children, changing them, going out for walks or into the garden.

Observing nurseries in operation and talking to staff we heard that the point in the day that is often described as 'chaotic' is the period at the end of the morning's activities, while the children are using the bathroom, the room is being cleared up and tables set out for the midday meal. This is the ideal time for each adult in every group room to become the focus for her small group of children until after their meal is finished. In a group of, say, twelve children, there would usually be three (or four) staff during the middle of the day. The four children in each group would then be sure that for that part of the day they would have the close attention of their key person. It will be different for settings where babies are in separate groups, as at present the ratios for under-ones require there to be a minimum of 1:3.

Island of intimacy or 'island time'

When play material and various activities have been tidied away, each member of staff, with the small number of children to whom she is the key person, withdraws into a quiet corner. The staff member should have her own space which, for this pre-lunch time, is what may be called her 'island of intimacy'. It should always be the same corner, made comfortable with a quilt or rug and cushions, giving her the opportunity for quiet and unhurried observation, conversation and listening time with her group. This builds firmly into the day's programme a period when she can give her undivided attention to them. Suggestions for ways to maintain interest and stimulate conversation during 'island time' with children aged 18 months upwards can be found in Chapter 6.

From bathroom to meal table

During this time, at some point agreed by the staff, each small group in turn goes with their key person to the bathroom. When bathrooms are shared between more than one group it generates a sense of rush and tension that is easily avoided by better planning.

Until the food trolley is actually in the room, the small groups remain with their adult in their own corners. This avoids the bad practice of children being made to sit down at the tables before the food arrives, inevitably creating noise and restlessness.

If possible a member of ancillary staff or a volunteer will bring the trolley to the room so that a nursery worker does not have to absent herself from her small group. When the food trolley arrives, the key person for each small group goes to the table with her children. Once she is seated everything should be so arranged that she does not have to get up again – essential if she is to get any enjoyment from her own meal.

Our own experience helps us to understand why it is necessary in creating a tranquil atmosphere for both nursery workers and children that the adult should remain seated. Imagine ourselves invited to a friend's house for a meal. If our hostess continually gets up to fetch things she has forgotten, there comes a point when the whole company choruses, 'For heaven's sake come and sit down!' As well as wanting her presence we are also a bit fed up that she hasn't prepared things properly. It is just the same in a nursery. Detailed suggestions about how the meal can be arranged to minimise disturbance are given in Chapter 9.

Benefits of a key person approach

As yet, there is no systematic research to show how the key person approach compares with the more usual arrangements and in what way outcomes for children are affected. It is interesting to note that Juliet Hopkins in the study already quoted found that, once nursery workers had formed close attachments, staff absence was much reduced because they felt it was really important for them to be in the nursery for 'their' children. This is certainly true of Ruth's personal experience of managing nurseries where the key person approach has been implemented, and Elfer *et al*. (2012, p. 38) also found that staff expressed a high level of satisfaction in their work and that there were fewer absences and less staff turnover when they took on special responsibility for planning and caring for a small group of children.

This was the experience of the head of a day nursery in north London, who wrote to us:

> Since we established a key person system here closer relationships have been developed between staff and parents, especially in the baby room. Children seem to settle into life at the nursery more easily. Some who had been at the nursery for a while and were still not happy, settled at once when they realised that one adult was their special person. Barry, who we had only seen tearful and withdrawn, became a smiling, outgoing, confident child almost overnight. For the first few days, he sat on her lap, then he took off and played with the other children happily, knowing that she was somewhere in the room.
>
> Staff seem to have a special closeness with 'their' children and this has increased their understanding of them. There are always the days when staff are ill or on holiday, and their children miss them for the day. On the other hand there are times when staff come into work even if they are not feeling too well because they care about what will happen to 'their' children. Parents like to have one person to talk to rather than fifteen, and seem able to talk more freely knowing that that person takes special care of their child. The key person appointments, a regular time set aside for a parent to talk in peace to their child's special person, have worked particularly well to establish a partnership between parents and staff in the best interests of their children.

Peter Elfer and Dorothy Selleck have undertaken very detailed observations of the operation of the key person approach in a range of nurseries and childcare centres (Elfer *et al*. 2012). They found, as we suggested above, that it was essential for the early years workers at every level to be fully involved in the decision to introduce the approach and to understand the reasoning behind it. Otherwise it might operate in a tokenistic way that had little meaning for the children and did not result in a closer relationship between any individual child and his or her designated key person.

Ruth's experience of introducing the key person approach to a large organisation was that the benefits to staff, parents and children were immeasurable. It involved the whole of the organisation, the marketing team, human resources, learning and development. Administrators talking to parents and responsible for bookings understood the reasons behind settling-in visits and openly discussed and raised these as part of the booking system. Nursery staff felt more valued by the parents, as they got to know the children better, to understand the stories behind the young children, and were privy to details about the family and extended family. One staff team was fortunate enough to meet Elinor as part of their induction and were able to talk with her about the ethos of the approach and ask questions about how it works in practice. Dorothy Selleck, a close colleague of Elinor's, worked with another team to support their early learning about the key person approach and used a vivid metaphor to introduce staff to the concept. Imagine that the key person has a piece of elastic attaching them to their special child which at times is stretched to full length, but also allows the child to 'spring back' to the practitioner as often and quickly as he needs to.

Summary

This chapter discusses the importance of close personal relationships for children's development and happiness. It suggests an approach which allows warm attachments to develop in a group care setting, taking full account of the impact on parents and early years workers. Problems are acknowledged but can be overcome, provided the principle is agreed.

Once the approach is established, the key person takes on many important functions, such as managing the child's settling in, easing separation, fostering language and cognitive development, home visiting, relating to parents, assessment and record-keeping and liaison with outside specialists and agencies. The role becomes more demanding and responsible but also offers far more interest and opportunities for learning, to the benefit of children, staff and parents alike. Secure attachments, made possible in a childcare setting by the key person approach, foster resilience, and resilience predicts mental health and social competence in childhood.

From our own experience of implementing the approach, both with new and established teams, the practical and logistical challenges are the same in most settings. Making time for staff to question, reflect and then be part of decision-making for implementation is crucial. If the setting's vision is to have an effective key person approach in practice, then all the staff must want to work towards that vision, understanding that the triangle of a close personal relationship between key person, parent and child will be the reward for all.

3 | Planning spaces for living, playing and learning

Our experience confirms that children need a great deal of freedom . . . to appreciate the infinite resources of their hands, eyes and ears, the resources of forms, materials, sounds and colours . . . without anyone arbitrarily setting the timing, rhythms and measures for them.

(Loris Malaguzzi 2004)

In this chapter we will consider:

- The importance of the physical environment;
- The design and appearance of the setting;
- Creating a welcoming environment;
- Planning the best use of space;
- Special areas for people under three.

The impact of the physical environment

Development Matters (Early Education 2012, p. 2) identifies enabling environments as those that offer 'stimulating resources, relevant to all the children's cultures and communities, rich learning opportunities through play and playful teaching and support for children to take risks and explore'.

The physical environment exerts a major influence on how early years practitioners feel about the job and on the quality of experience they can offer the children. Spacious, well-designed buildings can make life easier for everyone and more welcoming and interesting for those very young children who might be spending a full day in them. Unfortunately day nurseries and childcare centres often have to operate in premises that are far from ideal. Whatever the limitations of the building, however, there is always something that can be done to make it more comfortable and attractive to the adults and children who spend long hours of the day there. A few purpose-built centres have adopted an open-plan design, with children free to use the whole floor space but with 'home' areas enclosed on three sides. We have seen this working very well, allowing different play activities to be concentrated in separate areas and avoiding isolation of staff. On the other hand, if not well managed, it can be a recipe for chaos. A very successful design is to have group rooms opening out of a wide corridor with doors to the outside area on the other side.

Ofsted (2012) sets out the minimum requirements for the registration of an early years setting, detailing, amongst other things, space requirements and health and safety requirements (pp. 23–25). Part of the inspection in an early years setting looks at how well the provision meets the needs and contributes to the well-being of the children. There are detailed regulations enforced by inspection about the physical aspects of nursery buildings, but these are concerned with health and safety, not their aesthetic qualities. Even the space requirements are minimal – for example, having an outside play area is not a requirement, although having daily outdoor activities is. However, we have seen some of the most creative work with under-threes going on in what appear at first glance to be quite unsuitable buildings.

Practitioners both in home settings and out of home settings will need to consider the environment and how to ensure the child engages with and uses it. The way the environment is planned and organised (and re-ordered during play and exploration) supports and enables the children's play and their motivation to explore and question, and to think critically.

The entrance area

The entrance area is a public statement by the centre about its values and priorities. What messages does it convey? We can see that some nurseries create an artificial child's world with no reference to anything that goes on outside, while others make a positive attempt to build bridges with families and the community. There are welcoming messages in the different languages of families using the centre, pictures of local neighbourhoods and family life, photographs of the members of the nursery staff with their names, so that parents and visitors can easily identify them, and photographs of children engaged in play activities.

On the other hand, the amount of information provided in the entrance area may conflict with the aim of keeping it looking visually attractive. Too many notices can give it an institutional feel and create an overcrowded effect. Notices should be carefully designed and non-authoritarian in tone. Digital cameras make it possible to go beyond the familiar displays recording outings and expeditions to produce narrative sequences illustrating children's projects and activities. Early years staff are usually highly skilled at presentation and know that successful wall displays require time and effort.

Careful thought is needed if the space that people first come into is going to be genuinely welcoming, just as the hallway does in most homes. Coming into a bright, carpeted area with comfortable chairs for waiting or conversation, and plants, well-displayed photographs and pictures on the walls feels quite different from a dark

Figure 3.1 A welcoming reception area (Photograph: Shaftesbury CC Nursery)

passage with a narrow bench, prohibitive notices and stacked-up equipment. Special attention needs to be given to the visual impact of this area, both on those visiting the nursery for the first time and those who enter it every day.

The impressions we receive on entering a new place do not only come through the eye – we need to give attention to the auditory as well as the visual environment. Anyone who has visited a friend in hospital will know that one of the most distressing aspects is the incessant clatter. We need to do everything possible in a nursery to keep the noise level to a minimum. This means attending immediately to crying babies, an absolute prohibition on shouting or calling across rooms, music only as part of the planned programme and surfaces designed to be sound-absorbent. Noise creates stress for staff and inhibits children's speech development.

Another important aspect of the sensory environment is smell. We have something to learn here from the commercial world. Estate agents often advise their clients to have bread baking in the oven or freshly brewed coffee on the stove when people come to view their houses. Bunches of dried lavender, sage and other herbs hanging where babies and toddlers can smell them, and flowers safely displayed in vases or pots with a little water add to the homely feel of a centre. Pots of herbs and flowers growing in and outside can be looked after even by the very youngest children. Practitioners need to be very alert to the risk of unpleasant smells permeating the setting – from damp coats, nappies or spilt milk, for instance.

Organising the group room

The way in which the group room is planned makes a big difference to how far activity can be child-initiated and self-directed. Practitioners have to manage the daily task of keeping the room in reasonable order. Lack of floor and storage space and the constant shifting of furniture can make this a very trying aspect of the job. Careful thought needs to be given to how these problems can be minimised. The unalterable fact that playing, eating and sometimes sleeping must be provided for in the same space can bring feelings of stress and restriction which affect both children and adults.

Resources, storage and seating

It is important that all staff should feel that their group room is attractive and well organised and for everyone to experience some pleasure and satisfaction as they enter it each day. Unless a really critical eye is maintained, it is easy for people to get used to a room with a chaotic and uncared-for appearance. This can have a profoundly

Figure 3.2 Storage allowing children to make their own choices (Photograph: Coram Early Childhood Centre)

depressing effect without people being consciously aware of it. A useful way of initiating improvement in appearance and organisation is to have regular discussions with everyone who uses the room, with the theme, 'What I would like to keep in this room and what I would like to get rid of'. This can result in some energetic throwing out, allowing storage space to be used more efficiently. It also ensures that resources that are meant to be in the baby room or toddler room remain there, and those that have 'wandered' to other places are brought back. It is also a good time for checking equipment in need of repair.

Effective arrangements for storing play materials in good order are essential. To enable the staff to operate as facilitators, the storage should, as far as possible, be on open shelves so that children can choose and select for themselves or see what is available and ask for what they want.

Another most important point, often overlooked, is the need for at least two adult-sized chairs in every room so that a staff member and parent can sit down and talk in comfort. Every group room needs a chair which is suitable for an adult holding or comforting a child. Nursery practitioners who habitually hold children in their arms while standing up put themselves at serious risk of developing back trouble. Chairs for toddlers are not a priority. Better to offer them lots of floor space where resources can be set out on rugs or mats, or low-level furniture on which they can pull themselves up and practise cruising. Chairs for mealtimes should be at a height that enables toddlers to place their feet comfortably on the floor.

The most successful kind of group room has the appearance of spaciousness, but with cosy corners. People who design the interior of restaurants and pubs know that their customers prefer comfortable, secluded areas and that no one likes to sit at tables out in the middle of the floor. Children feel the same way.

Walls and windows, the importance of light

It is best to be selective about the number of mobiles, hanging decorations and paintings or drawings that are displayed on the walls. More is not necessarily better. Small children's paintings can look very attractive but need to be properly mounted and fixed at a height for children to see them. Responsibility for wall displays should be clearly allocated to a particular person for an agreed period. The importance of light in a nursery cannot be overestimated: clean windows make a great difference to the appearance of the room. Windows left without any decoration allow maximum light, give a sense of more space and, if the windows are at child height, enable even the smaller children to see what is going on outside. Staff should be discouraged from painting or sticking pictures on the windows to brighten things up or, in the case of some commercial day nurseries and childcare centres, to indicate the function of the building and attract enquiries. Unfortunately the result often reduces the available light and gives a cluttered effect, especially in small spaces.

Creating a facilitating space

The role of the adult

Except in centres with open plan arrangements, day care usually involves two or more adults spending large parts of the day in a 'group room' with a number of children. Most centres have designated spaces for different age groups. Childminders may be able to use several parts of their house for their work. However, they will still plan and consider how the spaces are used and how they supervise children, using different areas of the home.

During the day the practitioner takes on a number of distinct but interrelated roles on which the functioning of the unit (or home) depends – those of **organiser, facilitator** and **initiator**.

As **organiser** she is responsible for use of space, ventilation, arrangement of furniture, storage, the appearance of the room and keeping things clean and in good repair, in cooperation with domestic staff (if any). Time for starting and ending activities, for clearing up and putting away, sharing a bathroom with other groups and setting up tables for mealtimes, are all matters for precise organisation, while allowing flexibility to accommodate the unpredictable needs of individual children.

All practitioners (including childminders) need to be good time managers, and aware of the pitfalls of poor time management. This has to be coupled with the need for flexibility and spontaneity. For example, it starts to snow just before lunch. What is the practitioner to do – delay lunch by half an hour and share in the joy of an unexpected snowfall? Or carry on and hope it settles and can be enjoyed later? Choices of this kind have to be made constantly by the staff. In this case, if all the children have rushed to the door or window and are desperate to go out, the decision is obvious. Organising shifts, rest breaks and time to meet or talk with parents or visiting specialists all add to the complexity of the day and cannot happen smoothly without detailed planning. Add to this after-school pick-ups which happen for many childminders and nurseries and we can understand why time management is an essential skill for organisers.

Rodd (2006, 2012) suggests that the major obstacle in early childhood services is interruption. Leaders have to work around phone calls, external and internal meetings, visitors and staff supervision, so planning, prioritising and managing their day, week and month is essential. It is much the same for the practitioners working in the group rooms. They are having to adjust every day to the fluctuating and changing moods, growth spurts, wants and needs of a group of small children, but the temptation to plan too rigorously means that moments in the snow are missed or the child who is desperate to show you the shiny damp slug on the path is told to hurry up and come in because it's lunchtime.

Quiet moments can be used to fold up the washing whilst watching a busy group of toddlers – the washing can always be abandoned, or perhaps some of the older toddlers will help sorting and classifying – bibs in one pile, the towels in another and their own clothes back in their basket or bag. The experience will support language, maths, self-awareness and self-esteem. Real tasks like this offer the sort of experiences small children would have had at home, and need to be seen as important and valuable. However we need to remember not to miss the pure enjoyment and texture of everyday life. Greenman and Stonehouse (1997, p. 219) remind us, 'if you are constantly articulating, enhancing, elaborating, reflecting, classifying and counting, genuine pleasures and authenticity will fade, and children – and you – will overdose from teachable moments'.

Successfully carrying out the second role, that of **facilitator**, depends on this planned organisation of time, space and materials. By imaginative provision and arrangement of play equipment, the adult enables children to choose and develop their play, on their own or with others. Her attentive presence provides emotional anchorage to the group of children, who know that, if necessary, she will intervene as referee or comforter. The children are encouraged and enabled to decide how their play should develop, by observing other children and adults, imitating what they see and through first-hand experiences (as in the clay or cooking below).

In the third role, as **initiator**, the adult more directly leads the play, and ensures that all the resources are ready and that an appropriate space is available to set up whatever equipment is needed. She may work with a small group which requires her undisturbed attention, giving help and encouragement in activities such as baking biscuits, making a collage, footprints with paint, making music, reading a story or gardening. This kind of initiator is not to be confused with what might be called 'the ringmaster', which is sometimes necessary if there is a large group to control. Here the worker risks finding herself in the role of entertainer, dominating the group in a charismatic way. It is important to clarify the difference, because large-group orchestrated activity is generally inappropriate for children of this age, restricting and distorting their play and learning. With the key person approach fully in operation, this should no longer occur.

Supporting staff and balancing the roles

Staff teams will discuss and plan how best they can work with the children in their care. Bruce (2011, p. 63) suggests that they will need to organise the day to support 'the natural ebb and flow of play scenarios'. The aim should be for the practitioner to be the secure figure, the point of reference for the children in her group whilst they explore and immerse themselves in the available opportunities and resources for play. The three key roles of organising, facilitating and initiating will be spread across the staff, worked into their daily plan, each taking on one of the roles at different points of the day, depending on the needs of the children. Staff need to remember that they (the adults) do not always have to be in charge of what is happening – there needs to be a balance of adult-led and child-led activities. In an experienced staff group the workers will complement each other, with different members giving more emphasis to one of the three roles, and support to those staff new to post or newly qualified. Managers and supervisors can encourage workers to bring the three roles into better balance by helping them to become aware of their own preferences and work style.

Planning the best use of space

Unlike a nursery school, a childcare centre is a place for living as well as working and playing. The physical environment must take account of this dual function. It has to combine comfort and homeliness with the practicality of a well-run nursery classroom. Its overall appearance should offer interest and pleasure to children and adults alike.

Banks, shops and restaurants pay huge sums to interior designers to create a visual environment which is attractive to customers during their brief visits. Yet we are often content for children to spend their most formative years surrounded by ugliness and clutter. It is noticeable that this is not generally true in countries like Italy, which give far more importance to visual and artistic education than we do in Britain. In Reggio Emilia nurseries the central piazza is fundamental as a meeting place, a place of communication. Ruth is fortunate to have worked with colleagues who had visited Reggio Emilia. The sharing of their experiences and observations afforded much discussion and debate across the staff teams, and contributed to small but effective changes of practice and the environments for both children and adults – such as introducing real crockery at mealtimes, and in the home corners, and a much wider range of creative materials set out in workshop areas.

Brookson (1999) recalling her visit to Reggio enthused:

> I got really excited in the music room in Diana school, it had a complete drum set, hanging lengths of wood that made a satisfying resonant sound when struck . . . All this with a magnificent garden full of scents and sights through open French windows. It was truly an assault of all the senses.

The physical environment in Reggio is often described as the 'third teacher' and those who have visited will attest to this.

However, rather than try to reproduce the 'Reggio approach' we should use our reflections and observations to help develop our settings' own culture and approach. All too often we see childcare centres decorated with crude cut-outs of Disney cartoon characters which add nothing to the appearance of the room and hold little interest for children after the first pleasure of recognition. 'Real' paintings are rarely seen in British nurseries or childcare centres, though in other countries this is regarded as an aspect of introducing children to their cultural heritage. Of course, much of the wall area in a nursery will be needed to display children's work or for notices and information to staff and parents, but there is usually space in entrance areas, passages or the staff room. It is also worth thinking about places where the wall space is usually thrown away, such as kitchens, bathrooms and cloakroom areas.

Some local art galleries run loan schemes, and may have basements full of once-despised Victorian narrative paintings and water-colours, now to be found reproduced in every greeting-card shop. These can be very appealing to children and offer much scope for conversation. Children tend to be eclectic in their tastes and are also intrigued by non-representational art – paintings by twentieth-century artists such as Picasso, Miró and Chagall, for example. Chinese, Persian, African and Indian paintings and wall hangings also offer much interest. Pictures of instruments, musicians and dancers act as a stimulus for these kinds of activity (Pound and Harrison 2003). Some local authorities offer access to a range of multicultural artefacts on a loan system, through toy libraries or the Early Years Consultants team and can be useful when practitioners are putting together displays to support children's learning.

Parents are of course the practitioner's most accessible resource. Most families will be delighted to share artefacts representative of their cultural heritage, knowing that they will be valued and respected by the setting. Elinor was a great believer in asking parents to contribute to displays, enabling parents to play a fuller part in the planning and delivery of their children's learning and making the setting a richer, more beautiful space to be in.

Creating a satisfactory visual environment is not a once-and-for-all job, but something that needs to happen continuously. Just as at home we are constantly making small adjustments and improvements, changing pictures from one room to another, moving a lamp or a plant, a nursery will only look inviting and cared for if the same kind of process is going on. If a nursery unit is being created or furnished from scratch, it is best to stick to plain colours, not too bright, for basic items, so that staff and parents can exercise their creativity in the wall displays, hangings, mobiles, cushion covers, pictures and other easily removable and replaceable objects. Fitted, hardwearing, stain-resistant carpets are a good investment and can create the effect of more space, absorb noise and are pleasant to sit on. Rugs that can be brought out to enhance an activity, such as a special round carpet for circle time, can help children to identify different points in the day and add to the 'specialness' of the activity (see 'islands of intimacy' in Chapter 6). Ruth used a round rush mat for babies to sit on at her Treasure Basket, signalling a change in the environment, and introducing the babies to new textures (Forbes 2004).

Work by Elizabeth Jarman, founder of the Communication Friendly Spaces™ programme, identifies ways in which practitioners and parents can re-think the environments they currently have in their settings and put children at the very heart of the setting. Jarman's work concentrates on de-cluttering spaces for young children and reminding practitioners of the importance of lighting, natural colours and sensory materials. The use of easy-to-access resources such as clothes airers (to make into tents or dens) and large pieces of net curtain to make hideaway places or peep-bo spaces, encourages practitioners and families to look at what they have around them, how it is currently used and how it can be re-ordered and used in a more imaginative way.

A child's eye view

In planning the available space to the best advantage, a good exercise is to observe the children's movements carefully during different times of the day. We can often identify a 'dead area' where, for some reason, children do not go, increasing crowding in other parts. Once this is recognised, the space can be brought into use by making it more accessible or by putting equipment for a popular activity there. Practitioners can ensure that mirrors, mobiles and pictures are at the right height by lying on the floor – after all this is the viewpoint of the very youngest children. So, does the mirror enable them to see themselves and their friends? Can they kick or reach out to the mobile and practise their hand-eye coordination to make it move? Can they hear the wind chimes in the garden? This is probably most important during the design phase of a new nursery or centre, ensuring that windows in the areas for the 0–3s are low enough for children to see out of, that doorways are accessible to the garden for crawling or tottering toddlers, ensuring free flow between inside and outside (see Chapter 10).

Involving children in care and maintenance

Maintaining order in the group room is an essential task for the practitioner, when replacing and replenishing resources. Constant unobtrusive re-ordering, enlisting the help of individual children whenever possible (as with the laundry basket discussed earlier), is much better than a single 'clear-up' time.

Involving the older children in tidying and cleaning up can mean more effort for the staff as it is usually quicker for the adults to do it themselves. But if we look on everything that happens in the nursery as part of the children's learning, this is a short-sighted approach. A supply of small dustpans and brushes, and cloths for wiping tables, will encourage children to take part in 'real' tasks, and encourage a sense of satisfaction and achievement, as the sand area is kept in order or spilt milk from snack time is wiped away quickly and without a fuss.

Of course, it is particularly important that boys should see clearing up as their job as much as that of the girls. Even today we are aware that it is mainly mothers who are responsible for organising childcare, managing the household and doing most of the domestic tasks, whilst working full- or part-time. Numerous studies of family life and the division of domestic work between men and women show this. Because the staff of childcare centres are almost all female, boys can easily get the idea that clearing up is 'women's work', especially if that coincides with what they see at home. It is especially important in the twenty-first century that we as childcare professionals do all we can to dispel this misconception.

Organising a group room for under-twos

A baby room needs to combine a sense of spaciousness with intimacy, allowing free movement for mobile children and a quieter area for babies not yet able to move by themselves. We still sometimes see baby rooms almost entirely taken up with cots. A better solution is to use suitably covered mattresses in one corner, where babies can be put to sleep (or put themselves) when they are tired. Many centres now use large wicker baskets with soft sheets and cushions for babies and toddlers to crawl into and rest or sleep, as and when they feel the need. If there is space the area can be screened by a curtain or carefully positioned furniture. Mattresses are also useful for babies at the stage of sitting, either propped up by cushions or unaided, and rolling or levering themselves about. But as soon as they begin to crawl they need the firm surface of a carpet.

The general layout of the room for this age group needs to give maximum scope for the gross motor activity which occupies so much of the children's energy as they progress from crawling and pulling themselves up to taking first steps. Carpet is essential for children at this stage so that they can have bare feet, allowing them to grip in the process of achieving the balance necessary for walking. They also like to sit on a carpeted area to manipulate anything which comes to hand.

If you are planning a new space it may be possible to have only part of it carpeted. Having the flexibility of two floor surfaces helps staff to plan activities around the changing and developing needs of the under-twos. A carpeted area has the advantage of quietness but for some purposes a hard floor is preferable.

If possible, the hard floor area should lead to the outdoor space. Direct access to a covered outdoor area and/or garden is a great advantage, allowing free movement in and out of the room and enabling babies to sleep in prams in the open air (always of course under close supervision). The garden area for under-twos should be separated by a low fence or hedge from the general outdoor space so that, while this age group is not cut off from the rest of the nursery, they are protected from accidental bumps and knocks by bigger children using tricycles, prams, cars and trolleys in their outdoor play. More suggestions for planning and equipping an outdoor area for under-twos are given in Chapter 10.

Storage

Adequate, well-planned storage space is just as essential in a room designed for under-twos as for older children. This becomes obvious as soon as we start to give real thought to play objects for this age group. For example, it is most important that each child's personal cuddly toy or love object has a designated place for when it is temporarily discarded, so that it can be quickly retrieved when wanted. Baby rooms are too often cluttered up with bulky containers or plastic baskets into which everything is indiscriminately flung at clearing-up time. As well as occupying valuable space, this often encourages thoughtless accumulation of mass-produced plastic toys and grubby stuffed animals, which have nothing to contribute to the children's development.

As with a group room for older children, it is best to have earmarked 'corners' for different types of play material. There is a difference, however, in that, as soon as they can move freely, children of this age will roam about, exploring energetically, carrying with them whatever they happen to be holding and dropping it wherever they are when something new catches their interest. They will play with the available material all over the room, not focusing their activity as the older ones do. Provided various types of equipment are based (and replaced continually) in specified parts of the room, even very small children will quickly learn to respond to the adult's request to 'put dolly back in her cot' or 'this goes with the other books in the book corner'. These simple instructions, related directly to an action, and evoking the smile and thank you of the adult, provide genuine experience in collaboration which need in no way be oppressive. A sense of self and the beginnings of personal autonomy are built up in a myriad of small ways by the practitioner's understanding of such daily opportunities.

Special spaces for twos and over

We assume as standard practice that a group room for over-twos will have most of the following designated areas, though there may not be space for all to be in permanent fixed positions.

The quiet corner

In the long nursery day it is essential to arrange a quiet, enclosed space for resting, daydreaming or looking at books, magazines, catalogues or collections of cards. Book corners are not always sufficiently protected to provide such a refuge. If there is not an actual corner available, this can be created by placing a sofa or divan at right angles to the wall, combining it with low shelving or the back of a cupboard facing the other way.

Because the staff usually have the opportunity, however limited, to withdraw to their staffroom, it may be forgotten that children also need a space away from the pressure of the general activities of the group. The aim should be to create and maintain an atmosphere of cosiness and safety. The essentials are a proper carpet, and cushions in abundance, large and small (but not random, and with carefully chosen covers). A covered cot mattress on the floor and another placed up against the wall are very welcome for sitting or sprawling, as are a low armchair or sofa if there is space. These can form part of the protective 'wall' together with a wooden book rack on which a changing selection of books is kept. Alternatively, books can be placed in a wall rack with easy access so that children can take them out and put them away themselves or kept in attractive baskets on the floor. There must of course be a firm rule that no books are to be thrown about or left on the floor to be trodden on.

When there is an opportunity, an adult can spend time with one or two children seeing that the books are in good order, not torn or with frayed bindings, so that maintenance is a continuous process. It is more effective if a particular member of staff takes responsibility for this.

Mail order catalogues are interesting to small children, but need regular checking so that they can be discarded before they become grubby or torn. A shoe box or a rectangular wooden box filled with well-chosen postcards can form another point of interest. The smallest children will enjoy looking at postcards of single subjects, such as animals, flowers, cars and ships. If there is a suitable shop nearby, a small group can be taken to choose for themselves. Parents and friends can also be invited to contribute to the collection, which needs regular weeding and new additions.

Other items for quiet, small-group activities can be stored on shelves out of the children's reach. Examples would be a collection of finger puppets, an assortment of large buttons in a clear container, a box filled with remnants of different materials – bits of lamé, velvet, lace, Indian and Chinese silks, pieces of embroidery and upholstery trimmings. Market stalls and charity shops are a good source for this kind of item. Other possibilities are shells, beads, shiny pebbles or tiny decorated boxes. They must be large enough to prevent a choking hazard, and carefully checked to ensure there are no sharp edges. All of these can offer scope for fantasy and imagination and lots of conversation. Because such collections are made up of small items which easily become lost, they should be enjoyed with a practitioner who has some interest in their care and replenishment. Very close supervision is also essential to ensure that children do not swallow smaller objects or put them in ears or noses. One period of the day when using such collections is especially helpful is towards evening, when only a few children are left and some kind of comfort and intimacy is what everybody needs. Similar items will be used by the key person during her special time with her small group before the midday meal, the 'island of intimacy' described in Chapter 9.

Imaginative and make-believe play

Imaginative and make-believe play is very wide-ranging and can occur anywhere, but seems to be particularly stimulated by what is usually called the 'Home Corner'. A purpose-made structure is not essential and may take up too much space in the group room, but it is important that the chosen area should be permanent and that the play in and around it goes on undisturbed. Low, solid screens will suffice, with a curtained 'window' on one side. A curtain can also be used for a door if necessary. The space inside should always be carpeted to create a sense of intimacy and comfort.

Finding detailed items for the Home Corner is a good opportunity for the practitioner, and her own 'play' in the area is a central factor in developing its full potential. One member of staff in the group room needs to take responsibility for assembling and replacing items and keeping them in good condition. The corner needs its own special furniture, a small low table and two chairs, not the standard nursery ones – small wicker chairs are ideal. The 'cooker' can be an upturned wooden box with hob plates, either painted or represented by glued-on cork or rush table mats.

Dressing-up areas should welcome and entice children. Clothes should be hung up at a height the toddlers can reach, and jewellery can be hung or be kept in attractive baskets or boxes to rummage through. Above all, the clothes should be kept clean and in good repair. The best things for toddlers are those most easily available from parents and charity shops – some suggestions are listed below. Catalogue or shop-bought outfits are expensive and unnecessary – and they are quite limiting and restrictive in their use. A fireman's hat is usually sufficient for a toddler and easier to put on in an instant than trying to pull up 'waterproof' trousers and a top from a commercial set.

A small dresser or set of shelves is needed for keeping pots and pans, cutlery, plates, cups and saucers. Kitchen equipment should consist of real, not toy items, which children can identify with and recognise from their own homes (see Figure 3.4). Of course this should reflect the range of cultural diversity in food preparation and eating customs. It will often be helpful to ask for advice from parents, or better still to visit them at home. They may also be able to offer packets and jars to stock the shelves and these can be filled with corks or dried pasta to represent food. Above all, the Home Corner needs to be kept looking attractive and orderly (but not over-tidy) to encourage enjoyable individual or sociable play. Charity shops are good places for a supply of china cups and saucers, teapots and plates – matching sets are not essential!

Figure 3.3 An enticing dressing-up area (Photograph: Coram Early Childhood Centre)

Figure 3.4
Make-believe
play with real
equipment

Suggested items for pretend play

Home corner

- Range of real saucepans (different sizes) as in photograph
- Colanders
- Sieves
- Measuring jugs
- Teapots/coffee pots
- Milk jugs
- Kitchen utensils – wooden spoons/pasta servers/slotted spoons/ladles
- Picnic sets/outdoor eating sets.

Baby equipment

- Baby bath/potty
- Real nappies – disposable and green reusable type
- Changing mat
- Small flannels or pieces of muslin to use as 'wipes' (cut up and put in a reusable wipes box for washing).

Dressing-up clothes

- Hats
- Handbags, shopping bags/haversacks
- Waistcoats
- Shawls
- Shoes and slippers
- Capes
- Elasticated skirts/petticoats.

Table play

The tables in a group room generally have three uses: for mealtimes; for small-scale manipulative play; or for an activity with a small group such as playing with dough, making biscuits or fruit salad for lunch, potato printing, tearing and shredding paper and pasting. Tables are not usually helpful in rooms where the children are all non-mobile, or only just mobile, as discussed earlier. Many toddlers simply enjoy sweeping things off the table, or the table will get in the way of space needed for practising crawling, creeping, pushing baby walkers along or scooting on small ride-on toys. Storage for tables can be a problem as they are essential for mealtimes and activities for older toddlers, but in baby rooms they can lead to babies – who should be on the floor reaching, stretching, grasping and rolling around – being pinned into chairs.

An important point for good maintenance of table play materials with slightly older toddlers is that each item should be kept in a strong, low wooden box or rigid plastic container, clearly labelled with a photograph to help the children put things away. A puzzle which is missing a piece is better thrown away as the point of it is its completeness.

Suggested items for table play

- Large coloured wooden beads. Younger children find it easier to thread these on plastic-covered electrician's wire. Older children will use the usual 'bootlace' coloured string with a long metal threader;
- Wooden insets and puzzles;
- Sorting trays with coloured counters;
- Soft boards with coloured wooden shapes, hammer and pin nails;
- 'Fuzzy-felt' boards;
- Deep meat-roasting tins filled with bird seed or lentils for scooping and pouring with small containers and spoons or cooks' small 'shovels' (only under close supervision);
- Blunt-ended scissors and catalogues or magazines for cutting out and pasting;
- Thick wax crayons and paper for drawing.

Floor play

A flat, carpeted area is needed – for tower-building and for using wooden blocks and construction materials of varying sizes. Each type of material should have its own box, and be kept on the floor space or ranged on open shelves close at hand. A car track with tunnels, bridges, trees and people will enhance and extend the play. Sturdy garages, houses and furniture all contribute to the development of the children's imaginative and role play. The small metal cars, buses, fire engines, ambulances, tractors, lorries, etc., should all have their own garage units close by into which the vehicles are put away after use. Cars found about the room should be regularly replaced, with children encouraged to share in keeping the floor play area looking inviting. A farm with animals can also be located here.

The floor play area should be protected from disturbing incursions by children not engaged in the play, and the number limited to a group of not more than four. 'Turns' need to be negotiated to permit concentrated and extended play.

Mark-making

The first scribbles and marks young children make are the beginnings of writing. We need to give them a range of tools to enable them to practise and develop their fine manipulative grasp, without curtailing the need for fingers and hands to be used primarily.

Although we have made practical suggestions for dividing the toddler room into 'areas' for different activities and for suitable resources, we should be clear that what is far more important is that the creativity of these very young children is recognised, supported and celebrated. This does not necessarily mean 'art activities'. Dorothy Selleck offers caution to practitioners about art activities for babies and children (Selleck 1997, p. 18). She describes how babies are deprived of the sensual creativity of using glue as finger paint when practitioners offer them glue pots and spreaders and paper to fix tissue or collage pieces. Bruce (1991) talks about the 'screwed up tissue paper syndrome' and the use of template outlines, something we have all seen and deplored. These are often about producing end products, mainly for parents, perhaps so that practitioners can demonstrate that their children have been busy during the nursery day. Far better that the babies' and toddlers' experiences are shared with parents through the use of the nursery camera – enabling practitioners to talk about the length of time spent engrossed in the sheer enjoyment of the play, the language and communication used to express pleasure, question and explore the materials offered.

We know these babies and young children would rather be smearing the glue or cornflour (gloop) across table top or high chairs, rolling their hands and fingers in it, pushing it, swirling it, rubbing their hands together and seeing the magic of changing paint colours. Tina Bruce (2004, p. 48) suggests that we seriously underestimate the creativity of children and we would argue that this includes the very youngest children, who we have observed being offered mundane adult-led activities with an 'end product' focus.

Providing for messy play

Lengths of wallpaper are useful for toddler rooms, rolled out on the floor or along the length of low tables. Paint may be offered or thick wax crayons. If paint, use wide pots or shallow buckets (recycled large glue buckets or readymade soup containers) and a

Figure 3.5 Providing for messy play

selection of brushes and rollers. This activity can be taken outside with buckets of water and large house-painting brushes to enable toddlers to 'paint' on the paving or patio areas, or 'wash' the walls and fences, delighting in the running of the water and the magic of drying times – where does the water go?

A two-sided easel is essential equipment, with a plentiful supply of paper securely clipped on. Easels can be of different heights, either commercially bought or a standard-size easel with legs cut off so that smaller children can reach. Aprons should be easily accessible. Paintings are best hung to dry on washing lines or clipped to the rungs of plastic clothes dryers with clothes pegs. Finger painting needs a Formica-topped table or the security of a high/low chair with its own tray. Hand washing facilities close by or a bowl of water and small towels will be needed. This is an example of an activity where even very young children can help to clean up afterwards. They will probably enjoy the clean-up just as much as the activity itself.

Sand play

A sand tray may be located in the group room if there is space, though it need not be available to the children all the time, and should be covered when not in use. If there is a 'wet' area available, this is obviously the best place to put it. To avoid waste, keep a clearly marked dustpan and soft brush together with a fine wire-mesh kitchen strainer hung up close to the tray. The children can be encouraged to brush up the sand regularly and sieve it back into the tray. Sand needs to be washed regularly. This is a task that children much enjoy. Using a diluted sanitizer or disinfectant will lengthen the life of the sand and prevent it from becoming smelly.

The equipment for use in the sand tray should be appropriate to its size, that is, not buckets and spades scaled to the outdoor sandpit, which are too large for an indoor tray. The small plastic plant pots from garden centres come in a useful variety of sizes and serve very well for filling and emptying of sand and making 'castles' and 'cakes'. Plastic scoops are less satisfactory than the metal ones used in hotel and restaurant kitchens for flour and sugar. Kitchen shops or pound shops are often a better source of items for the sand tray than educational suppliers' catalogues or toyshops.

The sand should sometimes be dry, but more usually kept damp to avoid the risk of it being flicked into eyes or hair. There must be an ample amount of sand if the children are to use it pleasurably. Most sand trays have too many implements and too little sand. Staff observing children in the sand need to take notice of this and frequently remove the objects that are less used, freeing space for other uses, such as making tracks and mounds. Equipment should be taken out of the sand tray at the end of the day and stored in a box beneath or beside the tray.

It is important that the sand play area does not become overcrowded. The adult who is supervising this part of the room needs to decide how many children can be comfortably accommodated at any one time and negotiate this with the children themselves.

Suggested items for the sand tray

- Colanders
- Sieves
- Plastic plant pots
- Metal/plastic scoops (from kitchen shops/pound shops)
- Measuring cups/spoons
- Small jelly moulds/cake moulds
- Patty tins
- Lolly sticks
- Pastry rollers (for mark making)
- Large pebbles (to bury)
- Shells (for mark making and burying)
- Other 'treasure' for burying.

Water play

This kind of play should take place throughout the nursery day: helping to wash and wipe toys and tables, washing dolls' clothes, watering plants and, above all, in the bathroom. The key person with her small group can allow the children unhurried time for experimentation with running water. Running taps provide the experience of trying to catch with finger and thumb the descending column of water and watching the swirl as it disappears down the drain. That experience is impossible in a crowded bathroom when any experiments are likely to lead to squirting and flooding, and may have to be firmly discouraged by staff!

When a water container is provided in the group room, as with the sand tray, it is helpful to provide a box for the smallest children to stand on, because if they are not at the right height, the water will constantly run down and wet their arms and elbows. Aprons should be hung nearby and be long enough to cover shoes, otherwise drips run down the front and soak the child's feet. Care should be taken to roll up cuffs and sleeves securely as wet sleeves can be very unpleasant. The water should be kept at a tepid temperature, with a towel accessible for drying hands. There should be a variety of equipment, not all in the water container at the same time as it is essential not to overcrowd it. Nursery workers should observe the quality of play and experimentation that the items offer and periodically weed them out and add new ones.

Suggested items for the water tray

- Cup with handle
- Small containers
- Tin with holes knocked in lower part
- Metal indoor plant watering can with thin spout
- Small metal teapot with hinged lid
- Funnels of different sizes

- Lengths of tubing, transparent and opaque
- Narrow-necked containers for filling and measuring
- Corks and ping-pong balls for floating
- Pebbles for sinking
- Small wooden bowl (for filling to sinking point).

One of the most dismal sights in a water tray is a 'drowned' doll floating face down. Bathing dolls should be a quite separate operation with its own equipment, consisting of a bowl, sponge, soap, a changing mat and small towels hanging neatly.

Summary

Because of the long hours that adults and children spend in day care centres, it is important to create an environment that is welcoming, comfortable and visually satisfying to all. Careful planning is needed to ensure that space is used to the best advantage. Ample, well-chosen materials, readily accessible, which encourage opportunities for child-initiated and self-directed play will enable the adult to choose the role of facilitator instead of always directing the children's activities.

Staff need to use their observations and knowledge of the changing and developing needs of the children to ensure that the organisation of the space for living, learning and playing is constantly reassessed.

4 Babies in day care

> The baby new to earth and sky,
> What time his tender palm is prest
> Against the circle of the breast,
> Has never thought 'that this is I'.
> (Tennyson)

In this chapter we will consider:

- The debate about babies in day care;
- Nurseries and childminders;
- Skills and attributes needed to work with babies;
- Building relationships and settling in;
- Feeding, nurturing and intimate care;
- Communication, play and learning;
- Creating a facilitating environment;
- Equipment and resources for babies.

It seems that hardly a week goes by without 'news' of research relating to babies and children under two in nurseries, and the possible effects of being in group care. As discussed in the previous chapter, research on brain chemistry has shown elevated levels of cortisol persisting through the day in young children separated from their mothers (Pereira-Gray 2013; Sunderland 2007). Belsky *et al.* (2007) found an association between early full-time day care, delay in communication and more aggressive behaviour, especially among boys. But the effects were not very great and much depends on the quality of the care setting. There is an extensive literature on the subject which can be most easily accessed on the 'What About The Children?' website.

Nursery or childminder?

A more perplexing question for mothers (usually) who have to return to work soon after having a baby is the choice between a childcare centre and a childminder. Fiona Fogarty and Helen Moylett, writing as mothers rather than professionals, describe how they made their different choices (Abbott and Moylett 1997). Typically, both were happy with the outcome, and their babies seemed to be happy too. It may be that this is more important than the particular form of care.

Our own experiences were also very different from each other. Ruth returned to work as a nurse doing some twilight shifts and sharing care with her husband. During the day she worked part-time for the Pre-school Learning Alliance both in pre-schools and then as a county organiser/tutor. She only started working full-time when her youngest child was in Year 3. Sonia has always worked full- or part-time, since her first child was born, except for one year, which she found the hardest in her life. Having experience of using both day nurseries and childminders, she has a strong preference for individualised care, especially for babies and very young children, but many mothers feel equally strongly that using a childcare centre with qualified, well-trained practitioners gives them greater security.

Whatever the decision, handing over your most precious possession to another adult is never easy, and for many parents working full-time and having to travel to work, the separation could be up to 50 hours a week. The workers' personal experiences of attachment and separation may influence practice and attitudes, both towards parents and their children (Manning-Morton 2006), and they will certainly have their own views about very young babies in group settings. In practice, the decision about whether, or how soon, to go back to work is seldom entirely within the mother's control. Economic pressures, conditions of employment and the still unsatisfactory provisions for maternity and parental leave often leave parents with very little choice. It is important for nursery practitioners to consider that families have to take decisions about childcare in the light of their particular circumstances. They should avoid the temptation to make judgements.

The skills and attributes of staff working with the youngest children

The most important quality for baby room practitioners is that they are interested in and enjoy being with babies. They must want to celebrate, and respond to the complexity of a baby's rapid development in the first year. As Elinor used to say, 'what a responsibility and what a privilege'. Practitioners will recognise and understand that the time they spend with babies is of value and importance: being able to observe objectively, record and talk to parents about what their baby has been doing during the day. And to do this they must develop a relationship with both parents and baby.

The key person approach was fully discussed in Chapter 2, so we will assume for this chapter that the setting is working to that essential principle.

If you were looking for someone to look after your new baby, and it couldn't be a close family member, what would you want that person to be like? What skills and knowledge would you expect them to have? The baby room practitioner under current regulations (DfE 2012b) has to have a minimum of two years' experience. In general, we agree that the baby room should be staffed by the most experienced and well-qualified practitioners. But we will all have known people who have a natural affinity with babies and they may not fit the 'most experienced and best qualified' label. Ensuring these staff members are offered opportunities for continuing professional development leading to a qualification gives a powerful message about the setting's commitment and how both staff and very young children are valued and respected.

When a group of mothers were asked how they went about choosing day care, they told Ruth that first impressions of the baby room and the staff at the time of their initial visit were crucial. One mother rejected a nursery when on a pre-arranged visit to look round the nursery, none of the baby room staff were in and there were no babies to be seen. She could get no idea of the people who would be responsible for her baby five days a week.

Certainly on a pre-arranged visit, at the very least, the senior practitioner in the baby room should have been available to talk to the mother, explain the nursery ethos and how the baby room works. Parents should be encouraged to look round several nurseries before making their choice, and organisations such as the Daycare Trust, Pre-school Learning Alliance, PACEY and National Day Nurseries Association all produce guides for parents about what to look for and what questions to ask. But perhaps one mother summed up her feelings best when she said 'I just want my baby to be loved'.

Being with babies is demanding, both physically and emotionally. As a nursery manager Ruth checked with the baby room staff regularly to make sure that they were not having a difficult time (especially if there were several new babies settling in), to offer support and if need be to suggest someone took a break. Simply to be another person in the room to help out for five minutes can be very important to reduce stress.

Building relationships

Settling in babies

Settling-in visits should be part of every nursery's admissions policy. Once a booking has been made, a start date agreed, and a key person allocated, relationship-building needs to begin. Paperwork is best done as part of the first visit, provided plenty of time is allowed. This enables the practitioner to extend the questions on the forms, and explain to parents the importance and relevance of the information requested. It is important that the paperwork is made accessible to families with limited understanding of English, or those with low levels of literacy. Some nurseries also schedule follow-up meetings with parents to discuss how the settling in is going, both for themselves and the baby. This provides an opportunity to get to know the parents on a more equal footing and find out how the nursery patterns and routines fit around home and work life. It should help the key person to begin to develop a bond with both child and parent, enabling them to begin to feel comfortable in the setting.

A new environment

The first few visits should include being introduced to all the new sights, sounds and smells that the baby will eventually encounter without the safety net of his familiar adult. Remember that the day-to-day tasks and routines that staff take for granted are the things that matter most to the baby – and naturally to the parent. The baby should be fed and changed during the settling-in visit so that staff can observe how parents carry out these important tasks.

He should be introduced to the place where he will be sleeping and be put into the cot or on a mattress by his mother initially and then by the key person. It is helpful for parents to bring in the baby's own bed linen to start with; the familiar smell will help reassure and settle him. Explaining to parents how a baby's powerful sense of smell links to emotional well-being reassures them that you have their baby's best interests at heart – not that the nursery is short of linen!

Feeding, nurturing and intimate care

Feeding

This is the basic experience for a baby. It not only means nourishment but sustained interaction with a close adult, an opportunity for communication that contributes to all aspects of his development.

Supporting breastfeeding

Breastfeeding has enormous health benefits for both babies and mothers. We know that babies who are *not* breastfed are at greater risk of a long list of medical conditions, such as gastro-intestinal infections, eczema and asthma, ear infections and obesity, and have an increased chance of developing type 2 diabetes later in life. The positive benefits for mothers of breastfeeding include lowering the risk of breast and ovarian cancer and using up more calories per day, helping them to return to a healthy weight. And, of course, breast milk is free.

It is important that childminders and nursery staff ask parents when they first visit how they currently feed their baby, and make it clear that they are fully committed to supporting breastfeeding, either through using expressed milk or enabling the mother to come into the setting during the day. With modern equipment for expressing milk there is no reason why babies in childcare settings should not be fed with breast milk using a bottle or a cup while they continue to be breastfed at home.

Childcare workers need to understand why this is well worth the small extra effort. When Ruth was managing a full day care setting, she arranged for a mother to come into the baby room every lunchtime to feed her baby. All the staff felt it important to support mum's wish to continue to feed when her son moved into the toddler room, and a quiet corner was found for her to do this, whilst the other babies and toddlers got on with the routines of lunch and nap time.

Respecting the baby's rhythms

When there is more than one baby to be bottle-fed, a real problem may face the nursery practitioner who has to harmonise as best she can the differing rhythms of each infant in the group. Although we no longer expect the sensations of a baby's stomach to correspond to the movement of hands on a clock, we still irrationally feel that it is unreasonable of a baby to demand a feed only an hour or so after the last one. We forget that he may then sleep for five or six hours without stirring. As the baby grows, his feeding rhythm will change, just as his sleep pattern does. It requires good observation and flexibility to ensure that it is the baby's individual needs and not nursery routine that sets the timetable, and that it is always the baby's key person who feeds him when she is present. In a busy room, there is a risk that she will be distracted from giving total quiet attention to him alone, which is as important as the milk he sucks. She needs to create an undisturbed corner to ensure that the experience is quite unhurried and comfortable for the baby as well as for herself.

When observing a baby at his mother's breast, or feeding from his bottle, we see that, of the nursing couple, it is the baby who is active, deciding the speed and the intensity with which he sucks, and the adult who responds to his movements, adapting the position of her arms and body to enable him to feed comfortably. The quality of their relationship is expressed in 'the primal gaze', the baby seeking intense eye contact as he feeds (Goldschmied 1974). An important question at this time is to see how his active role, so evident at the breast or bottle, can be fostered so that as soon as practicable he has direct contact with the food and can gain skill in manipulating it with fingers. This is the idea behind baby-led weaning, which may be requested by parents or introduced as part of the nursery's policy. If this is new to the practitioners it is crucial that they understand the principles and work closely with parents.

Baby-led weaning

Usually baby's mother will decide when to start complementing breast or bottle feeds with a first taste of solids. Baby-led weaning works on the principle that the baby is a competent learner and we should follow his cues. Most babies demonstrate when they are ready to try solid food. Rapley and Murkett (2008, p. 13) assert that 'most meals in any healthy cookbook can be easily adapted so that your six month old baby can share them'. It is, of course, essential that the family is eating a healthy and balanced diet. In the nursery, if meals are served using family service, babies sitting close to the table will be able to see what older children or the adults are eating, and they can be encouraged to try food if they appear interested.

As with all feeding, it is essential to talk with parents and ensure that the setting is following their wishes, respecting cultural and ethnic practices and offering babies a wide variety of foods to try as they move to a more solid diet (see also Chapter 9). Sarah, a practitioner in a baby room, told us about her first experience of baby-led weaning:

I was key person to two babies. Their parents were friends, and had met at the breast-feeding group held in the Children's Centre. When these parents came for their first settling-in visit, they explained to us about the baby-led weaning method and lent us the book – this helped our understanding. On the settling-in forms they did a separate sheet for instructions.

My first thought was it would be a high choking risk, and I was scared about offering and letting them choose 'chunks' of food instead of the purees and mashed food we would normally offer. However, once over the initial fear, we saw for ourselves how the babies had a choice of what to eat and how they ate, picking up their own food way before the spoon-fed babies do, and knowing what they like and don't like very early on. They also seem to have bigger appetites and enjoy their food more.

Compared with spoon-fed babies, those who are weaned on finger foods and feed themselves choose carbohydrates and vegetables over sweet things, leading to a lower BMI and a preference for healthier foods (Townsend and Pitchford 2012).

Figure 4.1 Discovering new tastes

Changing nappies

Changing nappies is a very intimate experience for both baby and practitioner. Most settings will have procedures related to this process regarding hygiene and how and where nappies are changed. However, for the baby new to the setting, it may be very different from what he is used to at home when nappy-changing might happen in the bathroom, on the floor, on the settee, or on a lap. Do the parents use commercial wipes, or cotton wool and warm water, creams and lotions? Is there a special song or rhyme that goes with their changing routine? The key person must find out all these details, and keep the information updated. Disposable nappies remain the most widely used, but, given the cost of disposables, both to the environment and to the family purse, more and more families are turning to modern cloth nappies, which are now far better designed and more convenient to use.

Enjoying and playing at change time
Having mirrors and mobiles at eye level or baby height, to engage (or sometimes distract) the baby while nappy-changing goes on, ensures it is also fun. The key person needs to find out from parents what baby's favourite changing song or rhyme is and learn it if it is new to her. Nappy-changing time is the perfect opportunity to have some face-to-face time and close eye contact, and 'tummy time' can be introduced, as discussed later.

Communication, play and learning

Understanding the communications of babies depends on intimate knowledge of their patterns of behaviour and close observation of their reactions from one moment to the next, very well illustrated by the picture sequences in *The Social Baby* (Murray and Andrews 2000). Parents develop this knowledge over the first few weeks after the baby's birth but nursery workers do not have the opportunity to do that. Exchanging information during the initial visits and settling-in period is therefore vital. Parents must be allowed time to talk about the ways in which they and the baby communicate. We know that even the very youngest do this through gestures, sounds and facial expressions. The photographs and observations in Murray and Andrews' book show babies from birth copying their parents' expressions and communicating through a range of sounds and gestures.

Crying: one of the 'hundred languages'

When they cry, babies are communicating that all is not well. But a baby's cry indicates many different needs, and only the adult with whom he is building a relationship of closeness, his key person, is likely to understand what it means. Elfer *et al.* (2003) question whether settings where many different adults interact with babies can reliably offer such 'attuned and sensitive responsiveness'.

There is great natural variation in the amount of time babies spend crying, and it also differs from month to month. Babies who hardly ever cried in their first few weeks will suddenly go through a phase of what seems to their parents to be continuous screaming. On the whole though, babies cry for a reason, and a persistent background of crying in a nursery indicates something lacking in the care that is being offered. Very little crying is heard in high-quality settings.

So why is this baby crying? He may be experiencing hunger, pain, physical discomfort, loneliness, overstimulation, or maybe just a general feeling of sadness at being away from his mother. When a baby's screams persist and he seems unable to accept our comfort, we sometimes feel an impulse to hand him to someone else, but this gives him the message that he is being rejected. Sometimes we just have to acknowledge his distress until it comes to a natural end. We can then reassure him by listening intently and by saying in our quietest, gentlest voice, 'I don't yet understand what you are trying to tell me, but be sure I will not leave you'. This is much more effective than the agitated pats, jiggling up and down and anxious chatter with which adults often express their own feelings when a baby will not stop crying.

It is worth remembering that some nursery staff, as infants, may have experienced the now discredited practice of leaving babies to cry until they stop from sheer exhaustion. We would not leave a deeply distraught friend in solitude if we could possibly help it, so why do this to babies who cannot even speak in words? Making connections of this kind may help to guide us in our handling of the babies for whom we care.

Listening to and learning from the baby

Goldschmied and Selleck's early publication and the video that accompanied it, *Communication Between Babies in Their First Year* (Goldschmied and Selleck 1996), showed how very complex babies' early communication is. Through verbal and non-verbal language they tell us about how they are feeling, how they offer friendship and empathy, and turn away to say when they have had enough (Murray and Andrews 2000). We know that babies can hear in the womb and that they respond to and recognise their mother's voice, long before they meet her. Very soon after birth they turn towards mother or father's voice and listen to the changing sounds around them (Trevarthen 2004). Fascinated by faces, babies need to be held close, where that close face-to-face contact shows affection and offers comfort. Babies are born with the ability to make their close adults engage with them. Who can resist the baby as he beams and coos in delight at our silly songs and action games?

Babies very early on learn to interpret cues and play conversational games, which contribute to later language development. Trevarthen (2004) termed these 'proto-conversations' which usually take place during the first three months of life. Our own observations of babies at the Treasure Basket show how older babies, from about six months, initiate conversations, offering or taking objects to and from other seated babies (Forbes 2004).

Babies who are talked to are talkative. It is important for practitioners to be tuned in to the gestures and signs used by babies before and as they become vocal and to be aware that not all babies come from homes which offer a good environment for language development. For some parents singing, playing rhyme games or simply talking to their baby does not come easily or naturally. For these babies, the key person plays a crucial role.

'Motherese' or infant-directed speech (IDS) will be recognised by most parents and practitioners as the way we spontaneously talk to very young babies. It tends to be slower than usual speech patterns and accompanied by exaggerated facial expressions. There are more pauses allowing for a response from the baby. Trevarthen (2004) describes it as having a rich musical quality with clear rhythm and melody. Babies enjoy this sing-song way of communication. They begin to respond and join in, and it is an important element of the face-to-face interactions between practitioners and babies that are a source of early learning and self-regulation (Whitebread and Basilio 2012).

Books and stories

Babies need and love books. From a very early age they enjoy the experience of looking at the book and hearing the adult's voice, as she describes the pictures and tells the story as they snuggle up together. Telling stories using the expressive language of 'motherese' will bring the book to life. Babies quickly learn to anticipate the turning of the page. Ruth (Forbes 2004) describes an observation where an eight-month-old is caught on

Figure 4.2 Never too soon to enjoy a book (Photograph: Ellen-Raissa Jackson)

video, holding a book with one hand, lifting the book towards her, turning the book 180 degrees and 'telling' the story to the room. The baby was imitating the exact hand movements of her key person.

Rudolph Steiner believed that engagement with books and reading and writing should be discouraged until what seems to us a very late age – seven at the earliest. In an imaginary conversation with Cathy Nutbrown he explains that before that children should be engaging with the natural world and each other, hearing stories told, not read, learning from their own exploration and first-hand experience (Nutbrown *et al.* 2012). However, because literacy is so central to our educational culture, it is very difficult for children not familiar with books to function in an ordinary primary school. It is an advantage for children from a very early age to see how adults handle books and recognise them as a source of interest and pleasure. We believe in offering access to books to the youngest children, from babyhood onwards.

Choosing books for the baby room

There should be an assortment of books with real photographs and others illustrated with sketches or drawings. The content should reflect the setting, community and society, and staff should check books for stereotypical and negative images. (See also Chapters 6 and 8.)

Bookstart offers many resources for parents to encourage an early interest in books, with suggestions for suitable titles. Many Children's Centres offer one-to-one work with families in their homes using the Bookstart resources as a way of engaging with families who might not ordinarily think of reading to their babies and young children. Both at home and in a childcare setting some books (regularly checked and maintained) should be easily accessible to babies, and can be kept in attractive baskets, or sturdy boxes covered in sticky-back plastic. The baby will then have the opportunity to make decisions about which book to choose, and whether to look at it alone or with an adult.

A useful tip for using damaged books is to rescue the good pages, and laminate them. They can be used as part of displays, as labels or simply as a single page to trigger a conversation.

Music and rhyme

We all have favourite pieces of music, and music that we play to match our moods; it can calm, soothe or stir us up (Turner and Ioannides 2009). Children respond to music from a very early age – in fact the famous Japanese violin teacher, Shinichi Suzuki, advocated playing Bach and Vivaldi to babies in the womb. This idea, originally treated with ridicule, has now become a commonplace. From about 22 weeks gestation the foetus is experiencing music and other sounds (Powers and Trevarthen 2009) and many mothers will tell of pieces of music that they listened to during pregnancy which have a soothing effect on their new baby. In fact, Sonia's youngest grandchild, Freyda, before she was born, reacted quite differently to Mozart and Steve Reich (whose music is very percussive) – the latter provoking vigorous kicking.

Babies in their first year respond to music by chuckling and crowing and by musical babbling, which is quite distinct from speech babbling. Moog (1976), researching children's musical preferences, found that when they are very small they seem to like simple instrumental music best, but by the second year most children prefer songs with words. Singing with babies is important and practitioners need to be encouraged to use their own voices and sing regularly with the babies in their care. There are many examples of children under one year joining in family songs, babies discriminating between sounds and recognising melodies. Mary Fawcett suggests that this confirms that music is a biological given and that everyone is born with musical potential (Fawcett 2012; Malloch and Trevarthen 2009). The babies and mothers in Figure 4.3 enjoy singing and using simple sound makers during their under-ones session, being introduced to new songs and bringing their family favourites to the group. 'Baby music' sessions are offered by many Children's Centres.

Practitioners might begin with songs already known, perhaps from their own childhood or family. Babies will enjoy a range of songs and rhymes; gentle lullabies that are slower in pace to soothe or rock a sleepy baby, lively dance or folk tunes at other times. In the baby room music should include a mix of improvised movement and dance, very carefully chosen recorded music and, above all, singing by the staff.

Trevarthen (2004, p. 19) suggests that very young babies express themselves through their hand movements, in a form of 'dance', especially when their mother is singing or

Figure 4.3 Mums and babies in a Children's Centre baby music group

speaking, and that deaf babies under one year may begin 'sign babble' just as hearing babies do sound babble. By about four to six months babies will be predicting the timing and rhyming of baby songs.

Movement – mobility leads to play and learning

During the first year, babies acquire and develop many movement patterns. This is how they learn about themselves and their environment. As Ouvry (2000, p. 12) reminds us, Piaget, Bruner and Donaldson all assert that for our youngest children movement is 'thought in action'. Children have to first experience the world actively before they can hold thoughts or memories of those experiences as ideas or symbols. Babies need space and opportunity to practise and develop these movement patterns. In addition to the five senses of touch, smell, taste, hearing and sight, the sense of movement of our body (the kinaesthetic sense) is a vital element in the growth of our own self-image. Movement, in a restricted space, is already very much a part of the experience of the infant in the womb (how often do we hear the laughing complaint that 'baby seems to have football boots on!').

In infancy this sense grows fast when freedom of movement allows the baby to take tiny risks, which create confidence as to what she can attempt and achieve. Through movement she begins to learn about herself and her environment. As she starts to stretch and kick out with busy arms and legs, she begins to find out where they begin and where they end – how long and how wide she is. A baby lying upon her back on a firm but comfortable surface – a blanket on the floor is safest – will use the opportunity to the full to stretch and squirm and roll and heave. In this way she can make contact freely with her feet and hands as understanding grows that they are her own extremities. Bare feet are essential for this so that toes can be grasped and sucked. This also allows the baby to use a big toe to lever herself in rolling on to her stomach and back again, to her evident delight and satisfaction.

Baby massage

Baby massage sessions, offered in many Children's Centres, and some nurseries, are a good way of helping mothers to stroke and touch their babies. Massage not only relaxes babies, it increases their emotional and physical well-being and strengthens attachment bonds between baby and parent. For some women with post-natal depression (PND), holding and touching their baby may be a struggle, and baby massage taught and demonstrated by a sensitive, qualified practitioner can be helpful. It is soothing and calming for agitated or restless babies. Massage releases tensions between baby and adult and offers an opportunity for them to get to know each other better. As the limbs are gently stretched and stroked, the beginnings of 'who am I, where do I begin and end and where do you (the adult) begin and end?' are explored. Baby massage sessions observed by Ruth in the Children's Centres are an oasis of calm and quiet, with some babies sleeping deeply by the end of it. The mothers make very close eye-to-eye contact with their babies and talk quietly, responding to their babies' suggestions from the tiny movements of an arm or a leg. As Veronica Sherborne (1990, p. 38) said, 'all movement play is a form of conversation'.

Baby massage, baby yoga and other movement programmes are already part of many baby room routines and provide intervals of calm and enjoyment in the busy day. Enabling a member of staff to train as a baby massage practitioner would be an excellent investment.

Back and front

Babies need to be put on their stomachs or have 'tummy time' from birth, for short intervals, always with their elbows bent beneath their chin, so that the head is free to turn about. This is particularly important for babies today as it appears they spend an increasing amount of time in car seats or bouncy cradle-type seats. Since the Back to Sleep Campaign was launched, recommending that all healthy babies should sleep on their backs to reduce the risk of SIDS (sudden infant death syndrome or cot death), it seems that parents and practitioners have been reluctant to put babies on their fronts, even for short periods of time.

'Tummy time' is promoted and encouraged by health professionals and recognised as important not only for physical development, but for neurological development as well (KCH-NHS electronic source 2012; O'Connor and Daly 2009; Sherborne 1990). Being on their front helps to build the networks in the baby's brain that lead to higher thinking (Goddard Blythe 2009). Tummy time during the first nine months, along with opportunities and encouragement for babies to crawl, creep, take part in rough and tumble play, songs and games are the essentials for developing the neural networks affected by movement.

Tummy time from birth to around nine months – some suggestions

- A few minutes per day for newborns, increasing to 30 minutes per day;
- Use an exercise ball – place baby on his tummy on the ball, support your hand on his back or bottom, roll the ball gently forward;
- Try 1–2 minutes of tummy time during nappy change. Placing a rolled up blanket under his chest makes it easier for him to look up – encourage this with something shiny to look at or a brightly coloured toy;
- Tummy down carry – one hand between his legs and one hand under his chest.

Moving onwards and upwards!

Babies should be given plenty of opportunity to be on the floor during their nursery day. They need a supportive adult to lie alongside them or in front of them to encourage them to extend their head and begin to roll over. Soon, if inviting objects are put close in front of her, a baby will learn to transfer her weight to one shoulder, leaning on that

Figure 4.4 Tummy time builds networks in the brain

bent arm to free the other to stretch out and grasp the object which attracts her. In her efforts to reach out, the baby starts to make humping 'seal-like' movements, inching forward as the idea of crawling seems to grow. Practitioners may feel self-conscious as they lie on the floor encouraging a baby to rock from side to side or roll from front to back, but these are all important movements, encouraging a baby to get on to all fours ready to creep.

Babies cannot sit until they have gained control of first their head and neck, then the trunk; sitting comes next, and finally standing. Similarly, their manipulative abilities begin with reaching, then grasping, then releasing.

Young children seem to know when they want to pull themselves to an upright position but they need secure points on which to do this, which in a nursery should be provided. Some adults have the tendency to pull children on to their feet too soon, for even the most efficient crawling seems to make them feel uneasy. It is worthwhile to pause and consider how much safer it is for the infant to remain crawling until he is physically more mature, and there will be a shorter period when he will need to make frantic grabs on the closest furniture or person to sustain his wobbling steps. If you ever tried to ice skate, think how it felt the first few times you went on the ice! The key person will naturally support the newly mobile baby in his quest for independence, recognising those moments when a hand is needed to walk across the room or when baby wants to be left alone to negotiate the space, no matter how insecure his balance.

When a baby has mastered crawling and is enjoying his new-found freedom to explore, it is wise to teach him how to manage stairs in safety. We show the child how to sit on the top step and turn himself around with hands on one step and bended knees on the step below. If shown a few times how to go down on hands and knees facing backwards he will soon become most proficient, protected from the risk of falling. It is all too easy for someone to leave a stair-gate open, and teaching toddlers to manage stairs themselves as soon as possible is an important safeguard.

Creating a facilitating baby room environment

There is no division between care, learning, play and work for the child, and knowledgeable practitioners are aware of this, recognising that a rich curriculum will underpin the whole of the baby room day. It is essential that the staff who will be working in the space should be fully involved; they will have a sound understanding of their key children's needs and stage of development. The aim for an excellent baby room, then, is one where the environment meets the individual and changing needs of the children, and where each child's well-being, sense of self and holistic development are nurtured and promoted. The 'curriculum' is not something that fills in the gaps between meals, nappy-changing and other key care routines. The close interactions that occur at these times *are* the curriculum.

The EYFS (DfE 2012b) requires that each area of learning and development for babies and children should be implemented through planned, purposeful play and through a mix of adult-led and child-initiated activities. Staff should use their knowledge of the individual needs, interests and stage of development of each child to plan a challenging and enjoyable experience.

Security and stability

Babies need most things around them to remain the same, to be constant, to know that their key person will meet and greet them in the morning, that their cot or favourite rest space will be there when they are tired, that the book they really enjoyed yesterday will be available today, and lunch is always served at the same time – or nearly always! This kind of predictability gives babies confidence to get the most from their day in an out-of-home care setting. It means staff should consider carefully how they set up the baby room and how often they change it round. The key person should be asking herself 'what does my special child need now, at this particular moment?'

The baby room should encompass spaces where babies can play together or be alone, develop a sense of self-identity, foster close relationships, interact with adults and other babies and toddlers and feel that they belong.

Safe spaces, play spaces, quiet spaces
We need to provide an active learning environment designed for both non-mobile and mobile babies. Spaces for:

Figure 4.5 A place to be quiet and watch (Photograph: Community Playthings)

- Physical play – moving and doing – inside and outside; opportunities for large and small motor experiences – babies need to be able to kick and reach at interesting items strung above them; mats for rolling on; slopes to wriggle or crawl up; low steps or platforms; opportunities to see the room from a different height or angle;
- Sensory experiences – lights, music, a range of tactile materials, flowers, herbs, resources to support the exploration of colour, sound, size, shape and weight (see Chapter 5);
- Quiet/social opportunities – where babies and adults can snuggle up, look at a book together or have a rest, or simply watch what's going on around the room;
- Cognitive experiences – investigating, thinking and imagination – this is where babies will have opportunities for exploring objects, collecting, sorting and classifying, beginning to learn about object permanence, and cause and effect.

Frame the room

Look at the space and think how to make the best use of it. Varying heights of dividers offer the opportunity for quiet spaces, hideaways, and dens. Partitions might be perspex, mirrored or solid; others might have a magnetic finish or a washable side for mark-making. A horizontal mirror on the wall just above the skirting board is helpful for non-mobile babies lying or seated to become aware of who they are and just enjoy their reflections. Ensure that it is positioned at the correct height; test it out on babies lying on their backs and tummies. Fixing a length of banister rail to a wall (perhaps with another mirror behind it) supports those babies beginning to stand. Spaces will be of different sizes and very dependent on the shape of the room – some large, some considerably smaller. Do consider, though, how much space a crawling, cruising or wobbly walker needs to get about. Use furniture and equipment to work out how you can 'close' areas at certain times by using gates.

Most important is to watch how the space is used by adults and babies alike. Do we give non-mobile babies the opportunity to lie close and get to know each other? This can only be tested by putting ourselves in the place of those babies and lying on the floor – what could a baby see and reach? Is it interesting, stimulating, are there things to encourage them to reach, swipe, listen to, and can they see out of a low-level window? Having to step over babies in the middle of the room on the way to the bathroom or main exit indicates that routes and zoning need some attention. It can be useful to have someone from outside the centre or room to observe during the course of the day. Monitoring what can often be reported by staff as the 'trickier' times of the day (arrivals, meals, preparation for going out for a walk or into the garden, departure times) can also help inform the use of furniture and resources.

Surfaces

Think colour, texture and purpose: does it need to be waterproof, soft and welcoming, or easy to clean? Floor areas might be a combination of carpeted for quiet areas and non-slip easy-clean for paint, water and sand play. A mixture of tables and easels, and possibly areas of the wall where paper can be fastened and wall 'painting' allowed. The floor space and surface should allow for small and large trucks, and for push-along toys and balls to be rolled.

Storage

Some storage will be open and accessible to the babies, some will be at adult height, and some will be locked. Staff usually have very clear thoughts about what is needed in terms of storage. It is useful to look around and see how the space is being used. Too much clutter and things being left on the side mean either not enough storage or a lack of care and pride in the workspace.

Sights, smells and sounds

Greenman and Stonehouse (1997) pose a seemingly simple question: 'How wonder-ful is your home-base?' The challenge is to walk into your baby/toddler room and get a measure of the sensory environment on offer. Is there the scent of herbs, flowers and plants or food cooking in the kitchen, or is the prevailing smell of disinfectant, or worse, of babies who need changing? Can we hear laughter (cooing and gurgling from young babies) from adults and children, 'silly voices and rapt silence' (p. 199).

They have a useful audit tool which we have adapted and used with staff during discussions about creating a sensory baby and toddler environment. Does the description of your baby room match theirs? Have you created places for:

concentration, creativity, hide-away places, quiet places, noisy spaces, empty spaces for daydreaming and daydreamers . . . astonishment, lovely, mysterious, transformations, thrilling, joyful . . .

(Greenman and Stonehouse 1997, p. 200)

Equipment and resources for babies

There are an increasing number of resources designed for babies, some of them very useful, but others which should be looked at with a critical eye. They may be intended to make the adult's task easier, but not necessarily to the benefit of the child. However limited the budget, it is worth investing in strong, high-quality wooden equipment.

Buggies

The folding pushchair or buggy has virtually replaced the pram and revolutionised mobility for parents and practitioners. However, a serious drawback is that they are mostly designed so that the baby faces forward. This means that the baby cannot keep eye contact with his adult and conversation is inhibited.

In a buggy, the baby finds himself in a kind of moving plastic limbo, carving a way between oncoming legs and feet. Any adult who has been pushed in a wheelchair through a hurrying crowd will tell you that the experience of meeting this human flood can be quite disturbing. A baby can only hope to hear the occasional disembodied adult voice to reassure him that he is not alone in space. Nurseries and childminders should try to obtain pushchairs that enable a baby to face the person pushing him and be sure of his adult's continuing presence. Research by Suzanne Zeedyk for the National Literacy Trust has shown that if the baby is facing you, you are twice as likely to talk as when your baby is facing away from you; there is the opportunity to make eye contact and offer instant reassurance (Zeedyk 2008, electronic source). The study also found that babies in inward-facing buggies were twice as likely to be sleeping as those in away-facing buggies. This could be related to the babies being more relaxed and their stress levels being lower.

Baby walkers – a health warning

A common type of baby walker to be avoided is a circular frame on small wheels. The child leans on the frame and propels himself with his toes. This activity may give an illusion to the adults that a child is learning to walk. In fact it may delay walking, as the child is not learning the essential ingredient of balance, and the feet are not well placed on the ground. In addition, this type of walker can be extremely dangerous because of the great speed with which an otherwise relatively immobile infant can move around. And of course, babies in baby walkers are unable to explore the environment fully. The Chartered Society of Physiotherapists advocates a total ban on the use of baby walkers

Figure 4.6 A durable wooden truck, with many uses

on the basis of research which shows an association between their use and a delay in development.

A much better form of baby walker or pushcart, is a strong low wooden truck, heavy enough not to tip up, with a handle at shoulder level which gives support and confidence and which will not go fast when pushed by a child who is practising first steps. The truck can also be used for loading wooden bricks or other objects and is sometimes used instead of a doll's pram. It is worth investing in the very best quality that can be afforded because this is a piece of equipment with really long-term value.

Play equipment for babies

An abundance of toys in the form of animals of all kinds, some attractive and others grotesque, find their way into nurseries. A clear distinction needs to be made between a favourite personal soft toy, animal, traditional teddy or doll, and the indiscriminate collection of such items which frequently clutter up a nursery.

The baby's or child's special object, which may also be a piece of woolly blanket or other material, has for a long time been understood by most adults to have a real significance for a child. Many parents will have had the experience of hearing a frantic wail 50 miles down the motorway as realisation dawns that Teddy has been left behind. There is nothing for it but to turn round and go back. Attachments to familiar and well-used objects persist into our adult lives. These personal objects should be treated with proper respect by caregivers and always kept where the children can have easy access to them.

However, nurseries and crèches often accumulate large numbers of poorly designed soft toys and animals with no personal meaning for the children. These animals are frequently of plastic, which by no stretch of the imagination could be called 'cuddly', or of synthetic materials with an unpleasant texture. Staff would do well to have a regular and rigorous sorting out and casting away of these items which use up valuable storage space. They can be replaced with a smaller number of good quality, realistic animals covered in natural fabrics with interesting textures.

The following items, many of them suggested in practitioner workshops, will engage the sitting baby's developing manipulative skill and produce an immediate result, encouraging repetition and practice.

What's inside?

For initiating this kind of play the adult needs various containers such as strong egg boxes, small baskets or boxes (with easy to pull off lids) and cardboard cylinders. Suitable items to put in them are ping-pong balls, golf-balls, shells, short lengths of chain, cotton reels, film containers (if these are still to be found – we found some in a recycling centre), pom-poms, corks. The baby will enjoy opening the container and discovering what is inside, first simply emptying out and later beginning to replace items or sliding them through the cylinders. These are very good toys for interactive play between babies and adults. The adult's job is to keep the collections in containers ready for use and not scattered about. By the end of his first year the baby becomes increasingly fascinated by the activity of putting objects into containers and emptying them out. This is a precursor to heuristic play (see Chapter 7).

Photo-tins
The key person makes the photo-tin with the help of the parents. Collect some family photos – Mum, Dad, Grandma, and siblings. Cover a large cylindrical tin with white paper and then stick on the photos. Remember to attach them with the tin in a horizontal position so that as it rolls the baby can see the images. Cover the tin with sticky-

back plastic and replace the plastic lid. Making one of these is also a useful thing to do as part of the settling-in process. Asking parents for the photos and talking about the other important people in the baby's life reassures families that their baby is being cared for in an environment that respects and values what is happening at home. This idea can be adapted according to the imagination and creativity of the practitioner.

In Ruth's baby rooms there were also tins with pictures or photos of familiar animals – dogs, cats, sheep, cows, etc. – and inside the tin were finger puppets or very small soft toys of the corresponding animal. As well as rolling the tin towards baby and making one of the animal noises, you could then open the tin and 'find' the animal. This initiates further conversations, promoting early language skills.

Crawling and creeping

Have a variety of large blocks covered in carpet, soft play-blocks, and big cushions/bean bags to offer a variety of height. Or fill a quilt cover with some partly blown up balloons – so that they are still quite soft – and let the babies crawl over it; the effect is like a soft mountain.

Introducing a range of textures

Cellophane scrunched up into a ball can be rolled towards seated or lying babies, for them to grasp and explore. Seated babies will enjoy reaching into small buckets or containers for the cellophane ball and enjoying both its texture and the accompanying noise. It will go into their mouths, so watch carefully and don't leave them alone with it.

One use for our collections of scarves is to push a couple of them into a kitchen towel cardboard roll, leaving a tempting piece hanging, ready for the baby to pull out. Small square tissue boxes can also be stuffed with scarves – nylon or chiffon types are best. A baby's hand will just fit in, so put some interesting things such as the pieces of scrunched up foil; a velvet bow tie; long lengths of ribbon and chain; strings of beads.

Summary

Caring well for babies in a group setting can be difficult and costly. The more we get to know about babies, the more complex the work becomes. To be truly responsive to their fluctuating needs, ever-changing rhythms and subtly varied communications requires an individualised approach or system of care so that the key person can get to know her special children and their families well. Practitioners need to be aware of the reasons parents have chosen to use childcare for their baby and avoid judgemental attitudes. They need to be sensitive to the mixed feelings that many parents experience in leaving their young babies. Making close personal relationships with other people's babies is demanding, professionally and personally.

Babies need interest and variety in their lives as much as older children, and careful thought should be given to the environment in which they spend their days and the playthings offered to them. Working with babies in day care has changed significantly over the last couple of decades. Advances in neuroscience, regulatory changes, parents working longer hours and the increase in provision across the sector have led to much higher expectations of what a quality environment for our youngest children should look like and how it should be delivered.

5 The Treasure Basket

When an Aboriginal mother notices the first stirrings of speech in her child, she lets it handle the 'things' of that particular country: leaves, fruit, insects and so forth. The child, at its mother's breast, will toy with the 'thing', talk to it, test its teeth on it, learn its name, repeat its name.

(Bruce Chatwin, *The Songlines*)

In this chapter we will consider:

- Introducing the Treasure Basket to parents, practitioners and babies;
- What's in the basket?
- First steps in decision-making;
- The adult's role;
- Questions and answers about the use of the basket;
- Collecting items for the basket.

Since the first two editions of this book were published, the Treasure Basket has become a staple item of equipment for every childminder and baby room offering care for the under-ones, and appears in the portfolio of nearly every early years student. However they do not necessarily understand the principles behind the model. This has resulted in the term 'Treasure Basket' being applied in ways that deviate very far from the original concept. The Treasure Basket is specifically designed for a particular age group: babies aged six to nine months, who are sitting up but not yet independently mobile. It is not simply a random collection of playthings in a container but a basket of a particular design, containing very carefully chosen objects designed to stimulate the baby's senses and brain development. In later chapters we suggest how the Treasure Basket principles might be extended for use with older children, but we reserve the name 'Treasure Basket' for its original function, as a means of engaging the interest and concentration of those youngest children before they can move.

The idea for the Treasure Basket grew out of Elinor's close observation of hundreds of babies over many years (Goldschmied 1987). She understood that babies were demonstrating very clearly that they were bored by the limited playthings typically offered to them. She suggested that, instead of making the assumption that the babies were simply 'grizzling' or 'teething' (the usual explanation) their close adults should look at what was being offered to interest them and support them in beginning to play and learn by themselves.

The Treasure Basket at its simplest is a basket crammed full of objects, safely selected and specifically chosen by an adult, with items generally not regarded as toys, but objects from the natural and the made world (Forbes 2004). Elinor was adamant that there should be no plastic in the Treasure Basket, as babies are exposed to so much plastic in their daily lives: feeding bottles, cups, plates, cutlery, toys, nursery furniture, etc. that she felt that the basket should be a 'no plastic zone'. We have passed this message on as part of training and introducing practitioners and parents to our own baskets. However Ruth was able to argue with Elinor for the inclusion of a coiled, blue fibreglass wine bottle stopper which had an interesting texture and added some colour to the basket. Clearly someone else agreed, as it disappeared during a training session and never returned.

Elinor told Ruth that she wanted to cry at some of the 'Treasure Baskets' she had been asked to look at in childcare centres she had visited. Some were filled with broken, uninteresting objects, too big for a baby to handle and in containers that ranged from a tiny basket left over from Christmas hyacinths with space for no more than four

Figure 5.1 Ruth's Treasure Basket

objects, to huge laundry baskets with contents that 'looked like the sale section of a kitchen shop'.

> if you put a common object in the Treasure Basket it has to be a very good one, not inferior, otherwise the Treasure Basket becomes the rubbish basket, and that is why a badly collected Treasure Basket is the worst possible advertisement because it denigrates something which could be, should be, appreciated – therefore it's got to be safe, it's got to be beautiful.
>
> (Forbes 2004, p. 65)

The actual basket, which we examine in more detail later, is as important as its contents. Elinor spent a lot of time observing babies, indeed this was her skill and her passion. Her observations and subsequent discussions with physiotherapists and colleagues trained in the Alexander Technique, resulted in her very precise specification for the basket (see page 90).

Introducing the Treasure Basket to parents and practitioners

Adults encountering the Treasure Basket for the first time quickly become fascinated by the notion of collections. They remember their own childhood experiences of playing with items from the kitchen cupboard or rummaging in their mother's handbag, and observe how their own babies enjoyed clutching at the bunch of keys that they carried around with them, or textured mats from the coffee table, finding things that were never designed for babies infinitely more alluring than the plastic or furry objects typically offered to them. Most parents immediately connect with the interesting objects and collections and the sensory element of the Treasure Basket. They can be assured of the safe selection and care given to the nursery baskets and be encouraged to contribute items or to develop their own basket for use at home. The nurseries and Children's Centres where Ruth worked lent out baskets, with instructions, after workshop sessions. This inspired parents to explore the possibilities around them, to encourage safe and sensible reuse of found and real household objects. Parents brought in items for the community baskets, describing how their own baby had enjoyed the object. The possibilities of bulk-buying were explored: someone bought a box of wooden egg cups and split them between several baskets. Other people found dolly pegs from a craft supplier, reasonably priced items from a discount store and lovely material from a market stall.

Choosing, sharing and being able to make confident selections for the Treasure Basket gives parents and practitioners a sense of ownership and responsibility for the selected objects and ensures that regular checks are carried out, whether at home or in a group setting.

Introducing the Treasure Basket to the baby

Between five and nine months, most babies will be sitting safely; this is the right time to offer the experience of a Treasure Basket. At first they will need to be supported, propped with pillows or cushions, to enable the muscles in their back to begin to strengthen. At this stage babies frequently topple over or flop forwards as they begin to gain control and are propped or supported to sit. This is because their neuromuscular control has not fully developed, and as it starts from the head downwards, control of head and neck comes before control of the trunk (McCall and Craft 2000). Once babies are able to sit unsupported they get a new sense of autonomy, are able to see things around them from a different perspective, and gain a degree of control over objects and events. However sitting also brings frustrations. Interesting things seem to be out of reach or prohibited by adults from further exploration.

Collecting safely

A list of suggested objects to begin collecting for your Treasure Basket is given at the end of the chapter; however there are a few principles that need to be observed when collecting. The most important thing to bear in mind is that everything in your basket

Figure 5.2 Involvement and concentration (but bare feet are better) (Photograph: University of Roehampton)

will go into a baby's mouth, and be licked, sucked, chewed and dribbled on. This means all items must be checked for choking hazard. Ensure everything can be washed or wiped, or is considered disposable

The Treasure Basket allows babies to use all of their senses – sight, smell, hearing, taste, touch and what Elinor referred to as the sixth sense, that of kinaesthesia, or the sense of movement. At the basket babies are encouraged and enabled to explore and begin to play with their whole body, especially using their mouths, and their feet.

The purpose of collecting these objects is to engage all the baby's senses:

- Touch: texture, shape, weight;
- Smell: variety of scents;
- Taste: more limited scope, but possible;
- Sound: ringing, tinkling, banging, scrunching;
- Sight: colour, form, length, shininess.

The objects should come from the natural and the real world, so good examples would be a small beautifully turned wooden bowl (think of the size of a baby's hand) or a piece of drift wood, warm to the touch, smoothed by the incoming tides and free from splinters; a large pebble, again smooth, always feeling cold, and different in colour depending on the area of country it was found in; an onyx or marble 'egg' maybe textured or smooth, again of a size that can be manipulated and handled by the small but eager fingers of a young baby; a bunch of keys, the edges smoothed by years of wear and use, not sharp or they will cut inquisitive lips and mouths.

Avoid objects that have been artificially scented, often shaped into fruit; these will, in the main, have had chemicals added to the wood, and should not be offered for babies to suck and mouth. Far better to have naturally scented pieces of turned wood, and real fruit (replaced regularly) such as a lemon, lime, apple or orange. Metal objects like whisks should be especially carefully selected. For instance, some of the cheap 'milk frother' type whisks are made of several thin pieces of wire that easily come apart and can be very sharp. Instead choose one, about 15 cm in height, from a good kitchen shop, in which the handle and whisk section are completely moulded together. Babies love them but they need to be chosen with great care (Forbes 2004).

It goes without saying that nothing in the basket should be chipped or broken. However, Treasure Baskets are not always treated with the love and respect they deserve and in extreme cases this can even be dangerous for the babies using them. Practitioners collecting and selecting objects for baskets in group or out-of-home settings must be extra vigilant about the maintenance of the basket and its contents.

Some questions for organisers and practitioners

- Have all the staff experienced some training and participated in discussion about the use of the Treasure Basket?
- Is there a named person to be responsible for the maintenance of the Treasure Basket(s)?

- Have parents been introduced to the concept?
- Where will the basket(s) be kept when not being used?
- Are the objects in the basket kept solely for the Treasure Basket or do they 'wander' into other rooms?
- Is the basket regularly checked – at the end of every play session?
- Do you change the objects or add new items to keep the babies' interest?
- Do you use your observations to inform future play or extended play opportunities for the babies? Are you matching your babies' changing and developing needs to your daily planning?

It is important to share the creation of the basket with parents, to explain why some objects have been selected and others discarded. For example, certain items, perhaps brought back from trips abroad, that are heavily varnished or brightly painted could contain substances that are very harmful to babies, who are going to put everything in their mouths. But you will soon find items for your basket everywhere you look: charity shops, car boot sales, around the home, and so will parents and other colleagues.

There are companies now selling complete 'Treasure Baskets' and this may seem tempting. In many ways, however, buying an already filled basket defeats its purpose, leaving aside the fact that the quality can be very variable. It takes away from parents and staff the responsibility of choosing objects with some meaning for the babies and families in a particular setting and makes it less likely that they will be properly cared for. In a group setting the named person responsible for the Treasure Baskets will ensure the principles are adhered to and the value and beauty of the basket is maintained. Treasure Baskets can become collections of cultural and family heritage; Ruth's own baskets are now nearly 20 years old and some of the objects are even older and were in her original 'bit' box (Forbes 2004). These were explored and enjoyed by her son and daughter, and are now delighting her grandchildren. Some of her 'treasures' carry significant memories – gifts and exchanges from other Treasure Basket users during training sessions, and from Elinor herself.

The baby at the basket: discovery and concentration

As we closely observe a baby with the objects in the Treasure Basket, we can note how many different things he does with them – looking, touching, grasping, mouthing, licking, waving, banging, picking up, dropping, selecting and discarding what does or does not attract him. He also uses an object in his hands and mouth as a laughing communication with the close-by adult or with another infant seated at the basket. It is striking to observe how the whole body is involved; if feet and toes are uncovered they respond in a lively way to the stimulus and excitement that activity with the chosen object induces. We often complain that babies seem to want to pull their socks off all the time. Perhaps they are trying to tell us something!

The concentration of a baby on the contents of a Treasure Basket is something that astonishes observers seeing it for the first time. Attention may last up to an hour or more. There are two factors which lie behind this and it is difficult to say which comes first; in fact they operate together. There is the infant's lively curiosity that the varied objects arouse, and there is his will to practise his growing skill in taking possession, under his own steam, of what is new, attractive and close at hand.

The use of the Treasure Basket is one way that we can ensure a richness in the baby's experience when the brain is ready to receive, to make connections and so to use this information. It is here that a well-stocked Treasure Basket, provided by a thoughtful adult, can offer experience of absorbing interest, enabling a baby to pursue vital learning for which he is ready and eager. When planning a baby's diet we give great attention to his menu, offering the range and quality essential for his daily nutrition and rapid growth. But what about his 'cognitive' diet, which nurtures his developing capacity to use eyes, hands and mouth in concentrated activity?

First steps in decision-making

Watching a baby as he explores the items in the Treasure Basket, it is fascinating to see the zest with which he chooses the objects that attract him, the precision he shows in bringing them to his mouth or passing them from one hand to another and the quality of concentration as he makes contact with the objects. We see his intent observation, ability to choose and return to a favoured item that attracts him, sometimes sharing his pleasure with the responsive adult. He is in no doubt about his ability to select and experiment.

We all know of people who, faced with a wide variety of styles in a shoe shop, are quite unable to decide which they want. It might not be too fanciful to say that if they had started off with experience of the Treasure Basket, it could have stood them in good stead in later life.

The adult's role

Sometimes adults feel that unless they are active at the Treasure Basket, offering objects to the baby, helping him to hold the 'right' end and so on, they have no role to play. They fail to realise the importance of the emotional anchorage which they offer, creating by their presence the confidence that enables the babies to explore, play and learn. The fact that the adult is not active does not mean that we put down the basket beside the baby and let him 'get on with it'. He needs the safety which our interested presence gives when he is faced with the challenge of objects that he may be handling for the first time.

Our 'interested presence' means sitting close enough to the basket to maintain eye contact; this offers the emotional anchorage and security needed. The adult's smiles and eye contact send out a reassuring message; there is no need for the adult to talk, and the baby will lead the play and initiate any interaction. The only time we should intervene is when he tells us in his own way that he has had enough, is visibly tiring or becomes upset.

This apparent inaction can be hard for the adult, who is used to initiating and leading young children's play experiences – she may feel that she is not 'doing it properly'. This is when working alongside a more experienced practitioner can help.

In any new experience we, as adults, have two kinds of feeling. We are curious and excited by a situation that is new and strange, but this also arouses doubt and anxiety. Some people seem temperamentally more willing to undertake something that might hold risks. Others are more cautious. But if we have a friend whom we trust to encourage us, we take on some of their confidence and find that diving off the side of the pool or climbing a steep cliff is not so frightening after all.

It is not that we need to encourage babies to handle the play material – given a chance they will do so. But in the unknown there is always some element of threat, and it is the adult's attitude of calm interest that allays a baby's anxiety and so frees his energy for concentrated enjoyment. Once the Treasure Basket has been assembled it offers infinite opportunities for infant decision-making with little effort required from the caregiver other than ensuring that the items in the basket are clean and regularly replenished with new objects.

The importance of this last point perhaps needs underlining. Unlike a bought toy that remains the same until it is outgrown or broken, a Treasure Basket should be constantly changing and evolving. Perhaps the closest parallel for adults might be the staff notice-board at work. If it is nobody's job to keep the board in order so that the current notices are lost among a jumble of old ones and each day we see the same things, we soon lose interest and eventually stop looking at it at all.

Protecting babies at the basket

In a group setting, when two or at most three babies are seated round the basket, they need close adult supervision. Babies also need protection from mobile children who come to investigate. If older children continually want to join the infants and use the Treasure Basket, this means that there is no appropriate play material to interest them elsewhere in the room, and steps must be taken to remedy this. The right of babies to be undisturbed, as well as the educational value of their play, needs to be properly recognised.

It is also necessary to take account of the possible danger to a baby seated at a Treasure Basket when there are mobile children about. An older child has the strength to lift objects that are too heavy for a baby, and in their hands a heavy pebble or a metal spoon, perfectly safe for a baby to play with, can do serious damage in an instant. This is no reason to deprive the baby of the interesting experiences that such objects can offer, but it does underline the importance of close supervision when children of mixed ages are present.

Interplay between infants

The Treasure Basket provides an opportunity to observe social interaction between babies at an age when it used to be said that infants are not interested in each other. Observing two or three babies seated at the Treasure Basket it can be seen immediately that this is not true, as the video, *Infants at Work* (Goldschmied 1987), clearly

Figure 5.3 Sharing the basket

demonstrates. Babies, though intent upon handling their own chosen objects, are not only aware of each other, but for much of the time are engaged in active interchanges. It is the availability of the objects that stimulates these exchanges, which sometimes develop into little tussles for possession.

The intense looking, glances, smiles, preverbal noises of great variety, touching each other and sharing objects, all spring directly from the experiences babies have with their close adults. Infants who have had multiple carers or those whose homes have not provided enough loving care and stimulation do not respond in this way. The 'abandoned and illegitimate' infants with whom Elinor Goldschmied worked in postwar Italy did not interact with each other at all, even though they spent all their waking hours lying or sitting together in a playpen. They remained silent, unsmiling, noiseless, only rocking to comfort themselves in their deep isolation. These infants, well cared for in physical terms, had no personal relationships or stimulus through play. Their contact with their natural mothers had been so short-lived that, having received so little, they were unable to give. They had had no opportunity to learn the beginnings of social behaviour, such a vital aspect of development.

Moving on to the next stage

Babies differ greatly in the speed with which they attain independent movement, and by eight or nine months some will already be making first attempts at crawling and beginning to move about, while others are still at the rolling and squirming stage. Mobility opens the way to every kind of exploration, and it is at this point that transferring things in and out of receptacles becomes an absorbing occupation. This interest appears early in some infants, and a good sized tin placed beside a baby seated at the Treasure Basket will offer him the opportunity to take the first steps towards that kind of play, moving objects from the basket to the tin and emptying them out again. Babies at this stage are in transition between what Corinne Hutt called 'epistemic play' (1979) when the question in the child's mind seems to be 'What is this?' and the next stage, which she called 'ludic play', when the child wonders 'What can I do with this?' as we see in Chapter 7.

Not the Treasure Basket

Baskets and boxes with miscellaneous objects are found in many settings and across age ranges. However, unless the term Treasure Basket is reserved for the model that we have described there is a danger that Elinor's original principles will be watered down, if not lost. Discovery boxes/baskets which are put together to support language development and involve the adult leading the learning, talking and encouraging the young child to name or describe the objects, are not Treasure Baskets. These are often baskets/boxes filled with themed objects – transport; self-care resources; things we wear; or all the objects made from one material, e.g. metal or wood. Christmas and other festival baskets have been observed, as have baskets with all the objects of one colour. Activity and vocabulary baskets and boxes have their place in the nursery and for children of different ages. Resources can be put together to support young children's schemas, and creative practitioners and parents can become involved in sourcing items and ensuring safe, appropriate use of them. We suggested discovery boxes in Chapter 3, which encourage fine and gross motor skills. Please just don't call them 'Treasure Baskets'!

Questions and answers about the use of the Treasure Basket

We have found that babies offered the chance to play with a well-stocked basket are almost universally appreciative, provided they are given time and the support of an attentive adult to overcome initial feelings of strangeness. The same cannot be said of caregivers, and we have often been surprised at the vehemence of the hostility expressed by some nursery staff and students. We can only speculate on the reasons for this, though the feeling that objects that cost so little (if anything) cannot have much value, is certainly a factor. Some questions and anxieties come up so often that they seem worth dealing with here:

Q: *Why doesn't the adult take an active part and talk to the babies as they play, so as to encourage language development?*
A: Observation of babies at the Treasure Basket suggests that their minds are very actively engaged and that the preverbal noises that they make in the course of their

play are a significant part of the process of language development. Talk by the adult at this time is merely distracting. The session at the Treasure Basket is only for a relatively short part of the day; close adult contact and conversation with the infant will take place continuously at other times, particularly during changing, washing and feeding.

Q: *What if the baby just sits and looks at the basket? Shouldn't the adult do something to start her off?*
A: It is not necessary for the practitioner to take the initiative to 'encourage' the infants, because they are well able to initiate their own learning and exploration by and for themselves. It is important to allow them to go at their own pace and spend as long as they like getting used to the appearance of the basket before they start to handle and explore the objects. They may just sit quietly gazing at the basket for as long as a quarter of an hour before they decide to reach out and investigate an object. They also need freedom to make their own choices. Sometimes a baby will spend a long period alternately sucking and waving a wooden spoon, ignoring all the other items pains-takingly assembled in the basket. That is his decision. Of course sometimes a baby will indicate clearly by crying or turning away that he is not in the mood for this kind of play at the moment, and that should obviously be respected.

Q: *Surely some of this material is very unhygienic and could cause cross-infection?*
A: Like any other playthings, the material in the Treasure Basket requires regular care and maintenance. All the objects suggested in the list below are washable, wipeable or disposable. Some (for example, the apple) will need to be changed after each session. Anything that cannot be satisfactorily cleaned should be discarded. With proper care there is no reason why Treasure Basket items should carry greater risk of infection than conventional toys.

We need also to remember that the group care of infants in itself must present increased risk of cross-infection. Bored babies without stimulating play material are unhappy and grizzly. There is evidence that when adults are in the equivalent state (that is, depressed and dissatisfied) their level of immunity to infection is lowered. The same is true of babies.

Q: *Aren't some of these objects dangerous – they could be thrown, or swallowed or used to poke another baby's eyes?*
A: Items for the Treasure Basket must always be very carefully selected with safety in mind. Obviously objects with sharp edges or points or small enough to be swallowed are to be excluded. The main protective factor is the limited capacities of babies of this age. They can wave an object or pick it up and drop it but they cannot throw or poke. Parents may need reassurance about this.

The great variety of potential items for a Treasure Basket (the list given below con-tains nearly a hundred suggestions and certainly does not exhaust the possibilities) means that there is no need for anybody to include an object which causes them anxiety about its safety – if in doubt, throw it out! But it is worth saying that, on the whole, people tend to be overcautious.

As we have already mentioned, the situation is different when older children are present, and the items for each session need to be selected with this in mind. Babies seated at the basket must always be supervised and not crowded up together. If too close, one baby might tap another with an object which has a handle, but they would not have the coordination to poke. Observation of trios of babies shows that they are very circumspect in the way they use an object with a handle, manipulating it with skill and judgement.

Q: *Isn't it likely that a baby faced with such a pile of objects might feel confused?*
A: The babies show us quite clearly that they know how to select and discard, often returning to a favoured item in the course of play.

Q: *Doesn't it take a lot more trouble to collect all these items than to buy toys or ready-made Treasure Baskets from catalogues or shops that are specially designed for babies by experts?*
A: Bought toys have their uses but good quality ones are extremely expensive and because babies develop so rapidly are likely to be used only for a short period. Some people find it easier than others to collect items for the Treasure Basket. Ready-made Treasure Baskets are expensive and take away the pleasure and skill of the staff to select objects, especially those relevant to the culture of the setting. It seems to depend upon developing one's 'imaginative eye' for what will interest and stimulate the senses. Once that happens, people involved in the care of young babies can become very excited by the search and it is a good way of engaging parents – fathers as much as mothers – in the educational work of a childcare centre.

Q: *Why are you so insistent on excluding plastic objects from the basket? Isn't plastic an inescapable fact of modern life?*
A: That is an important part of the reason. If we look at the playthings that are commonly provided for young children, both in their own homes and group care settings, they are almost entirely made of plastic or synthetic materials. We have to ask what quality of sensory experience these objects can offer, remembering that at this age touch and exploration by mouth are as important as sight. People sometimes object to the insistence on natural materials on the grounds that they are colourless. But most of the objects offered to babies are in very bright primary colours. Colour is better provided by fruit such as apples, oranges and lemons rather than painted objects which may be harmful when sucked or licked.

An exercise that we have used with parents and nursery workers illustrates this point. The participants, seated in a close circle on chairs or on the floor, are asked to close their eyes. We then distribute a number of plastic toys that each person is invited to explore for a moment and then pass on to their neighbour, so that everybody has a chance to handle each object. We ask them, with their eyes still shut, to share their impressions, which are usually sparse and hesitant: 'smooth', 'knobbly', 'hard', 'doesn't smell very nice'. Some people can't think of anything to say.

The exercise is then repeated with objects from the Treasure Basket. The passing of objects from one person to another does not proceed so smoothly; they are reluctant to give them up, wanting to rub them over their faces, tap, shake, sniff, even lick them. At the end the words pour out, with animated discussion of the different objects and guessing at what they could be. Finally the objects are set in two heaps on the floor and the participants told to open their eyes. Following this experience they have no difficulty in recognising the sameness of plastic toys from a baby's point of view as opposed to natural materials which can offer such an enormous variety of sensations through the mouth, ears, nose, skin and muscles as well as the eyes.

Guidelines for the use of the Treasure Basket

1. The basket should be not less than 35 cm in diameter and 10–12 cm high. It is essential that it is flat-bottomed, with no handle and strong enough for the infant to lean on it without tipping up. It should have straight sides and be made of a strong natural material (definitely not plastic). Elinor Goldschmied arrived at this specification from long experience, but baskets of this kind are not easily found and it will probably be necessary to have them made by a specialist basket-maker. This is a good investment, both for childcare centres and childminders, as a well-made basket will last indefinitely, whereas cheap substitutes will be less satisfying for the babies and usually fall apart quite quickly. (Ruth has all her baskets made by Roy Youdale, a master craftsman who also grows his own organic willow in different colours.)
2. Fill the basket to the brim with objects to allow the baby plenty of scope to sort through and to select what appeals to her.
3. See that the baby is seated comfortably with her body to the side of the basket, not leaning into it (with a supporting cushion if necessary). If there is a rim on the basket, see that it is near enough for an elbow to rest upon it.
4. The adult should sit nearby, not talking or intervening unless the infant clearly needs attention.
5. The Treasure Basket should be continually changing and evolving with the introduction of new objects. One way of introducing variety is to have a number of baskets stocked with different items and bring them out in rotation. Observe carefully though, as some babies like to return to favourite objects and may be upset not to find them in the basket.
6. The objects in the basket need care and maintenance – regular washing or wiping and elimination or replacement of damaged items.
7. If there are older children around, create a 'safe space' in a corner of the room with a piece of carpet or objects placed to mark a boundary for the babies seated round the basket. The adult should protect the infants from incursions by mobile children.

Suggested items for the Treasure Basket

Wooden objects
Small velvet-lined boxes; small drum on wooden frame; rattles – various types; bamboo whistle; castanets; clothes peg – two types; coloured beads on string; cubes; short lengths of wood; cylinders; bobbin; cotton reel; curtain rings – different sizes; napkin ring; spoon or spatula; egg cup; small turned bowl; foot massager; honey dipper; toad-stool darner; lemon squeezer (the sharp tip may need sanding down with glass paper); nut cracker; pastry brush; turned wooden eggs.

Metal objects
Spoons – various sizes; small egg whisk; bunch of smooth worn keys; small tins, with edges smoothed; toy trumpet; lemon squeezer; small funnel; large brass curtain rings; small harmonica; garlic squeezer; scout whistle; small metal frame mirror; key-rings linked together; bunch of bells; triangle; metal egg cup; firmly closed tins containing rice, beans, etc.; tea strainer; small tin lids – all types; metal beaker; bicycle bell; large scent-bottle top; tea infuser; costume jewellery; small moulds.

Objects in leather, textile, rubber, fur
Puppy 'bone'; puppy ring; small leather bag with zip; bouncy ball; velvet powder puff; length of rubber tubing; small rag doll; tennis ball; golf ball; leather spectacle case; bead-embroidered purse; bath plug with chain; small teddy bear; bean bag; small cloth bags containing lavender, rosemary, thyme, cloves; coaster-size rubber mats; stress ball; small knitted teddy/doll; satin-lined velvet ring box; small pieces of fabric; paperweight – acrylic and flat; small leather purse with popper; small kitchen spatulas.

Paper, cardboard
Greaseproof paper, scrunched up; small cardboard boxes; small paper gift-type bags with cord handles.

Natural objects
Fir cones – differing sizes; large corks; cork block; dried gourds; sea grass pear (or apple-shaped); large piece of loofah; shells (from sustainable sources please); marble eggs; large pebbles; large feathers; pumice stone; small natural sponge; a lemon; an apple; a lime; an orange.

Objects made of natural materials
Woollen ball; little baskets; bone ring; bone shoe horn; small raffia mat; wooden nail brush; toothbrush; cane bag handles; brushes of various types – check that they are well made and have bristles that stay put when pulled; large house painting brush; shaving brush; small shoe brush; cosmetic brushes.

Summary

Babies who can sit independently but not yet move need a wide variety of different objects to engage their interest and stimulate their developing senses and understanding. The Treasure Basket is a practical way to assemble collections of such objects and make them available to sitting infants. Two key points are emphasised: (1) the objects should be made of natural materials, not plastic; (2) the adult's role is to provide security by her attentive, but not active, presence. Once the baby is seated by the basket there is no need for the adult to intervene at all unless the child shows that he needs comforting or physical care. Sharing information through active sessions with parents and practitioners new to the ethos and philosophy behind the 'real' Treasure Basket experience for babies in home and group settings is vital. This enables parents to become active participants in choosing and selecting objects for the basket and provide their own basket at home (or borrow one from the setting) and ensures that practitioners are confident in the use of the Treasure Basket and explaining its benefits to parents.

6 The second year of life

I've forgotten the word I wanted to say and my thought, unexpressed, returns to the world of shadows.

(O. Mandelstam)

In this chapter we will consider:

- Independence and negotiation;
- Physical development, movement and manipulative skills;
- Health and self-care;
- Communication and language;
- A facilitating environment for playing and learning;
- Playthings for the second year.

Studies of childcare settings and childminders suggest that children between one and two may receive the least concentrated attention. In mixed-age groups they are often seen as disruptive, having lost interest in baby toys but still too young to be involved in the more structured activities provided for older children. During training sessions staff have often told us that they find this age group the most challenging to plan for and work with. Perhaps these were settings where the key person approach was not used or not used effectively.

As these children reach two years of age, those in a childcare setting will have a progress check as part of the EYFS, where possible to be carried out jointly between health professionals and the nursery. Practitioners will need to use their observations to inform the checks rather than allowing the prospect of the check to shape their practice. We consider the two-year-old check more fully in Chapter 8.

The key person will know and understand the rapidly developing toddler, and have a good relationship with her family, so that there can be mutual support and planning to meet her needs. The child needs to have a secure attachment relationship with her close adults to give her the confidence to explore and assert her curiosity. This can be a difficult time, especially for the parents and practitioner, as toddlers test out the strength of their attachment; this can result in behaviour such as biting, kicking, pulling hair and clinging on. Parents' feelings for their child can be challenged and it is important that they understand what is happening at this time (Dorman and Dorman 2002). Toddlers cannot make sense of or manage their own feelings and thoughts; they need a close adult or key person to do that for them.

As children develop the capacity to move around rapidly, they have to be watched, but this needs to be balanced by providing an environment in which they can move freely and safely. The second year is one of extraordinarily rapid growth and development. Their increasing mobility and language development are enabling them to find out and understand more about their world. This is all part of the symbolic explosion which occurs as the toddler turns into a talker and a player with symbols, pretending and imagining. Careful consideration and thought is needed by those responsible for their play and learning to ensure their experience is not negative and limiting, but rich and full of 'awe and wonder' moments (Bruce 2011).

Independence and negotiation

A child in her second year wants above all to practise her new-found skills of mobility, manipulation and speech. Consider, for example, what may happen when we take a toddler for a walk. To her, the immediate experience is that of moving under her own steam and responding to the myriad exciting things which she encounters, such as the cat sunning herself on the path or the hole being dug in the road. We, on the other hand, may have our own objective, which is to get to the Post Office before it closes. She sees a little low wall by the path on to which she clamours to be lifted so that, with our supporting hand, she can practise walking and balancing. This we know will cause a delay that we definitely do not want.

Faced with this situation there are a number of choices open to us. If we remember early enough the attraction of the wall, we can avoid her demand by taking another route. Alternatively, we can use our superior physical strength to pick her up and carry her, protesting, past the wall.

A third option is to say, 'Just once, because I'm in a hurry', promising a longer exploration on the way back. Of course 'on the way back' means nothing to her at that moment, but at least we have tried to find an honest compromise, to model an attempt to reconcile divergent interests. What makes dealing with an energetic toddler so demanding of our patience is that little incidents of this kind are happening all the time. The adult can either enforce her own wishes or negotiate a solution which also takes into account the child's perspective.

A young child's timescale is quite different from ours. As adults we have learned to switch quickly from one situation to another, and we develop an ability to do this, however unwillingly. Children cannot 'change gear' in this way and we must concede them time to adjust and to grasp what it is we want them to do. Many an upset and tantrum can be avoided if we remember this. Every tiny interchange where adult and child interests differ has significance in creating for the child a confidence in our respect for her and our understanding of her world. In moments such as these we might remind ourselves that the peoples of the world are also seriously engaged (not yet very successfully) with just this problem of how to resolve their conflicting interests. The urgent need for doing so may give our efforts with young children a wider significance than we may have previously thought.

This attitude certainly does not mean letting a child do just what she wants, for that can create anxieties and confusion for a child just as much as prohibition and control. It is aiming at a viable balance that takes so much of our energy and thought.

When a child is able to get about on her own and evidently enjoys her new-found power to separate at will from her adult, parents sometimes find it puzzling that at the very moment of moving away, their child also becomes more demanding of their closeness, even to the extent of 'clinging'. We have to remember that independence, though exciting and desired, can also be rather frightening. We need a secure base in order to have the confidence to venture out from it. Erik Erikson, in his classic book *Childhood and Society* (1955), identifies acquiring 'basic trust' as the first developmental task, which gives the child freedom to explore and learn. Children need to have secure relationships with close adults so that gradually they make their own kind of confidence which can enable them to tolerate doubt or stress and to take risks (Erikson 1955).

This enables the child to be more adventurous, leaving the security of the indoor play area and thinking about going outside. The door is open, there are voices to be heard and she can take the small risk – knowing that her key person will be there for a hug and a chat should she decide not to explore the garden this time, but to return to her lap.

There is an interesting similarity here with adolescents who, while they may test, sometimes aggressively, the limits of their parents' tolerance, still desperately need the secure base that the family provides and suffer if they do not have it (Parker *et al.* 1991; Stein 2008; Sunderland 2007).

Developmental lines

Anna Freud formulated an approach to assessing child development that she called 'developmental lines'. In the second year of life the child moves from almost total dependence to relative independence in broadly four ways: through movement and manipulative skill, in self-feeding, in early pre-verbal language developing into speech, and in self-care leading to bowel and bladder control (Freud 1965). The pace at which a child moves forward along these lines has clear connections with the quality of her relation to her close adults, at home with her parents or in the childcare setting with her key person.

There are many useful texts on child development for students (and for experienced professionals to update and refresh their knowledge). This book does not attempt to be comprehensive but focuses on the aspects that are most relevant to early years practitioners, many of which might be considered too mundane to be covered in more theoretical texts (see list of recommended further reading). However, in the second year of life there are so many notable changes and so many new demands that we make upon a child that it is useful to set them out, to remind ourselves how much is achieved during the period between 10 and 20 months.

The most important factors for healthy development are that you should recognise the skills a child has developed and provide plenty of opportunities to practise (Bruce 2010). One of the principles of the EYFS (DfE 2012b) states that 'children develop and learn in different ways and at different rates, at their own rates and in their own ways'. *Development Matters* helpfully suggested that the statements should be used to identify possible areas in which to challenge and extend the child's current learning and development by closely matching what they provide to a child's current needs (Early Education 2012). This document has been withdrawn and replaced with the Early Years Outcomes (DfE 2013), a non-statutory guidance for practitioners, which appears as a list of statements to see if children are developing typically for their age. The new document makes no reference to the characteristics of learning or pedagogy. We are concerned that this could lead practitioners to plan for assessment rather than for each child's individual developmental needs.

Physical development, movement and manipulative skills

Physical development is one of the 'prime areas' of learning and development, with two aspects: (i) moving and handling and (ii) health and self-care.

Once crawling has been established, at last an infant can attempt her objective of reaching the door through which her close adult has momentarily disappeared. She can move into the excitement of the descending stairs or open door leading to the garden. A quite new sense of 'I can do it for myself' can grow, but as yet with no sense of danger or of caution, and that is what can make this period so exhausting for the caring adult.

In the nursery, dangers are usually avoided but sometimes at the cost of creating an environment which is lacking in variety or has little to excite the child's capacity for curiosity. Most children have taken their first wobbly steps by about 13–14 months and at around 15 months are walking steadily. Kneeling, bending to reach toys, clambering on to furniture all follow, as observant practitioners will recognise, and signal the need for a more challenging physical environment – obstacle courses with tunnels promoting crawling, heuristic play encouraging bending to pick up objects, furniture that they are allowed to climb on, and raised platforms and steps to practise climbing, at which they become very expert.

> At 21 months Ruben tackles stairs using a range of options. The stairs in his Spanish home are marble; he only comes down them backwards using his hands and knees. Finding carpeted stairs in England for the first time, he tried out several methods. Bumping down on his bottom, sliding down on his back almost at full stretch, or standing upright, front facing, holding the banister (or an adult's hand) and taking one step at a time, putting both feet on the step before placing the other

in front of him. How he tackles the stairs differs depending on how quickly he wants to get to the bottom and the time of day.

We made suggestions in Chapter 3 about equipment and group room arrangement for this age, and in Chapter 10 we will make suggestions about how the outdoor learning area can be both safe and stimulating. Play material to satisfy these children's ceaseless interest in handling and experimenting with any objects close at hand is described in the next chapter.

Health and self-care

Feeding

The emphasis in our culture on children learning to use a spoon as early as possible can be a cause of stress. When young children are allowed to be active in feeding themselves with their fingers, this has two advantages: (i) they are not obliged to wait entirely on the adult's help and control; and (ii) handling food directly provides varied tactile experiences. When spoon-feeding is going on, the child, as suggested in Chapter 9, can be given her own spoon to 'help' in the process, even if not much food finds its way into her mouth at first. Toddlers who have been introduced to baby-led weaning will be far more confident in using a spoon, fork and their fingers, as well as probably eating a wide range of foods.

Practitioners will be aware that in some cultures it is normal for both children and adults to eat with their hands. In this case teaching the child to use implements in the nursery requires sensitivity on the part of the key person and discussion with parents.

One further important point for this age group is the need to ensure that children as yet without language can let the adult know that they are thirsty. There should be a jug of water and mugs at some place in the room so that the child can indicate when she needs a drink.

Respectful intimate care

For a child in her second year quite large parts of the day will still be taken up with caring for her personal and intimate needs. Perhaps in this area more than any other, respectful care, from a consistent key person, is essential. Too often this is regarded as a matter of routine, to be casually shared among whichever staff are available. It can lead to the kind of insensitive, depersonalised treatment of children described by Trudy Marshall (Marshall 1982). Given the changes to the EYFS and the requirement of a key person for every child, we would hope, but can't be sure, that such behaviour would be less likely to be observed today.

Respectful care is also about valuing the child and gives a powerful message about the attitudes of the nursery or childminder. This means that the environment for changing children's nappies is as carefully considered as the main play room; after all, they (and the adults) will spend a significant amount of time there during a nursery week. Routines should consider individual needs, and where care is seen to be an important part of the curriculum they will form part of the child's total experience of the nursery. Intimate moments of nappy-changing, or sitting on a potty or toilet, may offer some of the best opportunities during the busy day for one-to-one conversations between the child and adult. It is especially important for language development that, as far as possible, it should be the child's key person who provides her personal care, so that the practitioner can learn to respond to her signals and preferences in the way that sensitive parents do.

Toilet training is a subject that tends to arouse strong emotions among parents and staff. We now have a better understanding of the development of the nervous system, the growth of a child's ability to control and release her muscles, and of the way our bodily functions are connected with our emotional states. It is most important that family practice and the nursery approach are fully harmonised. The key person has the responsibility of seeing that the process is as smooth as possible for the child, otherwise she will be placed in a state of confusion. This underlines further the importance of the key person being responsible for the intimate care of her special children.

Independence in the transition period

While a child is learning to ask for and to use her potty, there will still be times of the day when she will be wearing a nappy – when preparing for a sleep, for example. She

Figure 6.1 A raised changing station

will need to be lifted onto the changing table, especially when she needs washing and drying before a clean nappy is put on. Children, asserting their legitimate independence, may reject any help and this again is where adults need to be understanding and sensitive to the child's feelings and not take it as a personal slight (Bruce 2011).

A positive way to deal with this daily occurrence is, as Ruth saw in Sweden, a raised changing station with steps which mobile babies and toddlers can climb with help as necessary, thus giving them an active part in the process (and protecting adults' backs from unnecessary lifting). Thus, both conflict and back strain for the adult are avoided.

There are times when a child will simply refuse to sit on her pot. Sonia remembers making a doomed attempt to bribe with Smarties a toddler who was going through this phase. After a couple of days her small daughter (23 months) looked at her coldly and said 'I don't like Smarties anymore'. The fact is, when it comes to a matter over which a child has control, there is no way that the adult can 'win' and it is wise to accept this gracefully. A child who persistently refuses the pot may be responding to over-severe toilet training at home, and tactful discussion with the parents is indicated.

Washing and wiping

Washing faces, drying hands and first attempts at brushing teeth, all form part of that basic care which adds up to feeling good about oneself. We hardly need to remind ourselves how different we feel after a tiring day when we can have a bath or shower. The unmistakable pleasure on a child's face during an unhurried bathroom time – as her key person gently combs or brushes her hair, helps her to wash, and tells her how nice she looks – underlines the value of this detailed care.

A key person can do this for her small group in a way that is impossible for a large number of children in an 'assembly line' atmosphere. We know ourselves how we feel

Figure 6.2 Growing independence in the bathroom

demeaned by the cry of 'next please' if we find ourselves waiting our turn in a hospital outpatient department. Recalling our own experiences of depersonalised handling in a range of situations can give us greater sensitivity in how we conduct bathroom time for young children. Our body image is something precious and entirely personal to each one of us, and our attitude towards ourselves is deeply bound up with our early experiences at the hands of adults.

Blowing noses

We can probably recall, in childhood, having our noses wiped roughly by adults, who often did not pause to notice that the delicate skin around the nostrils was sore. In the nursery, where the problem is multiplied by numbers, the gentleness and respect needed for this aspect of care can all too easily be overlooked.

Some children suffer from almost continuous nasal catarrh in winter, especially in areas where many families live in damp and inadequately heated houses or flats, and this may cause them considerable discomfort in breathing, and can also affect their hearing. One of the drawbacks of grouping young children together is the high incidence of cross-infection from respiratory problems and we should make every effort to reduce this. An important step towards self-care for children is for them to learn how to blow their own noses; this is quite a complex skill to master. The child will need support both from parents and the key person to help learn and practise this essential skill. We should note that there is a body of opinion, partly but not exclusively associated with psychoanalytic theory, which holds that using toilet paper to wipe noses creates a confusion in the mind of a young child who is at the stage of developing understanding of different bodily processes. Toilet paper should be kept in bathrooms and used for wiping bottoms, not noses. A second point has to do with reducing the risk of cross-infection. Used tissues should be disposed of in closed bins and not by putting them in a pocket where body warmth will favour the multiplication of bacilli.

Playing with 'messy materials'

A child who comes from a home where great emphasis is laid on keeping hands and clothes clean, may show doubt or anxiety about playing with materials that might be considered 'dirty' or 'messy'. This feeling must be respected, but it is the responsibility of the child's key person to discuss the matter with her parents and to gain for her their support and agreement that (with proper supervision and protective clothing) she may play with these things. Some toddlers prefer to be covered with protective overalls, others wearing just a nappy. Again, the key person will respond to the toddler's signs and signals in this.

Most babies and toddlers in nursery settings will have been offered the opportunity to play with 'gloop' (cornflour mix) or finger paint on the high-chair tray or at a table. The toddler in Figure 6.3 was playing with finger paint alongside an adult, swirling the paint round and round on the table top. Then he put his hands in the plastic plates containing the paint, chatting both to himself and to the adult, as the paint and his hands changed colour. Making the difference between 'allowed play' (with the gloop) and playing with food at mealtimes can become a difficult distinction for some children and practitioners. Dorothy Selleck in her reflections on 'Baby Art' (Selleck 1997)

Figure 6.3 Playing with finger paint

describes the pleasure shown by Samson aged seven months as he rubs a piece of Yorkshire pudding around his feeding tray, mixing juice from his sticky cup with the pieces of pudding and the gravy, rubbing his hands all over the tray. We are not advocating full-blown messy play experiences every time a baby or toddler is eating. In many circumstances it may not be practical or appropriate, but making time to talk with or comment on the food experience is something that respectful practitioners will allow for, and parents should be encouraged to do so too.

In later life there are people who find it most distasteful, if not impossible, to carry out a task such as gutting a fish, planting seedlings in mud, cleaning out a rabbit hutch, or working with clay or papier mâché. Maybe this strong aversion has its roots in a too severe denial in early life that such things can be not only legitimate but, in their way, pleasurable and creative.

Communication, language and cognition

'The strong silent type is not much good to a small child . . . From earliest infancy children need conversation' (Purves and Selleck 1999, p. 87). This reminds us that young children need to hear adults' and other children's conversations, to stimulate their developing communication and language.

The precise way in which language develops is still a matter of considerable controversy among psycholinguists, but it seems clear that there is a very strong predisposition to develop speech. Most children, except those who are profoundly deaf, eventually do so.

Hand gestures, posture, facial expressions and touch are just some of the many ways young children communicate non-verbally. Toddlers use clear signs for communicating – they point, look fixedly at an object or use what language they have persistently, until the adult responds by giving the toddler the language she needs. When the toddler looks out of the window saying 'Daddy car', we typically expand her utterances by saying, 'yes Daddy has gone out in the car, he'll be back soon' or 'Daddy has gone to work'.

Toddlers often use intense gazing to get their message across and this is beautifully shown in *The Social Toddler* (Dorman and Dorman 2002, p. 143) with photographs of Emily aged 15 months 'telling' her mother that she would like some raisins from a high kitchen cupboard.

The rate at which children learn to talk, as with other developmental lines, varies widely, although it tends to follow a consistent sequence. Gordon Wells, who carried out the most detailed longitudinal study of young children's speech development ever undertaken, concluded that the key factor was the extent to which close adults communicated with the child. Children who learned to speak early were those whose parents listened to them and responded to the meaning expressed by the sounds the child made. Parents who tried too hard to teach the child new words or corrected pronunciation or grammar were more likely to inhibit speech than encourage it (Wells 1985).

In the nursery the key person plays a major role in supporting and promoting the development of language, and having a close relationship with the parents will ensure that parents and nursery staff also communicate and share information about new sounds or gestures that the child is using. They can tactfully discourage parents who insist on prompting the toddler or correcting (as opposed to expanding) their attempts at speech.

By 12 months toddlers are pointing at objects of interest; they understand simple instructions – give me the cup, find teddy – and by 15 months they are using between two and six words. This jumps at 18 months to between six and 20 words but they understand many more, and children in language-rich environments may already by this age use around 50 words. Once they have a lexicon of 50–100 words, they will begin to combine them and form their first sentences (hello 2011). These are usually very familiar to parents and carers – 'bye-bye', 'all gone', 'please more', 'thank you'. We should be concerned if a toddler has no recognisable words by the age of two. Adults can support the young child's language development by providing a commentary. For example, when a child is playing with bricks, you might say 'you're building a tower, that's a tall tower'. Giving them a commentary rather than asking closed questions encourages a toddler to participate in the conversation.

Talking and listening to children – the right to be heard

Research has shown that 50 per cent of children reach school without the communication skills they need; some never catch up and these difficulties can continue into adult life. One child in ten has speech, language and communication problems (ICAN 2011).

Early years practitioners need to be confident in their knowledge of speech and language development and able to support children under three to develop the skills they need for learning to talk. The Speech, Language and Communication Framework (SLCF) lists the skills and knowledge that everyone working with children should have. There are a range of programmes and resources available to settings, and many local authorities have implemented the Every Child a Talker (ECAT) programme, Early Talk 0–5 or Early Language Development Programme (ELDP). These can support practitioners in assessing children's speech and language, as well as promoting communication-rich environments.

One of the drawbacks of a well-run nursery can be that a child in her second year who has not yet acquired speech can pass through the nursery day without much need to talk, and so lose out on the essential practice that a mastery of language demands. We also need to be vigilant about how much listening we do. The Listening to Young Children project (Lancaster and Broadbent 2003; Clark 2001) developed a framework for listening and responding to young children from birth to eight years. To enable children to have genuine opportunities to participate in conversation, we need to ensure relationships between adults and children that are based on the sharing of power and mutual respect. Lancaster suggests that these involve time, space and choice (Lancaster 2006, p. 66).

We should take the trouble to listen to young children because it acknowledges their right to be heard, and for their views and experiences to be taken seriously. Through listening we can learn more about how young children feel about themselves and the places and people they spend time with. Listening to very young babies and toddlers, where there is limited language but lots of non-verbal communication, takes space, skill and patience as their carers closely observe and become attuned to their signals.

The Mosaic Project and framework (Clark and Moss 2001) demonstrated ways in which we can better understand the experience of children under two in the nursery. Observations provided the opportunity to 'listen' to pre-verbal children, through the child's body language, their different cries, facial expressions, noises and movements. For example, one 22-month-old child was able to communicate to the observing adult the aspects of the nursery that were important to her, which included the garden, the water play area, playing with a particular friend, and activities with her key person.

Keeping down the noise level

When there are many children who have not yet learned to modulate their voices this can cause the surrounding adults to raise their voices too, adding to the clamour. In some nurseries young children have to struggle to make themselves heard and understood above the background noise of music on the radio. The radio is sometimes justified on the grounds that this is what the children hear at home, but we think this is a good reason for not providing it in the nursery. It certainly inhibits conversation, even between adults who are fully in command of language.

We can probably all remember occasions in a noisy café or pub when we shake our heads in exasperation and exclaim 'There's such a racket, I can't hear a word you're saying', and we give up trying to carry on a reasonable conversation. Even more so, children who are unsure of their own speech will tend to retire into silence, feeling that they just cannot compete.

In addition to being very important for the development of children's language, keeping the noise level down helps to create a calm, unflustered atmosphere. 'No calling across the room' needs to be one of the ground rules of nursery life, applying to children, staff and parents alike. Just as gaining the ability to move independently is a great personal liberation so also, for a young child, having words to make herself understood is a vital part of dealing positively with the many frustrating experiences that she must face in growing up.

Returning to the leaps in language development that this age group will be making, the whole toddler area needs to be 'communication friendly'. Our world today is very noisy – mobile phones ringing or registering messages all day (and night!), people constantly chatting on phones, televisions permanently on as background in many homes, and the usual domestic sounds of washing machines, tumble-dryers and dishwashers. Many toddlers miss out on moments of quiet. Try to make some time for concentrated listening, to a specific piece of music, for reading or looking at a book in a quiet space. For some children their time in the nursery may be the only opportunity for this.

To support a communication-friendly environment the practitioners might reflect on particular aspects of the provision and resources:

- Try to keep background noise to a minimum;
- Create welcoming places for play with puppets, songs and stories;
- Display well-mounted photographs and pictures at child eye-level;
- Have baskets and boxes accessible, labelled clearly with photos and full of interesting and different things;
- Use photographs to signpost doors and gates that lead to other zones – to the changing area or garden;
- Have space where places to hide and play with a friend can be easily created with blankets, frames, milk crates.

Words and objects

One important aspect of language development is the attachment of words to objects, acquiring a vocabulary. This is something we find very difficult when learning a foreign language at school or in an evening class, but it becomes much easier if we spend time abroad and have, for example, to go shopping and ask the name of the object we are seeing and handling. In the same way the child's innate drive to learn about the nature and behaviour of objects around her is a key element in her acquisition of language.

As she gains in mobility she has the opportunity to handle and manipulate an increasing variety of objects. Observation of children during heuristic play sessions (see Chapter 7) shows clearly how direct sensory experience enables them to gain precise knowledge of objects. A child will, for example, choose a length of chain, put it into a tin, slide it out again, and repeat the action over and over again with undiminished concentration and enjoyment. The self-directed action, with the feelings and bodily sensations that go along with it, mean that the words 'tin' and 'chain' eventually become imbued with the meaning that this experience brings to it. First, the child needs to have direct contact with objects during her play, and only then will the word attached to the object become meaningful. This process enables her to build her rapidly increasing vocabulary into the tool of language in the context of her overall learning and relationships.

Language development and television

Dr Linda Pagani and colleagues (2010) in Montreal conducted a study to determine the impact of TV exposure at age two on future academic success, lifestyle choices and general well-being. She found that every additional hour of television the child watched predicted a future decrease in classroom engagement and poorer achievement in maths, and poorer language development at school entry. Advice is generally that children under two should not watch any TV at all, and whilst this might not be possible, it is important to limit exposure for the 2–5 age group. Settings need to have a clear policy on this issue. There is no need for children to watch any television in a group childcare setting – they will very likely see more than enough at home.

Creating an environment for play and learning

The environment for these young children aged between 12 and 24 months should reflect their developing and changing needs. In this section we suggest the areas or zones that might be included in a toddler room, recognising that layout and provision of resources will be dependent on the space and funds available. Having said that, the essentials for this age group should always be on offer, and we have seen beautiful and stimulating environments created by practitioners in spaces not designed for under-threes as well as in high-quality purpose-built accommodation (Community Playthings 2013).

Toddlers thrive on continuity and repetition, as we know from their never-ending demands to hear their favourite book or action rhyme again and again. The environment needs to be secure, so that they learn where to find the baskets of curlers or corks to 'cook for dinner', the dolls and the home corner are always in the same spot and the water and sand trays are positioned by the window. This way the child gets to know the layout and route round the room, and is able to make choices about what she wants to do next. As in the baby room, there should be plants and flowers, and interesting objects from the real world, both to look at and talk about with an adult or to gather and use independently for sorting, collecting, transporting and beginning to use symbolically.

Practical requirements and the need for space

We have discussed the need for the changing and bathroom areas to be considered as places where one-to-one conversations and playful games and songs might take place, to ensure that care and learning are not seen as separate. Nappies and clothes can be stored in baskets from which the toddler can be encouraged to select her own. Places to hang coats and bags with spare clothes should be labelled with photographs and names. This demonstrates the importance of the individual child and supports a strong sense of well-being and belonging. We have found this is even more important for those children attending part-time, who may have to share their pegs.

There should be plenty of space in the toddler room for pushing the buggy and going off 'shopping', to sit teddy in a chair and feed him tea or drape a box with a blanket and create a hidey-hole. There needs to be somewhere safe for non-mobile babies if the space is a mixed-age group. Height is important too – platforms to clamber onto, hide behind, sit on and watch from, or window seats that allow toddlers to see what is going on outside. Reflecting on what this age range like to do, who they like to be with and how they get around will inform how the space might be set up and used. Toddlers like to be on the floor with their key person, looking at books, examining puzzles, creating masterpieces with fat wax crayons and big circular arm movements. Tables and chairs are not essential for toddler rooms, other than for mealtimes and occasional use for painting on. Better to have a couple of pieces of furniture at their height that allow them to stand to mark-make, to line up the cars, sort out the tea-set and play with construction materials or bricks. If you are using tables, let children stand at the table, rather than be seated. Sitting can make toddlers feel 'penned in' and may restrict their play.

Music and rhyme

At this age what children enjoy most is repeatedly hearing familiar nursery rhymes or songs. They can often be heard attempting to join in, and they love to fill in a missing word. Although they like repetition it is good to introduce them to new rhymes and verses from time to time. One tends to hear only a very restricted range of nursery rhymes in childcare settings, mostly the ones reprinted in mass-produced illustrated books. In fact there are many hundreds of songs, rhymes and finger-plays traditionally sung to young children (Opie and Opie 1997). Many nurseries and Children's Centres share favourite rhymes and action songs with parents, so that they can sing along on the way home in the car or buggy. Some childcare settings offer parents the opportunity to join them for rhyme time or music sessions, introducing parents to the vast wealth of songs around and perhaps to hear live music from local musicians.

Nursery staff do not need 'good' voices to give children pleasure by singing to them. If recorded music is used this needs to be selected very carefully. Many commercial recordings designed for children are of poor quality, with inappropriate accompaniments. They also tend to use unsuitable adult voices. Really it is far better to show children that singing can be spontaneous and informal. Children love made-up songs about themselves and the things that they do every day. This is something the key person can do regularly in her small group, or while in the bathroom or changing a toddler, either using a formula ('David wears blue shoes' to the tune of 'This is the way we wash our hands') or completely freely.

Some children in their second year will sit and listen intently to a piece of music for quite a long time, and often want to hear it over and over again. Others have an attention span of only a few seconds, but may still enjoy moving and 'dancing' to music, though usually without much reference to the rhythm. If there is a staff member with a special interest in music, she might start recording a collection of different pieces for nursery use. There is an enormous variety of recorded music to choose from, including the whole range of non-western music as well as European medieval, renaissance, classical and contemporary music.

In the group she can also help children to listen to different, quiet sounds, building on the experience of sound they will already have had with some items of the Treasure Basket and in Heuristic Play. If she can play an instrument, such as a guitar, the children will delight in listening and then having a go at gently plucking the strings and reproducing the sounds themselves.

Books and stories

Children love to hear stories long before they can grasp their full meaning. By the age of two they will gaze at books for quite long periods. Looking at books alone or with an adult needs to be encouraged in the setting, especially whilst they are learning to turn pages without tearing them. Practitioners should sort and repair books regularly to keep them looking attractive, whether in the book area or the book basket.

To make indestructible picture books

Babies and toddlers will enjoy and appreciate their 'own books'. With a digital camera and a laminator, these are easy to make, and if held together with treasury tags, can be easily added to. Take photographs of the child's family, pets and favourite things, both from home and the setting. This is a good way of involving parents. Books like this can also be made to welcome and introduce the child to the setting, whatever their age.

Harry, aged 16 months, was observed turning the pages of one such book and looking intently at a colour photograph of a plate of chocolate-covered biscuits. After looking for several moments he bent down his head and licked the page. Then he said his first word – 'bikit'.

When we get on well with somebody, the conversation flows, while with other people we can think of nothing to say. Young children are no different from us in this. If we try to speak to someone who is looking over our shoulder all the time, obviously only half listening, then we can become very cross and frustrated. Giving full attention to a child as she tries haltingly to express herself, can be difficult for the practitioner amidst the distractions and demands of a group, but is essential if we aim to help a child gain command of language.

Island of intimacy

This activity falls between the two age ranges, from about 18 months to 3 years of age, but we have decided to include it in this chapter.

Elinor Goldschmied created the term 'island of intimacy' to describe a short period of time when the key person for each small group of children gives them her undivided attention. Children require time and space and an available adult to develop their power of speech. Essentially, 'island time' is when the key person is available to support the child with the appropriate language to identify and share with the other children the materials that she has provided. Recalling our own childhood we can probably bring to mind playing with 'Granny's button box' or with a collection of shells and coloured pebbles. There seems to be a special fascination in containers – small purses, bags or boxes with different things inside them. Elinor had a large collection of beautiful, interesting and unusual purses, small boxes and a large collection of often quite tiny objects, to go inside them.

This special time for the key person and her children should last no more than 15–20 minutes, and the aim is to give every child time and space to talk about their chosen treasures. Use an attractive quilt cover or rug to create your 'island' so that the children will recognise it as a signal for this activity. If using the purses or small boxes, have one item in each purse or box – a shiny shell or a beautiful button, for example. Let the children choose a purse or box from your big tin or basket. The adult should begin to describe the child's chosen treasure, with a sense of wonder and anticipation, 'Charlie has chosen the beautiful little red satin purse, tell us Charlie, what does it feel like? I wonder if there is anything inside the purse . . .'

The adult's role

As in Treasure Baskets and heuristic play, the adult's task is to accumulate a collection of safe but interesting objects and to replace and replenish them regularly. Once you have decided to start making your own collections, involve all the staff team, because they will be able to find lots of treasures at home or in charity shops. This is a good activity for involving parents; they will be able to contribute with postcards from holiday locations, cards from visits to museums, art galleries, exhibitions, etc. This is a good opportunity to follow children's interests and schemas, finding things that you know might encourage a child to begin to talk. Two of the favourite items in Ruth's purses were cake decorations: a pink ballerina and a racing car.

The collections should only be used during 'island time' or they will lose their 'specialness', and the children need to be closely supervised when using them. When the children see the adult handling the objects sensitively, it will encourage them to see the objects as precious and encourage them to care for, touch and describe them. Have enough collections or sets of objects, just as you do for heuristic play, especially if you do the activity daily.

The role of the adult is to facilitate and promote conversation in the group. This is done by careful listening and responding to the children's questions and comments about the objects. It may be necessary to encourage shyer children or those with less vocabulary. Use open-ended questions, asking permission to touch their chosen object or commenting on the way the child is holding or exploring it.

Store the objects in attractive tins or containers. Ruth keeps one of her collections in a very large decorated tin that originally held a panettone (Italian Christmas cake). As the children become familiar with the collections they may request particular elements – 'the shells today please', or 'small balls' or 'pictures' (postcards).

Suggestions for 'island time' collections

- Small purses, with a range of fastenings, zips/clips/press studs/Velcro;
- Lipstick cases (often beautifully covered in material, we found several in Oxfam shops);

Figure 6.4 A collection of purses and small treasures for 'island time'

- Little boxes of differing shapes and sizes;
- Assorted buttons in boxes or basket – the children just choose one button. This can take longer than you would think. Find large unusual buttons as well as an assortment of small and medium-sized ones.
- Sets of small toys – animals, fish, insects;
- Photograph/postcard/card collection – you will be astonished at what they choose and why. Collect postcards of Old Masters, old-fashioned toys (from museums), landscapes, funny cards, animals, children, people and scenes from other countries and cultures.
- Coins, stamps, marbles;
- Shells, feathers, stones, fossils, large seed pods, small cones;
- Nuts, bolts, screws, Rawlplugs, small pieces of piping, tubing, small reels;
- 'Jewellery' collection: badges, brooches, necklaces, bracelets, rings, chunky costume-type jewellery.

Playthings

The second year spans a period of very rapid development. At the beginning of the year the mobile infant will still find satisfaction in exploration of textures and shapes by mouth and hand and in the simple toys described in Chapter 3. By the age of two some children will already be engaging in most of the kinds of play described in Chapters 7 and 8 and beginning to use more structured materials. Below we give some suggestions for play equipment for children in their second year designed to help them practise both physical and manipulative skills. Most of these are easily available from suppliers such as Community Playthings. Investing in good quality large equipment pays dividends, as it will be robust and stand up to the strains and stresses of group use over time.

1. Slide. A simple solid wooden structure with three low steps leading to a small platform with a slide on the other side. Low rail supports on both sides.
2. Playbox. A solid, 60 cm square box with a large round hole in one side for crawling in and out of. A curtain can be fixed to cover the hole, allowing 'hiding and finding' games.
3. Stacking boxes. A strong, wooden box with two smaller boxes inside. The measurements of the largest box should be about $28 \times 43 \times 28$ cm – not too high for a child to climb in by herself. The smallest box can be filled with wooden building blocks. This is probably the most versatile piece of play equipment of all and will certainly be used well into the third year. It is worth having two or three sets if at all possible.
4. Hollow bricks. Have two sizes if possible – about $18 \times 10 \times 8$ cm, and $23 \times 18 \times 8$ cm.
5. Baby-walker. This should be of the trolley type, described in Chapter 3 – a low wooden box with a metal handle at shoulder height for easy pushing. It must be sturdily built so that it will not tip up when a child leans on the handle, and the wheels should be slow-moving to avoid children bumping into each other.

6. Large, simple posting box. Commercially available ones, often made of light plastic in garish colours, are too complex for very young children to use satisfactorily. Choose a well-designed one made in polished wood. It should have three apertures in the top side: a round hole, a square hole and a slot. Wooden cubes, cylinders and rectangles, at least six of each, are needed for posting, and these should be kept in their own basket or tin so that the children can always find a ready supply when they want to use the posting box. Of course they will experiment with trying to post other shapes as well and should be allowed to find out for themselves what will and will not go through the holes.

Summary

During the second year of life the child's growth proceeds along a number of developmental lines. She moves towards independence in mobility, manipulative skill, feeding and self-care, and acquires the ability to communicate in words. The key person plays a crucial role in enabling this process to occur smoothly, in close consultation with the child's family. Careful management of the environment can reduce conflict and enable workers to offer a model of compromise and negotiation which demonstrates respect for the child's individuality.

This period sees the transition from intimate care carried out by others, which is such an important part of a baby's daily experience, to self-care, which is beginning to become possible in the second year. It is a time of rapid growth towards independence in every aspect of life, yet the child's physical ability to move away from her caring adults at the same time holds for her the duality of her need for them. She experiences a change in her relationships as more of her own life comes under her control. The growing sense of self finds clear expression when the words 'me' and 'mine' emerge into daily use. Along with this goes an intense urge to explore and experiment with any object that comes to hand, which is the basis for 'heuristic play', as described in the next chapter.

7 Heuristic play with objects

There can be no effective and satisfactory work without play; there can be no sound and wholesome thought without play.

(Charles Dickens)

In this chapter we will consider:

- The underlying principles of heuristic play with objects;
- The organisation and setting up of a heuristic play session;
- Heuristic play with older children and those with additional needs;
- Suggestions for objects and materials.

In this chapter we describe an approach to the learning of children in their second year of life, which was developed and put into practice by Elinor Goldschmied[1] in collaboration with childcare workers in England, Scotland, Italy and Spain. Heuristic play has become an important part of Elinor's legacy to early years practitioners. When used following Elinor's principles it is no exaggeration to say that it changes practitioners' thinking about the environment and the resources they use with very young children. This approach is not just part of a generally rich environment that we would want to provide for children in their second year, but a special component of the day's activities that needs to be organised in a particular way for maximum effectiveness. This is the reason why it is called here by an unfamiliar term, 'heuristic play with objects'. Put simply, it consists of offering a group of children, for a defined period of time in a controlled environment, a large number of different kinds of objects and receptacles with which they play freely without adult intervention.

Learning by exploration and discovery

Heuristic learning is defined in the Oxford Dictionary as 'a system of education under which the pupil is trained to find out things for himself'. The word 'heuristic' means 'allowing or assisting to discover or proceeding to a solution by trial and error'. It has been a dominant strand in English primary education for many years (though at the time of writing under political attack). Up till now not much thought has been given to how the principle might be extended into educational provision for very young children. By using the specific term 'heuristic play' we want to draw attention to the great importance of this kind of spontaneous exploratory activity, giving it the significance and dignity which it merits. The practitioner, by means of setting out an environment and a rich range of resources, will support and enable young children to discover, explore and find or create solutions by trial and error.

Increasing mobility is the central factor in the child's developing abilities in the second year of life. The newly acquired skill in moving is practised ceaselessly throughout the waking day, and it is often this passion for moving about which creates anxieties for the responsible adults and causes them to restrict the child and limit her opportunities for learning. If the family lives in overcrowded or cramped accommodation, where there is little or no indoor or outside space, this can compromise the young child's experiences. Recognising that some children have little or no access to an outdoor environment will mean practitioners have to be very creative in how they offer play and learning opportunities to the newly mobile child. Even when housing is good, very few people are prepared to redesign their living space entirely to suit the needs of a small child. How many times a day do we have to say 'No, don't touch' when they want to grab and handle our most precious or dangerous (for them) objects. The urge to use their increasingly precise eye–hand coordination, combined with lively curiosity, becomes a source of conflict.

It is often said that the concentration we observe in infants seated at the Treasure Basket is lost once they can move about. Typically, caregivers comment that children between one and two 'flit from one thing to another', that the play material available does not hold their attention for more than a few minutes. They are not interested in puzzles or putting pegs in their 'proper' holes, and would usually rather throw them on the floor. In fact the child is saying to us 'there are other things I want to do first'. Their level of competence cannot be satisfied by play material where there is a 'right' answer, determined by adults. Children in their second year feel a great urge to explore and discover for themselves the way objects behave in space as they manipulate them. They need a wide variety of objects with which to do this kind of experimentation, objects that are constantly new and interesting, and that certainly cannot be bought from a toy catalogue.

Watching children of this age brings to mind the ancient story of Archimedes in his bath. When he discovered the law of the displacement of water due to the volume of his body, he is said to have leapt out of the bath crying exultantly, 'Eureka – I have found it!' The Greek word 'eurisko', from which our word heuristic is derived, means 'serves to discover or reach understanding of'. This is exactly what young children do of their own accord, without any direction from adults, provided they have the

Figure 7.1 What is this?

Figure 7.2 What can I do with it?

materials with which to pursue their explorations. Far from losing the ability to concentrate, it becomes clear that, given the right conditions and materials, the child in her second year can develop concentration in a new way.

Heuristic play in action

Heuristic play is an approach and not a prescription. There is no one right way to do it and people in different settings will have their own ideas and collect their own materials. Indeed, one of the great merits of the approach is that it releases creativity in adults and makes working with young children more stimulating. However, the practical advice in this chapter is based on many years' experience in different countries and on detailed observations of a large number of children, many of whom have been filmed on video and subjected to close analysis.

Here are some brief descriptions of children engaged in heuristic play in groups of about eight. The children are of four nationalities but there are no obvious differences in the way they use the material.

> Antonio (14 months) crouched between two smallish buckets, one filled with bottle corks, the other empty. With quick, neat hand movements, he transferred the corks one by one into the empty bucket. Among the ordinary corks there were two champagne corks, larger and with a shiny covering, and a sauce bottle cork with a red plastic top. Finding a champagne cork, he looked at it intently, threw it aside, and continued transferring the ordinary corks. When he came across the second champagne cork and later the red-topped one, he discarded them without hesitation, showing his developing ability to discriminate and categorise. Once the second bucket was full he tipped it up, emptying out the corks on the floor.
>
> Noel (16 months), standing holding a large red hair roller, picked up a smaller, yellow curler from the floor and slotted it through the red one. He repeated this action with evident pleasure, his eyes fixed on the objects in his hands. Then he looked about and chose another red roller of the same diameter as the one he was

holding. He tried to pass the second red roller through the first. He paused and squeezed the two rollers together, trying to put one inside the other. Unable to do this, he dropped the second red roller and looked about, picked up a smaller, yellow roller and passed it through the original red one. He repeated this action three times, then, with a satisfied air, dropped both and moved elsewhere.

Jacqueline (17 months) was seated with her legs together in front of her, near a collection of ribbons of different colours and textures (satin, velvet, lace). She chose a length of red ribbon, laid it across her ankles, then took a length of fine chain and laid it parallel about two inches above the ribbon on her leg. She took a yellow ribbon and laid it parallel to the chain, repeating the process until the arrangement of alternating ribbon and chain reached to just above her knees. She looked intently at what she had done and smiled to herself.

Clemente (17 months), sitting on the floor with his legs apart, took a broad-based tin, turned it upside down, placing a slightly smaller tin, also upside down, on top of it. On this 'tower' he placed a yellow hair roller. Turning to look at

Figure 7.3 Beads are endlessly fascinating (Photograph: University of Roehampton)

another child nearby, he accidentally touched the lower tin and the roller fell off. Clemente picked up the roller and replaced it on the tower. He looked at it carefully and with his right hand gave a very gentle tap to the upper tin. The roller wobbled but did not fall off. He gave a slightly harder tap with the same result, then a harder one still, causing the roller to fall. He replaced the roller and repeated the process.

Janet (19 months) sat on the floor close to a nursery worker, holding a shallow box with a lid. She picked up four corks, one after the other, and placed them in a row to fill one part of the box. She took another cork and tried to make a second row below the first. There was no space to do this, so she placed two corks sideways, leaving an unfilled space in the box. She looked about, took a short length of chain, held it up until it stopped its dangling movement, and let it gently down to fill the space. Then she closed the lid of the box and turned to the adult with a smile. The adult smiled back without comment.

Some important points are illustrated by these observations. The children made their spontaneous selection from a wide range of materials (described below). They worked with purpose and concentration. Their physical energy and developing manipulative skill were an essential part of the satisfying and pleasurable activity. This led to constant practising and gaining in competence. These babies displayed many of the signals of concentration, persistence, precision, facial expression and posture, complexity and creativity described by Laevers *et al.* (1997). They were deeply involved in their learning, and they were also given opportunities to be self-directing and to initiate the learning themselves.

Antonio, at 14 months, clearly discriminated between the different types of corks, decided which he wanted in his receptacle, and rejected the larger champagne corks. Jacqueline made a pattern, a series of alternating chains and ribbons, a very deliberate and complex action. Janet solved the problem of how to arrange her corks in a given space with the resources she had to hand. The smile she gave to her key person was one of satisfaction, not having the language to say 'Look at this, I created it, I made a pattern, I solved a problem'. These babies were all involved and engaged at a high level and they had the security of an adult who was also engaged but not involved in their exploration. The adult who was the emotional anchor for these children returned Janet's smile, acknowledging her achievement but not needing to comment. She would be using her observations later to share with Janet's parents and inform her planning for Janet's developing skills and interests.

In the process of exploration of the material the question of right and wrong ways to use it does not arise. The children observe directly as they handle the object, what it will and will not do. Everything they undertake is successful; the only failure to carry out an intended action is when the nature of the material itself obstructs the child's efforts – as in the example of Noel who discovered that two hair rollers of the same diameter will not slot into one another.

This element of guaranteed success creates a very different experience for the child from much of the 'educational' play material often given to children of this age, which has a result predetermined by the design devised by an adult maker. This is not to say that materials of this kind have no value, but they have a different function, appropriate to a later stage of development than the one we are discussing here.

Children engrossed in their own discoveries do not come into conflict with others in the group, largely because there is so much material available that they are not required to do any sharing, which it is premature to expect at this age. This is in sharp contrast to the normal experience of nursery staff who often have to intervene in the course of the day to keep the peace amongst children too young to have language or negotiating skills. Moreover it has been observed during heuristic play sessions that children, as they approach the age of two, begin to engage in cooperative exchanges with others which arise from the exploration of the material, initiated originally for themselves.

The descriptions of the children's activities given above illustrate how they will move items in and out of spaces and fill and empty receptacles. From the mass of objects available, they select, discriminate and compare, place in series, slot and pile, roll and balance, with concentration, growing manipulative skill and evident satisfaction.

Of course, all this also occurs spontaneously in the process of play with anything that happens to be available, but usually in spite of adults and not because of them. These patterns emerge from children's naturally developing bodily activity provided that they are facilitated by the environment. What is different is the recognition that we should create space and time to cater for this type of play, acknowledging that children in their second year have specific educational needs just as much as four-year-olds.

Apart from the obvious pleasure that children find in the materials, heuristic play may have a major role in developing the ability to concentrate. This is strongly associated with cognitive development and educational progress, as research by psychologists such as Jerome Bruner and Kathy Sylva has demonstrated. Very young children engaged in heuristic play have been observed playing intensely with a group of objects for up to an hour. Superficially this activity may appear to be random or pointlessly repetitive, which is probably why adults are often tempted to intervene. In fact, close observation shows that the play has its own internal logic. The repetition is very like the activity of scientists who develop their knowledge by carrying out the same experiment over and over again with tiny variations. Indeed, Alison Gopnik and her colleagues suggest that children create and revise theories in exactly the same way as scientists (Gopnik *et al.* 1999). Sometimes great advances result from accidental observations, as in the case of Fleming's discovery of penicillin. The same is true for children. For them one thing leads to another in a pleasurable process of discovery, which in turn leads to further practice and the growth of skill.

Introducing heuristic play in a group setting

It is important that staff understand the purpose and thinking behind this type of play, that it is intended to enrich and not to replace the work that they are already doing. In order for it to succeed the staff as a group need to be committed to the idea. This is much easier if they can see it in action, ideally by visiting a setting where it is already happening or, failing that, by watching heuristic play on video and meeting people who are using it in their work with young children (Goldschmied and Hughes 1992; Froebel Trust 2013).

Because time and space have to be created to make an effective heuristic play session possible, even those not directly involved may have to make concessions and adaptations. That makes it essential that anyone thinking of introducing heuristic play into their setting should carry the whole staff group with them (Holland 1997).

There are some basic organisational points which should be observed if there is to be maximum satisfaction for the children:

1. At least 15 varieties of play materials should be provided, with a separate draw-string bag for each kind. This may sound a lot, but there are so many possibilities; a childcare centre in Barcelona where heuristic play has been in operation for some years has accumulated 36 different types of object. A row of hooks, labelled with the name of the object, is needed to hang up the bags when not in use, or an alternative arrangement that we have seen is a trolley with hooks and storage space used not only to store, but to wheel the resources to the room or area of the nursery where the play is taking place. The trolley also made it easier for small children to put some of the larger tins and receptacles into the storage space.
2. There must be plenty of items – this is a prerequisite for a good heuristic play session. When we have observed sessions where practitioners have complained that they are not seeing the concentration or engagement with the materials or when the creative and exploratory element of the play does not seem to be happening, it is often due to the nature of the objects or there being too few of them for the number of children involved in the activity. Practitioners often find it hard to believe how many objects and receptacles are needed for a heuristic play session for, say, eight children – 50 or 60 items in each bag and at least 20 tins or boxes. Suggestions for materials to be provided are given at the end of the chapter.
3. A clearly defined space is needed for the session, large enough to allow the children to move about freely. Quietness is an important feature of the session – carpet helps to reduce the noise level. If you are using the general play space for a heuristic play session, it is helpful if you can block off or cover other areas or resources, so that there is minimum distraction from the heuristic play objects (Forbes 2004). Where there is space, it works best to set up heuristic play in a separate room. This allows practitioners to set out a wide range of receptacles and objects. It can also mean that when children have had enough, they can return to the group room and other children can have a turn.

All other play material should be put away during the period chosen for this activity. A limited period of the day should be selected and reserved for heuristic play with objects. A good length of time is one hour, allowing for getting materials out and putting them away. It is important to select a time when the maximum numbers of staff are present so that one person can devote her full attention to a small group (eight children at most).

To avoid the children crowding together, the whole of the space available should be used. The adult preparing the session distributes tins and other receptacles of varying sizes around the area. How many tins are needed depends on the number of children in the group, but there should never be less than three per child. We have found different kinds and sizes of tins and baskets are much appreciated by children. They seem to like rummaging through the heuristic play objects, selecting a few of each to put in their basket, and then sit alongside it, examining and exploring the properties of the objects. Perhaps they are creating a 'treasure basket' of their own as they collect items from the various piles on offer.

When setting out the room for the session, the staff member selects a number of bags of objects (say five) to make a good combination – for example, chains, cardboard tubes, pompoms, tin lids, strings of beads and necklaces and curtain rings. These items are placed in separate or mixed heaps from which the children will make their own choice without needing direction or encouragement.

The adult's role in heuristic play

Children need time to consider how they will play with the material. As we explain below, the role of the adult is to give unobtrusive attention, and, as with the Treasure Basket, the concentration that the children show makes talking superfluous. As the children become absorbed in exploring, the objects will be spread over the floor. They need to be quietly reorganised from time to time by the observant practitioner so that the material always looks inviting. The worker keeps the empty bags beside her chair until she decides it is time for the items to be collected up by the children at the end of the session. Sufficient time, say about 15 minutes, should always be allowed for tidying up without rush so that this is as enjoyable as the activity of playing.

Much of the adult's work is done outside the heuristic play session. She will plan for the session, ensuring the space allocated is appropriate. She will be collecting objects, caring for them, ensuring that damaged ones are repaired and washed as necessary or thrown away, and thinking up new types of interesting items. At the beginning of each session she selects and sets out the objects and receptacles as described above. During the session she will be doing some inconspicuous re-ordering, and finally she will initiate the collecting up of objects by the children, putting them away in the bags and hanging each bag back on its peg.

Beyond this she is essentially a facilitator. She remains quietly seated on a chair (not on the floor), attentive and observant, perhaps studying a particular child and noting what he or she does with the material. The adult does not encourage or suggest, praise or direct what the children should do. The only exception to this is if a child begins to throw things about and disturb the others. In that case the best plan is to offer a receptacle and encourage her to place the things in it. She will also respond to any signals of children who are becoming tired or need a nappy change or other personal care during the session. If a second adult is available as an observer during the activity, then the observations can be used to inform future planning for individual children.

Involving children in clearing up

The other task for the adult is to keep an eye on the clock, to allow time for an unhurried end to the session. When the adult decides that it is time to start clearing up, it is a good plan first to tidy away the receptacles. Then show an object, say a hair curler, to the children and indicate by a gesture that it should be put into the open bag.

   The children should collect the items from the floor, bring them to the adult and put them into the individual bags which she holds open for them. As each article is put in, the adult can check to see that it is in good order, eliminating any that need replacing. In this way she shows that she cares for the playthings even if they consist of common household objects or scrap materials.

Clearing up

The adult can then use simple comments ('there's one under there', 'behind the chair', 'one by your foot') to show that all the objects of the same kind are to be put into this bag. Each phrase is linked directly to an action, so that even very small children have no difficulty in accomplishing the task. If there are several adults in the session each one will be holding a different bag, so that if the child picks up an object other than the

Figure 7.4 Clearing up: an integral part of a Heuristic Play session (Photograph: University of Roehampton)

one being asked for, she can be directed to the other person. In this way the whole floor is cleared and there is a general feeling of satisfaction in having done the job together. Even the youngest children of 12 or 13 months will understand very quickly that the adult wants the items collected. Only later will they grasp that the adult is asking for specific objects. Enabling the children to select and see differences and similarities is part of the adult's task as she directs the collecting up of the items.

There are three reasons for emphasising that the adult should remain seated while the children collect up the items.

- First, and perhaps most important, it protects the adult's back from the strain of picking up large numbers of objects from the floor.
- Second, it reinforces the policy of 'tidy up as you go'.
- Third, it provides a natural way of expanding the children's developing vocabulary as they identify by name each item that they bring to put in the bag. In addition, the children are practising selection and discrimination between different categories of objects, the first stage in sorting, leading eventually to the mathematical concept of sets.

Practitioners meeting heuristic play for the first time occasionally find it difficult to accept the apparently passive role of the adult, and especially the fact that there is no unnecessary talk. But what would an adult say to a child absorbed in heuristic play? Inevitably she is tempted to comment and make suggestions, inhibiting the discovery process and interfering with the child's concentration. There will be other times of the day when the adult will sit on the floor close to the children for cuddles and conversation.

Of course, there are also times when speech is necessary during heuristic play sessions, most usefully during the clearing-up stage. We would emphasise, too, that none of these guidelines are absolute and should never be taken to the point of causing the adult to behave in an unnatural or rejecting way towards a child. We have, for example, seen a young nursery worker, anxious to follow the rules, ignore an obviously distressed child who was holding up her arms and crying for attention. Clearly a child who is upset for any reason cannot play and must be comforted. If the upset is temporary, the child may return to play after a brief cuddle.

More usually, staff who have experienced conducting this kind of play session have noted that an atmosphere of quiet concentration develops. Conflicts between the children rarely happen because there is abundant material, but many friendly interchanges are observed, both verbal and non-verbal.

For the adults it can be an interlude of calm in a busy day which gives them a chance to observe the children in a way not easy at other times. However, the inactivity of the adult is largely deceptive since it is her quiet but attentive presence which makes the whole thing work.

Heuristic play in different settings

It is not suggested that a heuristic play session should be offered to children every day, and the staff should use their discretion about this. There are advantages in giving it the feeling of a special treat, which will remind adults of the need to create a clear time and space, when they are not to be interrupted by ringing telephones or other distractions. Similarly, it underlines the need to treat the material with care and respect, to keep it in good condition and pack it up carefully at the end of each session, not leave it lying around underfoot.

In childcare settings heuristic play can provide a special activity for an age group that is otherwise often overlooked. It is the equivalent of the common practice of withdrawing the older children for more structured activities outside their group rooms. In 'family' groups where the under-twos often have to compete for attention with the older ones, it can enable a staff member to give special attention to a small number of children.

Sessional playgroups taking funded two-year-olds might find heuristic play a useful element in their planning tool-kit, and if staff have not previously used the approach, support from their local authority adviser might be helpful, or a visit to a setting where heuristic play is well embedded. Parent and toddler groups could make use of the fact that there are always plenty of adults available, to offer heuristic play with objects to the one- to two-year-olds in some sessions. Conditions may not be ideal, but even in community or church halls it is usually possible to create a quiet space and make a welcoming corner with a piece of carpet or large rug. We know of a Children's Centre that offered a heuristic play session as part of an under-twos group that met in the local medical centre. Parents who had never heard of or experienced heuristic play before enjoyed a session and started to collect items to expand the experiences for their children.

In Children's Centres, early years settings and nurseries caring for children from homes where play is not a priority and perhaps there is much pressure on the available space, or whose parents may need help in building a better relationship with them, heuristic play has an invaluable contribution to make. These children are especially likely to have been denied the freedom to explore and experiment in their home environment. For the parents, a heuristic play session provides a unique occasion when they can sit quietly and observe their child without feeling any obligation to control her behaviour.

Heuristic play also depends on resources that are mainly from the real world. Often these things are considered as 'junk'; however we like to think of them as being 're-found' and then reused, part of the commitment to recycle as much as possible. Collecting materials for heuristic play is not expensive and the resulting enjoyment and learning, as we have already said, is far beyond what can be obtained from most commercially available toys.

Heuristic play for older children

Elinor Goldschmied designed the heuristic play model specifically for children aged
between one and two years, but we have seen it used very successfully for children in
their third year. Sonia was able to observe two successive sessions at Eastwood Day
Nursery in Roehampton, the first with younger children and the second with children
coming up to three. The difference between the two groups was fascinating. The young
children mostly played individually, exploring what they could do with the objects
they chose and paying little attention to other children. The older ones, though equally
absorbed and concentrating, formed little alliances, playing together in groups of two
or three. Some of them built elaborate structures with the materials available and
enlisted the help of others to carry out what was clearly a preconceived plan. Because
the resources were abundant there was no conflict, and the children played for 40
minutes very quietly and harmoniously. When one of the two attendant adults indicated
that it was time to clear up, the children themselves fetched the storage bags and started
collecting the objects to put in them with a minimum of adult assistance.

Figure 7.5 Heuristic Play is equally appealing to older children (Photograph: University
of Roehampton)

Adapting heuristic play principles: does it change our perceptions of very young children's play?

Some practitioners (Holland 1997) have taken the principles of heuristic play and considered how the approach might be applied to other areas of provision for young children. Many centres now include natural materials and objects from the outside world as part of the everyday resources offered to children under three. In some of the settings we have visited, baskets of pinecones, cotton reels, large seed pods, wooden curtain rings and many other 'found materials' are stored in baskets on open, low-level shelving where the children are encouraged to choose and select which particular objects they would like to explore further. In the same settings the adults expected and encouraged the children to replace the objects in the baskets and return the baskets to the shelf. Just as clearing up is an integral part of heuristic play, so it should be encouraged across as many areas as possible of young children's play and exploration.

Materials required for heuristic play

One part of the organiser's role is to collect, buy or make a good quantity of the items listed below. Many of the objects can be collected by parents, staff and friends – empty tins, metal jar caps, pinecones, for example. Others, such as woollen pompoms, can be easily made. Recycling centres are good places to find resources – one visited in Somerset provided film reels, knitting machine cones (plastic and cardboard), short lengths of tubing and piping.

Bought items, from hardware stores, shops selling kitchen equipment or haberdashery departments can be quite inexpensive. Also needed are drawstring bags in which these different items are kept when they are not in use. The bags must be large enough to take the number of objects required for the group (40×50 cm is a good size) and made of a material which is tough enough to stand up to heavy use but not too stiff. They must open wide at the top to allow children to drop in the objects at the end of the play session.

The adults need to search continually, with an imaginative eye, for different objects suitable to add to the bag collection. This is a good way to involve parents and volunteers and can become a strong interest for them. Many of the items are similar to those included singly in the Treasure Basket, providing the widest possible variety of size, weight, colour and texture.

One of the attractive and creative aspects of these varied materials lies in the infinity of possible combinations that go far beyond the imagination of any one person. It has been calculated that four bags with 60 items in each allow for the possibility of 13,871,842 combinations!

Christmas and other festivals offer a good opportunity for parents to help stock up for heuristic play. The range of tins and gift bags available increases, with wonderful variety of shapes and size. This following list incorporates items from many different sources, including some suggested by students and practitioners and others seen at various settings or suggested at training days.

Receptacles

Tins (as many different shapes as possible – round, square, oval, with and without lids); baskets, variety of shapes and sizes, with handles and without; very small buckets with handles (often found in garden centres); whisky-bottle cylinders, with metal bottoms; crisp cylinders; hollow cardboard tubes – carpet rolls cut down are good; cardboard cylinders of all kinds (such as the insides of kitchen paper, cling-film and aluminium foil rolls); wide-necked plastic bottles – varying sizes; flower pots – ceramic and plastic; nests of boxes or baskets; money boxes and other containers with slots in the top – shoe boxes with lids can have a slot cut out.

Things to drape objects around or hang from

Mug trees; kitchen roll holders; small gift bags; knitting cones.

Objects to collect or make

Woollen pompoms, not too big, in primary colours; ribbons of velvet, silk and lace; wood offcuts; old keys, tied together in small bunches; metal jar tops; cockle or snail shells; larger shells; corks, varying sizes; pinecones.

Objects to buy or acquire

Curtain rings, wooden and metal; cotton reels; electric cable spools – varying sizes; wooden laundry pegs; hair rollers of differing diameter; ping-pong balls; golf balls; stress-type balls; rubber door stops; furniture castors; varied lengths and weights of chain; costume jewellery – lengths of beads, large bracelets and bangles; ice cube trays; door knobs; drawer handles (knob design); measuring cups, bowls and spoons; colanders.

Summary

As they acquire mobility, children have an increasing need to explore and experiment which may be frustrated by their home environment. This chapter explains the theory behind heuristic play with objects, a particular way of offering a planned learning experience to children in their second year and beyond. Providing heuristic play in group settings requires careful working out of practical details: time, space, materials and management. The adult's role is that of organiser and facilitator, not initiator. Given generous supplies of well-chosen objects, children in their second year will play with concentration and without conflict for extended periods. Heuristic play offers the young child the opportunity to find out through first-hand experience what the objects will and will not do. Nursery collections should reflect the developing and changing interests and mobility of the young child.

There is no right or wrong way in heuristic play, unlike with most manufactured toys, and that is its most important benefit. It is inherently inclusive and can be a valuable approach to offer older children with learning difficulties, who can play with the material at their own level, or to those with mobility problems. Practitioners can sometimes feel defeated by the problem of how to offer adequate and appropriate activity to children in their care who have additional needs; heuristic play may offer some answers.

Note

1. Elinor acknowledged the contribution of Katrin Strohe and Thelma Robinson, based on the ideas of Dr Geoffrey Waldon, to the model of heuristic play described in this chapter.

8 Children in their third year

All mothers should keep a book wherein to write the sayings of their children –
when a child speaks of honey as beejam, it reveals the creation of language.

(William Barnes, Dorset dialect poet)

In this chapter we will consider:

- The child's sense of self;
- Development in the third year of life;
- Communication and language;
- Children's thinking;
- Play and learning;
- Two-year-olds in early education settings.

'An explosion of self-awareness' is one of the ways in which the experience of a child in the third year of life can be described. In a nursery group, the practitioner has the demanding and interesting task of adapting herself to the tempo of children at various stages of development and with a wide range of interests and experiences.

Children in their third year are very interested in their own appearance and love to inspect themselves closely, especially if there are full-length mirrors available. They will also compare their skin colour and hair texture with those of other children and ask questions about differences. In fact, good use can be made of the opportunity to re-inforce children's positive images of themselves, pointing out that people come in all kinds of beautiful colours, and they should be offered a range of skin-coloured paints and crayons with which to represent themselves. Children need to see themselves and their families reflected in the images around them, their jigsaws, picture books, dolls, puppets and, most importantly, in the people who look after them.

Children aged between two and three need to feel valued and respected and we should give them increasing opportunities to make their own choices and decisions.

Their speech is emerging but at times they still experience the frustration of not being able to make themselves understood. Their craving for independence – 'me do it' – may conflict with adult priorities, hence the negative terms often used to describe this period, 'the terrible twos', 'tantrum toddlers'.

Shanta Everington (2010), writing both as a mother and an early years professional, suggests that parents think instead about 'the terrific twos' and make a list of ten positive things about life with their two-year-old. This would be a good starting point for anyone working with children in this age range and their families.

Development in the third year of life

In his third year, the child moves with a certain degree of autonomy into a period of consolidation while seeking a vast amount of information about his immediate world. He tries to interpret how this relates directly to himself, and strives to respond to the often inexplicable demands that both his adults and his peers make upon him. Because a child often does not have sufficient information to make sense of what is happening, he has to deal with anxieties and frustrations that need imaginative understanding from his adults. Happenings that cannot be explained take on a mysterious and magical quality. Children are not alone in this for we, as adults, often have similar feelings when, for instance, we have conversations on Skype or FaceTime with family living abroad or when we consider the miracles of genetic engineering. We always need to respect and not laugh at the child's attempts at understanding.

Physical activity

Penny Greenland (2010) suggests that just as 'five a day' should be part of our healthy eating regime, a healthy movement diet should also be recommended. The analogy with a healthy diet is helpful when planning physical activities and promoting an environment that supports movement, and where children's sensory needs are met, especially those lesser recognised senses – proprioception and vestibular sensation. Proprioception is the sense of movement of limbs and joints, location of parts of our body, and spatial orientation. It is the sense which enables us to walk along an imaginary line, or to drive a car without constantly looking down at the pedals. Vestibular sensation relates to gravity, being aware of where our body is in relation to the floor and how to maintain our balance.

By the age of two a child will run safely in a straight line, and later round corners, negotiating obstacles. As he practises climbing up and getting down from furniture and apparatus, his ability and judgement rapidly increase. At two years he walks upstairs two feet to a step, but by three he can do so with alternating feet, though going down he will still use both feet on each step. At three years he walks and gallops with enjoyment and control.

Exploration and experimentation sometimes arouse great anxiety in adults. The question is always how to balance legitimate risk-taking and safety. For instance, how high should we let children build towers with large blocks and at what height should we intervene? Do we allow them to stand on a chair to continue building, knowing they might fall off it? If not, are we curtailing the learning of future engineers and architects or preventing them from developing their own sense of balance and stability? Instead we could reduce the risk of a fall by providing the right kind of chair, firmly placed, with someone holding it.

In one setting we observed children confidently using a deep barrel as an adjunct to the climbing frame. These children helped each other, were protective of their own and other children's safety – 'hold that bit there', 'move your leg over more', 'hang on to that rail' – and greatly enjoyed being hidden completely from view when they dropped into the barrel. Clearly they had practised these movements many times, and now were using and demonstrating their skills.

Many nurseries and Children's Centres have 'movement areas' or offer opportunities for 'Developmental Movement Play' (Jabadao) which is a neuro-developmental play-based approach to support development, learning and well-being. After staff have been introduced to the principles they are encouraged to look at their environment and think how they might offer an indoor movement space (see also Chapter 13).

Figure 8.1 Enjoying developmental movement

Self-care in the third year

Toilet training

There is great variation in the speed at which children achieve bladder control, and, as is well known, this area of development is extremely sensitive to any kind of stress or anxiety. An upset in the family or an illness can easily cause a temporary regression, and it is very important for nursery staff to accept this without reproach or impatience. For a child who has been dry for some time, wet pants are uncomfortable and sometimes embarrassing. Treating the incident in a matter of fact way is most likely to avoid a setback becoming a long-term problem. Nursery staff and childminders should resist pressure to give too much importance to the matter, for instance by constantly interrupting the child's play to suggest a visit to the bathroom. By this age there is no need for communal 'bathroom time' and children can go as they want throughout the day, though they will probably need reminding, and most will still require supervision to ensure hands are washed. This point could be reinforced by displaying an appropriate photograph.

The bathroom should be planned and maintained to encourage independence, with low-level hand basins, toilet paper, soap, paper-towels or driers within reach, and bins accessible and emptied regularly. Cubicles should have half or three-quarter height doors, providing some privacy for the child, but also allowing the adult access to those who need help.

Dressing and undressing

Children of this age are constantly taking off their clothes and dropping them wherever they happen to be at the time. This is all part of their growing drive towards independence. Parents should be asked to dress children for nursery in clothes that are both practical and easy for the children to manage by themselves – using Velcro instead of buttons or laces, for example – and that can stand the rough and tumble, paint and play-dough of a nursery day. Ensuring there is somewhere to hang children's coats, with photos under the pegs, is a good starting point for independence.

Figure 8.2 Here's my coat

Communication and language

Language and social development are interlinked; adult–child relationships are key and we know that the main way children acquire language is by listening and talking with the people that they love and trust, including their key persons in the childcare setting (Elfer *et al.* 2012). Spoken language, however, is only one of the ways we represent ourselves and communicate. Others are 'dance, drama, painting, sculpture, music, facial expression, body language, eye contact and touch' (Bruce 1991, p. 117). These non-verbal forms of communication are particularly important in working with children with language delay or learning difficulties.

Vygotsky's (1978) work on play and its relation to language and children's ability to self-regulate their gradually emerging cognitive and emotional development has been very important to the body of research in early years. Language, play and cognition are linked to young children's social skills. In their play, children practise the words they are learning. Vygotsky argued that it is through their play that children develop and use symbols and the early sounds linked to meaning (from about 10 months onwards). Those first 'words' used consistently and repeatedly with a familiar object or person, supply the connection between pretend play and early symbolic development (Whitebread and Basilio 2012). Vygotsky observed that it is often in their pretend play that we hear self-directed or private speech, a running commentary on what they are doing.

It is through Vygotsky's work (1978) that we recognise the importance and support of people, including other children, in the development of thinking. The 'zone of proximal development' is when young children move from being supported by an adult or another child, when involved in a task, to being able to perform the task alone, either through questions – 'possibility thinking' – or modelling – introducing a new skill. We heard the children in the climbing frame and barrel observation, talking to each other – 'turn round', 'try it like this' 'let me help'. Children can then repeat and practise the skill or action demonstrated. They go on to internalise, learn the behaviour and then use the skill later.

Listening and talking in the nursery

In earlier chapters we have shown how meaning becomes attached to words through a child's direct sensory experience and play. If the key person approach is operating effectively, the 'island of intimacy' (see Chapter 6) provides a significant time when the small group of children are sure of their close adult's full attention. This is a point when the key person can make a note of how each child's language is progressing, which can be shared with parents and as part of the individual planning for the child.

It is particularly important that occasions of this kind are built into the structure of the day for children in their third year, when feelings and ideas often come faster than words and a child will sometimes stutter in eagerness. It helps if the adult gently holds the child's hand, showing her genuine consideration for what the child is struggling to say. Barbara Tizard showed in her comparison of children's talk in nursery and at home that the quality of conversation in the nursery tends to be inferior because it depends on how much the adult knows about the context, which of course is taken for granted by the child (Tizard and Hughes 2008). The authors also noted that in the home the adult was typically responding to the child's questions, whereas in the nursery it was the other way round.

Iram Siraj-Blatchford (2011) proposes an effective pedagogy, which she calls 'sustained shared thinking' (Sylva *et al.* 2004). This is when two or more individuals (adult/child or child/child) work together to solve a problem, extend a narrative, or clarify a concept, both parties contributing to the thinking which then develops and broadens. This is far removed from the sort of dialogue – it can hardly be called conversation – when we often hear adults asking children meaningless and intrusive questions ('what colour is that bucket?') when the child is engrossed in pouring and filling, carefully using a shovel and a sieve.

Children, even those with a wide vocabulary and a good command of language, cannot be expected to appreciate the subtler aspects of adult speech. This can lead to misunderstandings. For example, Jan, a childminder, had been visiting a friend with Sally, a usually amenable two-year-old who she had been looking after for several months. As they were leaving she said to Sally, 'If we have time on our way home perhaps we'll go to the zoo.' Sally, who had much enjoyed their previous trip to the zoo, picked up the last few words of the sentence, not grasping the significance of 'if' and 'perhaps'. When it turned out that there was not after all time for the zoo, she was understandably disappointed and frustrated, and promptly had a tantrum.

We now know that language development at the age of two years is a good predictor of children's performance on entry to primary school (Roulstone *et al.* 2011). By two years a child will understand between 200 and 500 words and use more than 50 words, putting together short sentences – 'bye bye daddy', 'come on mummy'. At this age they generally understand more than they say, but by three we will be hearing new words daily. However, there is considerable variation in the rate at which children acquire language. In a sample of 1127 children, using the data from a large longitudinal survey (the Avon Longitudinal Study of Parents and Children), 55 per cent of children aged 25 months were using sentences of three to four words, 27 per cent were using two words and the remainder were at or below the single-word level (Roulstone *et al.* 2011).

This is the age of endless questions, the child constantly asking 'What's that?' as he moves about handling different objects and demanding a response. The overstretched adult at home may exclaim 'Oh do be quiet' or, as we have all done, 'Can't you keep still for a minute?' If the child could only explain the urge which drives him to move and to talk he might say, 'Can't you see I have to practise this difficult new thing I can do if I'm to get better at it?'

At times their very strong urge to communicate may be inconvenient to adults, especially at the beginning and end of the day when the parent and practitioner may need to share important information but the child is also desperate either to relay some of the day's events to the parent or to share something equally vital with his key person. Early years practitioners play a key role in supporting parents, by modelling positive responses to children and demonstrating diversionary tactics.

As observed by Vygotsky, children in their third year often talk to themselves continuously as they play. If we listen carefully, we hear them rehearse or play back conversations about events or situations that are significant to them. Sometimes children's self-talking gives us very important information about their situation. Alessio, two-and-a-half years, was a child that adults found very difficult and he was constantly reproved at the nursery. He was observed sitting alone on a small swing in the garden murmuring in a sad rhythm 'Alessio is a bad boy, Alessio is a bad boy', painfully internalising the negative image he was constantly receiving from the world. As Elinor Goldschmied noted, if such a cry for help falls on deaf ears, the adults are failing in their job.

How language reveals children's thinking

The daily care of young children in this age group, with all the testing out and challenge to adults that growing awareness of self and others rightly involves, can be very demanding. One of the compensations is that it can also be utterly fascinating. Marco, on a beach for the first time, gazed at the sea and commented, 'It's too full up.' Rebecca, also a month or two past her second birthday, asked, 'Can I go in the big bath?' Matthew, waking after a night of heavy snow, exclaimed, 'There's an all white outside.'

Emma, at nearly three years, was standing beside her grandmother watching a plane crawl across the sky at a great height. The adult commented, 'Perhaps that's the plane I shall go to Italy in tomorrow.' Emma gazed at the plane, tiny in the clouds, and said, 'But how will you get in?' The adult's simple, but serious, explanation enabled her to begin to understand the connection between size and distance.

Anna, at three years, announced in the nursery bathroom, 'I'm going to eat lots and lots and lots, and then I'll get fat like Mummy and have a baby.' Anna was using the information she had about eating and weight, applying what she knew to a situation of which she was ignorant. At that moment it was important that no one laughed, which might easily have happened. Ruben, at 20 months, has been told that there is a baby in his mummy's expanding tummy, and that he will have a sister. He often strokes the tummy gently saying 'baby' and offers it his toys and cup.

Adults may be unprepared how to respond to children's comments about sex and reproduction. Practitioners should discuss these matters in supervision or with colleagues so that they can answer children's questions without embarrassment. It is also important to talk with parents about how they respond to their child's increasing curiosity on subjects that they may perceive as difficult. This will help to alleviate miscommunications which simply confuse children. As they use their newly acquired language, children are constantly giving us vital clues about what is important to them and what they need to understand.

Communication difficulties

As we noted in Chapter 6, there has been a drive to improve the language-learning environments of young children, especially those who are socially disadvantaged or living in poverty. Interventions such as Every Child a Talker (ECAT) and the Speech,

Language and Communication Framework all focus on improving services and provision for children and young people with speech and language and communication needs, in which childcare settings can play a valuable role. For example, how far do the adults in the setting organise the day so that they have opportunities to listen attentively to children? This needs to be a subject of regular staff discussion, with a special focus on the needs of children whose family language is not English or those who have language and speech delay.

Some children may stammer or be hesitant in their speech, they may have limited vocabulary or be unable to put more than two words together. They may not be able to use language to play or interact with other children, leading them to become socially isolated. Speech delay in a child whose development is otherwise normal may be an indication of a hearing loss, often due to 'glue ear' when the child's hearing is reduced or distorted. Careful observation and discussion with parents is required, so that they can share this information with their doctor. Practitioners will be aware of the variation in speech development among the children they work with and make an assessment of when a referral for extra support, or advice from a speech and language therapist or a health visitor, is needed.

Supporting creative thinking

We need to be constantly mindful of how much learning in the nursery is adult-led and directed, and how much is child-initiated. We have already identified how sensitive adults can support the storytelling and narratives of young children through additional props and being part of the story. However we should also think about where and how we might join their play (and learning) and not get in the way. Whitebread (2007) points out that some adults are much more effective than others in doing this. Bruner's concept of scaffolding is helpful here, where the adult is supporting the learning through careful intervention to enable the child to be successful in a task and thus internalise the understanding and be able to reuse it in the same or a different situation at a later point (Wood *et al.* 1976). We recognise children, as Bruner did, as active learners, who construct their own knowledge and become able problem-solvers.

The skill of a good 'scaffolder' is to know when to engage with the child and when to withdraw. Bernadette Duffy describes this as 'well timed, well tuned intervention, to be able to stand back, observe, listen and reflect before diving into children's play', becoming aware of children's interests and 'fascinations' (personal communication 2012).

Another useful concept is 'possibility thinking' (Craft *et al.* 2011) which is about supporting and enabling children to shift 'what is this?', to 'what can I or we do with this?' as, earlier, in the progression from Treasure Basket to heuristic play.

Questions that constrain children's thinking and creativity are the 'possibility narrow' ones, for instance those with yes or no answers. Detailed observations of children's play episodes enable us to think about our engagement and the questions we ask, to recognise unwelcome or unnecessary interruption of the narrative or play that is happening, and to reflect on how we might enable children to follow and build on their interests and ask their own questions.

Figure 8.3 Going shopping with a friend

Self-regulation

Whitebread and Basilio (2012, p. 20) describe this as young children learning to 'interact with others in increasingly more complex ways in accordance with social rules'. Self-regulation develops gradually, and research is demonstrating that these skills can be learnt. The key person will ensure that young children have opportunities to practise them, both with adults and other children. Children in their third year are becoming more cooperative with other children as their language develops, but often need a sensitive adult to help them. Whitebread (2011) suggests that children who are best able to self-regulate are those who have had a good early attachment and adults who have nurtured them.

Schemas – helping us to understand children's thinking

A 'schema' is the term coined by Chris Athey (1990) to describe a pattern of behaviour which can be repeated and generalised, and is used in different situations (Bruce 2004). They are initially linked with movement, being dynamic and active. Athey observed that children could be seen trying out the same action across a range of places and with a variety of resources. For example, Ruth came across a mother standing on the edge of the children's bathroom, and overheard a plaintive 'Come on Lucy, it really is time to go home now'. When Ruth enquired how long Lucy had been in the bathroom, her mother replied, 'Oh, she's long finished, she is just turning on and off all the taps'. What bliss for a child with a rotational schema, a line of low-level hand basins! When Ruth asked Lucy's mum whether this was something she did often, her mother reinforced the staff's hypothesis that she had a rotational schema. Lucy also spent a lot of time spinning herself round and round on the spot, or watching the driver of the family car intently when using the steering wheel, and she was fascinated by washing machines. Recognising schemas can help us support children's interests and learning. Lucy's key person will be observing closely for her preferences which might include circle games, wheels and cogs of all descriptions, spinning tops and roundabouts when visiting the local park. Some settings have developed 'schema bags' with resources to support and extend the most commonly observed patterns of play behaviour.

Stories and rhymes

Through this third year a child has a growing pleasure in listening to repetitive jingles and nursery rhymes and in hearing favourite stories over and over again. Story-reading can make a useful contribution to language development but only if it is carefully handled, with attention to the individual experience of each child. Stories need to be rhythmical and read with intonation – children love stories with alliteration and enjoy making up nonsense words. Every time we read with a baby or older toddler we are showing them how books should be held. Letting them help to turn the pages from a very young age encourages them to show care and respect for books. We need to hold the book correctly, promote left-to-right eye movement by using our finger to follow the print. This will help in the development of literacy and could be the first step towards a love of books and a lifelong passion for reading.

Reading stories encourages us to talk to the child about the book and its wider context. Books that show different cultures and countries give an opportunity to talk about different places and people we know, perhaps people in our own community.

Bruce and Spratt (2008) suggest using 'prop boxes', materials that can be stored in boxes or bags to enable children to revisit and retell rhymes or stories, making their own versions and variations during their play. These are also available commercially, and many settings we know use a combination of 'home-made' and bought-in resources. Prop boxes or story bags are a way of putting some of the more attractive soft toys, action figures or animals that accumulate in a nursery to good use. It also gives children the chance to search for appropriate objects, such as the bowls and beds needed for Goldilocks.

Many of the Children's Centres we know have story boxes or bags for parents to borrow, encouraging them to spend time reading with and talking to their children about favourite stories or rhymes that they have heard in 'Play and Learn', 'Bookstart' or 'Rhyme-time' sessions. Some settings operate a library system where books can be borrowed, and this is a good way to introduce books to homes where they might not be seen as important.

The local children's librarian is usually very willing to advise, and it may be possible to arrange to have a rotating collection on loan. Nurseries still need their permanent stock, as children like to return to their favourites again and again. Of course, as well as being read to, they need to have free access to the book corner so that they can look at books whenever they want to in their own time, being encouraged to return the book to the shelf when they have finished with it.

Storytelling

In some settings story time involves reading stories to a large mixed age group, perhaps numbering up to 15 children. In a group setting this is usually done with the object of releasing staff to do other things, but rarely works like that since extra adults are needed to keep order, hush the child who wants to start a conversation with his neighbour, or bring back the little ones who would rather wander off and play. Inevitably in a large group some will not understand what it is all about, some would prefer a different story, and others just do not feel like sitting still at that particular moment.

Children are likely to get far more out of story-reading (or storytelling) if the large group is split up among the available staff, who each use a separate space and judge their choice of story by the age range and interest of their small group. In this way the children can have a chance to express their own thoughts and reactions to the story. The story becomes a trigger for interesting conversation that can be related to other experiences, and the reader is able to find out what the children have understood (or often misunderstood). Stories do not have to come out of books; a nursery worker who makes up and tells her own stories can have a special kind of direct communication with her small group. Collections of folk tales from many different countries are readily available and usually have the repetitive structure that is so popular with children of this age.

The book corner

How the book corner or reading area is set up and maintained sends a strong message to parents and children about the relevance and value of books and literacy. The space should be light and airy, with large floor cushions and ideally a comfortable adult-sized sofa. The main requirements of a book corner are that it should:

* Be cosy and welcoming – with places to snuggle up with a book, as well as sit at a table;
* Have lots of good quality books, with some non-fiction as well as fiction and books that reflect both the children's interests and their culture;
* Be an inviting and interesting space – perhaps with a small display, posters about the books (often available from publishers or bookshops when they take down displays) or a story bag on display for children to use.

The book corner is a good place for collections of postcards (kept in an attractively covered shoebox) which can also encourage discussion and perhaps some story making.

A postcard from someone on holiday might prompt a story about being at the seaside, swimming or the fishes to be found in the sea. Children coming up to three can understand the idea of other countries and are often very interested in hearing about them, later recounting their new-found information to the amazement of their parents.

Photographs made into books by practitioners can offer children the opportunity to revisit places they have been to on outings or be reminded of visitors to the setting – important times to lay down memories and talk about 'what happened when . . .' These photograph books can also be helpful for new children or those just settling in, to see and hear about what exciting experiences the other children have had and suggest what they might do in the future.

Good quality books are not cheap, and an adequate budget needs to be allocated for additions and replacements. Books need selecting with the same care as toys; they should be checked regularly to ensure that they are in good condition and ruthlessly thrown out when they start to look scruffy and grubby.

There is a wonderful range of books available for this age group, and no excuse for tolerating the feeble stories and crude or confusing illustrations often to be seen. Early years workers need to read reviews in specialist magazines or quality newspapers. Suggestions for a 'good' library of children's books can be got from Bookstart, the local library and catalogues. Sharing information on children's preferences for particular books makes a good topic for a discussion with staff and parents. The range of books should include 'old favourites', new publications, anthologies of poetry and rhymes and

Figure 8.4 A book corner in the reception area of a Children's Centre

a selection of non-fiction books, which are often most popular with boys (Bruce and Spratt 2008).

When looking at new books, practitioners should ask – just as we would if selecting a book to buy for ourselves – is this a good book? What is the storyline, are the illustrations attractive and appropriate? Is it humorous, does it contain repetitive and rhyming dialogue? Is it a story that the children can join in with? The best books are ones that give as much pleasure to the adults as the children. We all have our particular preferences, perhaps books we remember reading with our own children. Ruth's was *Don't Forget the Bacon!* by Pat Hutchins, Sonia especially enjoyed Julia Donaldson's *The Gruffalo*. The book corner should contain some books that the children will be familiar with from their home and culture, such as those that accompany children's television programmes, and others that will introduce them to new ideas and contexts.

Music

Sadly, music is an area that tends to be rather undeveloped in many early years settings and most of what is written about it focuses on older age groups. However, music is a vehicle for expression and communication, just like language, so that no child is too young to benefit from musical experiences. Music gives us an opportunity to express our feelings and emotions at whatever age.

Practitioners are often unsure how to introduce and develop 'music' in their setting. This may be because they are not confident about singing or are unsure of what to offer young children. Linda Pound suggests that there are three elements to make music education in the early years more fun – improvisation, song writing and physical engagement. Young children as young as two years of age can be heard improvising songs as they engage in other forms of play (Pound 2010, p. 148).

Sophie, 21 months, was playing at her childminder's with her tea set. The adult gave her some play-dough which she began rolling between her hands.

> She flattened it slightly and placed it carefully on the tea plate. She then reached for the teaspoon, held it vertically so that the bowl end was uppermost and pushed the end of the spoon into the dough. Sophie then very quietly began in a sing-song voice, 'Happa birday oo u' and pretended to blow out the 'candle'.

Most of us can think of a particular piece of music that arouses strong memories or feelings. As practitioners we should give young children a varied musical diet that nourishes their emotional development and encourages them to listen and respond, whether it is jazz, opera, folk, classical, early music or world music.

By the age of three, children who have had a rich experience of music with their close adults will be able to sing a recognisable tune and will often have an extensive repertoire of nursery rhymes. They love dancing to music, and especially dancing with adults, being held and 'danced' with, and they are very interested in making music themselves and in seeing adults play instruments. Musicians are usually delighted to be asked to play and talk to young children. Tina Bruce (personal communication) tells of a group of three- and four-year-olds who, whilst watching their parents enjoy a barn dance, set up their own 'barn dance area', copying the adults, including one child acting as the 'caller'. It is good for young children to play with, listen to and enjoy musicians from a range of musical traditions. There may be parents who are able to share their musical talents and skills, whether through story, song or instrument.

Duffy (2010, p. 127) believes that 'musicality is an innate human characteristic and that involvement in music making not only gives children a chance to develop musical concepts and skills but also encourages self-esteem and well-being'. She describes how the staff team at the Coram Children's Centre wanted music to be something that was embedded in the life of the Centre, not reliant on a visiting weekly teacher. They worked with an experienced music-maker to support their own musical development alongside that of the children. By having regular music sessions attended by staff, children and parents, confidence grew and staff gradually took over leadership of the sessions themselves.

In whatever way the setting develops its musical offerings, what matters is that young children see familiar adults making music – not only outside musicians – and that they have ample opportunities for individual musical play and exploration apart from adult-directed activities (Pound and Harrison 2003).

Using and looking after musical instruments

It is important to differentiate between the musical instruments that are kept accessible in a music corner where children can experiment with sound independently or in the pretend play box for occasions when children act out 'being in a band', and those instruments that are only used when an adult is involved. The more expensive 'real' instruments such as drums, tambourines, shakers and xylophones should be kept in a safe place and used in a planned way, like the objects for heuristic play.

Musical possibilities for young children have been extended by the availability of instruments from other cultures. These are available from catalogues, local ethnic shops and from colleagues or families holidaying abroad. Often these instruments are ideally suited to this age group, enabling children to make and hear a great variety of different sounds. We just need to be mindful that 'instruments' brought back as holiday souvenirs do not always sound or play as they should, and may have paint or varnish that does not conform to our standards. The other drawback is that some of them are rather fragile.

A small group of children approaching their third year, with adult help, can learn to play different rhythms, choose instruments, take turns and create a satisfying musical effect. They can also learn to listen to each other and to different kinds of short pieces of music and talk about what they hear. However, what matters, as with all kinds of play, is the child's experience, not necessarily any kind of end product or performance. Music at this age should be a natural extension of playing with sound as described in Chapters 4 and 6.

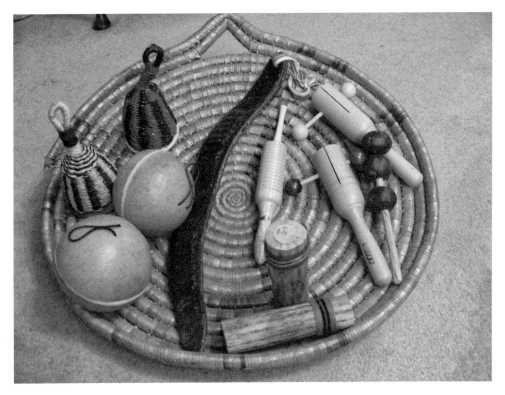

Figure 8.5 Multicultural instruments for 18 months onwards

Outdoor music

Just as we take books and stories outdoors, so the potential of the garden for music-making should not be overlooked. Pound and Harrison (2003) point out that the outdoor area can be used to explore and discuss the sound effects of natural phenomena like wind, rain and trees, or to use larger and noisier equipment than would be feasible indoors. Mobiles can be made or bought and hung from pergolas, using metal and wood to make chimes. Recycled cutlery can hang and will blow in the wind, and bells can be hung through the trees. Planting schemes can also be designed to produce interesting sounds, as described in Chapter 10. Outdoor space can give us more room to link music and movement; we should be braver about bringing music outside for the children to listen and move to. Children usually need little encouragement to dance. Many will have experienced local festivals and events where music and dance take place and they love to join in. Practitioners who are prepared to start the dancing can be helpful for the less confident children.

Social development

To encourage the development of social skills, practitioners must have realistic expectations of children's behaviour. Children in this age group need time to get to know each other and develop friendships. Small-group activities with their key person are still an important part of the day, especially for language development, as is snack time in key groups or using a café system (see Chapter 9). It is important to provide ample play materials to go round, organising the space and activities to ensure that the children do not have to wait to access areas or resources. Expecting two- to three-year-olds to share is not realistic and simply leads to conflict, although by the end of this year they are beginning to understand the concept of taking turns. They will still need help with developing these important social skills, so here the adult's role is to model positive behaviour and language and to show interest and enthusiasm.

A two-year-old at home or with a childminder can learn so much by observing and participating in the 'real' work of running a home. The child who spends all day in a childcare centre can easily miss out on this experience. That is one reason why it is important for them to participate in essential domestic routines such as setting or clearing tables, sorting washing and sweeping floors. The practitioners can also maintain a really well-stocked and attractive home corner and dressing-up area as a permanent feature of the group room, and this will result in much imaginative and sociable play. First-hand experiences with real objects and responsive adults who support and model will enhance the play experience on offer and stimulate the child's development (Bertram and Pascal 2010). The two-year-olds will play with pots and pans, filling and emptying receptacles in a way which echoes their previous absorption with the activities of their heuristic play with objects, talking and interrelating busily as their imaginative play develops apace.

If one adult, as suggested in Chapter 3, takes responsibility for the area of the nursery where this type of play provision is set up, she is present as a point of reference. In this role she can see that the practice of 'tidy up as you go' is followed, using simple indicators such as 'Let's put the clothes on this dolly' or 'Which bed do you think teddy would like best?' She will know when to stand back and listen, observe the play and only 'dive in' or mediate when needed. By her unobtrusive intervention and consistently maintaining a quiet contact with these youngest ones she enables the play to go on smoothly, led by the children. Where children in their third year are part of a mixed age group, staff need to give particular attention to providing opportunity for this kind of imaginative play, which is so closely related to the growth of language.

Writing, drawing and painting

Mark-making

Mark-making is the beginning of drawing and writing. We need to provide ample opportunities for it, and to recognise and celebrate the marks made by people under three, rather than dismissing them (even in our own minds) as 'just scribble'. Mark-making is often accompanied by singing or self-talk – in line with Vygotsky's theory that 'inner speech' becomes the director of language and action. It is interesting to note that children in their writing and drawing reflect the society, community or culture they come from. For instance those from non-western cultures make marks from right to left or top to bottom. They sometimes realise that adults may have difficulty in decoding their marks and ask the childcare worker to translate what they have written into grown-up writing, or they may explain what a drawing or series of marks represents, describing it as 'mummy' or 'my bike'. But at other times their interest lies in the activity itself and they should not feel under any pressure to share their ideas unless they want to.

As they draw, children increase their 'graphic vocabularies', using their pictures to express meaning. Through their drawings they tell us their stories, feelings and what is going on in their lives (Mathews 2003; Whitebread and Basilio 2012). The progression in children's drawings and painting is a fascinating subject that has been much studied by psychologists.

For children in their third year a mark-making area should have a selection of:

- Thick wax crayons;
- Chubby pencils;

Figure 8.6 Mark-making over a large space

- Round-ended scissors (including left-handed ones);
- A range of paper – textured, coloured, lined, plain;
- Envelopes;
- Glue – both in stick form and pots with spreaders;
- Hole punches;
- Sellotape;
- Sticky note pads.

To these could be added old diaries, address books and calendars.

The mark-making area will enable these young children to practise and become skilled users of the crayons, pencils and pens offered. Home-made pads using recycled paper can easily be put together, and at this age children like nothing better than having their 'own' pad on which to draw up shopping lists.

Painting and drawing

In using paint, the two-year-old experiments with colour, passing the brush from one hand to another, scrubbing the paint on to the paper. By three years he is beginning to paint pictures, matches primary colours and may 'name' what he paints. Parents who have not had the opportunity to use paint themselves may find it difficult to appreciate the pleasure that children experience from their early attempts. One of the more distressing experiences for a practitioner is to see a child's treasured painting stuffed into the dustbin on the way home. Staff need to spend time and thought on the best way to help parents give recognition to their children's achievement and not to judge a child's work by inappropriate standards. Practitioners can show their own appreciation by careful mounting and display of selected items. It may sometimes be best to give parents the option of keeping the child's work in a folder at the nursery, which provides a later opportunity for discussion as parent and key person together look at how the paintings change over time.

Useful resources for the painting area include:

- Easels – of an appropriate height;
- Tables – paint behaves differently horizontally and vertically, and children should experience both;
- A variety of brushes including long ones, chunkier short-handled types, house-painting brushes and chunky shaving brushes;
- Men's shirts to use as aprons – some children strongly dislike the feel of plastic painting aprons. Old shirts can be supplied by parents or bought from charity shops and simply binned when no longer usable.
- Rolls of lining wallpaper;
- Other things with which to apply paint and make patterns – limited only by the practitioner's imagination – straws, string, sponges, construction blocks, root vegetables.

Figure 8.7 Deep concentration at the easel

Figure 8.7 is one of a series of photographs. This one shows how the toddler used her hand to support the paper on the easel; she painted over the magnetic buttons, on the easel itself and the paper. She used one hand to hold the paint pot and her concentration was such that she was oblivious of the observing adult and camera.

Malleable materials

The equipment for play with malleable materials, such as sand, clay, mud, dough and water, needs to be well maintained and attractively presented. Having a zoned workshop area for water, paint and malleable materials helps to keep the resources in one place and makes maintenance easier, especially if there is a sink (preferably one for the adults and one for the children) for ease of clearing and cleaning up. The two-year-old has fun discovering the behaviour of the various substances by pouring, slapping, kneading, poking and manipulating them directly with his hands (often trying to eat them too). He does this before going on to use the variety of tools available. He needs scope to do so freely within the limits of mess that the environment and the adult can permit. He may go on to making castles or puddings, mixing dry materials with water, shaping and moulding things to which he may or may not give a name. At a later stage, boards, rolling pins and metal shapes can be provided – then dough becomes biscuits that can be cooked and eaten and there is a recognisable end product. The staff member observing will note how important it is to allow the first exploratory play to take place, not falling into the trap of making objects herself or imposing adult perceptions on the child, but waiting for him to make his own imaginative leaps as his skill increases.

Water play also progresses, and in the later stages can encompass such useful activities as washing items of play material such as Lego, or dolls' clothes and cot sheets, wiping down tables, and washing and drying one's own face and hands.

Learning new skills

As they approach their fourth year, children develop the ability to use simple tools and learn different techniques. A group of three children with staff supervision can make a fruit salad, cutting up the fruit with knives and squeezing juice – activities around which a great deal of lively conversation will take place. If shared with the wider group as part of tea or a picnic in the garden the activity becomes all the more relevant and real.

Using scissors, pasting, making collages, selecting and threading beads, all increase manipulative skill while providing a sense of achievement in a task completed.

As with a heuristic play session, the principle of tidying up alongside the adults when finished gives a sense of pleasure in order. The practitioner offers a model of someone who cares for the materials – in every area of the nursery, be it puzzles, building blocks, construction sets or painting materials.

Two-year-olds, free places and the EYFS progress check

Settings judged good or outstanding by Ofsted may find that they have more children in their third year in future as a result of the government's offer of 15 hours a week of free childcare to 'vulnerable' two-year-olds (see Chapter 1). It is essential that practitioners have access to training in order to provide the best care and learning opportunities for these children, who may come from families under severe pressure and with multiple problems, or alternatively be living with foster parents and have a history of abuse and neglect (see Chapter 14 for further discussion). Early years practitioners may find themselves as part of 'Team Around the Child' meetings for children with a Common Assessment Framework (CAF), contributing to discussions and plans with a range of professionals to ensure that the child and their family have the appropriate level of support and safeguarding. Some practitioners might be part of a Core Group for a child with a Child Protection Plan, and additional support from other services may be needed for the practitioner and the family.

Early years settings are also responsible for carrying out a two-year-old developmental progress check, which is a statutory requirement of the EYFS. The check should provide parents with a summary of their child's learning and development in three prime areas: Personal, social and emotional development, Physical development, and Communication and language. Settings should ensure they have permission from parents to share this information with other professionals. It has been suggested that the EYFS progress check should coincide with the Health Visitor two-year-old development review to provide a more holistic picture of the child. Settings may be involved in discussions with colleagues from their local authority early years team and health professionals to ascertain how the check will be offered and monitored locally.

Summary

In their third year children are constantly striving to assert their increasing autonomy and to make sense of the world around them. The tool of understanding is their growing command of language, which they need ample opportunity to practise. To ensure that this happens in a group care setting requires careful attention and planning, based on the key person approach. Language and social development are interlinked and we know that the main way language is acquired is through communicating and hearing language from and with their parents or close adults; it is an active and interactive process. Supporting and extending children's thinking is a key responsibility of the early years practitioner.

The third year is also a time when awareness of diversity develops. Early years practitioners have a unique opportunity to counter prejudice and discrimination, to help all children feel good about themselves and develop positive attitudes to the different groups of people who make up our society. The government's two-year-old childcare offer is likely to bring new challenges to settings without previous experience of caring for and educating 'vulnerable' children of this age. It is the responsibility of the centre leader to ensure that the staff have appropriate training and support for this demanding task.

9 Mealtimes: promoting healthy eating and enjoyment

> Where there is no enjoyment and no fun the food is beige coloured.
> (Raymond Blanc, chef)

In this chapter we will consider:

- Planning and organisation of meals;
- A child's eye view of food and mealtimes;
- The role of the key person;
- Ways to lay the foundation for healthy eating;
- An inclusive and multicultural approach.

When friends tell us about their holiday, describe where they stayed and what they did and recommend that we go to the same place, perhaps the first thing we ask is, 'What was the food like?' Food is not only to do with survival but also with enjoyment and companionship. We need to give mealtimes special consideration both for the children's sake and for our own. Greenman and Stonehouse (1997) suggest judging the quality of a childcare setting by the level of attention given to these matters.

Feeding gives the opportunity for the baby or toddler to have some intimate time with her close adult. For the key person who knows just how the baby likes to be held, at what angle to tip the bottle and the baby's signs for 'had enough', it is a real privilege to feel the move from alert hungry infant to one who is drowsy and sated in her arms. As the baby moves into a high chair next to the table with the other toddlers, mealtimes become a more social affair, not just eating, but learning and practising motor skills, developing a sense of autonomy and having conversations. However, only someone who has actually conducted mealtimes for a group of young children fully understands the kind of stress that this can mean and the detailed and complex organisation needed.

Baby and toddler rooms will probably have a mixed age range of children between six months and 18 months, possibly up to two years of age. This will mean that there will be a range of bottle-fed-only babies, mixed feeders, babies that need to be held for feeding, and babies sitting in high chairs or low chairs at the table. It can almost become like a military exercise. So planning and managing mealtimes is something that requires a great deal of thought.

Food at the hub of the nursery

In most families the kitchen, or the room adjoining it, is the hub of the house. In nurseries and childcare centres it is usually separated off from the teaching and learning spaces. This contrasts with the pre-schools in Reggio Emilia where the cooks and cleaners are seen as integral members of the teaching staff. The kitchens there are located so that the preparation and cooking of food is observed by the children and the smell of cooking can permeate the building. 'The role of cooking is seen as bringing authenticity into the life of the school and the kitchen as a place of warmth and domestic security' (Bishop 2001, p. 77).

We have visited nurseries in this country where architects have taken on that message and planned to bring the kitchen into the heart of the setting. A lower serving hatch enables children to see and smell what is happening and engage with the staff preparing and serving meals. In many nurseries ancillary staff are fully integrated into the team. Cooks usually have regular contact with parents to discuss specific meals for children with allergies or special diets (see below) or simply to receive feedback on the menus.

At the other extreme are settings which do not have their own kitchens and parents have to provide the meals for their child, or the food is centrally provided and delivered in containers, with little direct control over the content. Worst off of all are those whose meals come frozen in individual portions, bearing no relation to personal preferences and likes or dislikes. For them the following points may at least offer a basis for negotiating better arrangements.

Raising awareness and changing practice

In order for practice to change, people first have to become aware of what habit may have led them to take for granted. As an illustration of how this might be done, here is Elinor Goldschmied's account of an exercise she ran as part of a training course for senior staff in charge of day nurseries in a social services department. This was very typical of Elinor's imaginative style of teaching. On this occasion she had the help of the two under-fives advisers who had invited her to run the course as well as the collaboration of the kitchen staff in the day nursery where the course was taking place. It was agreed that the participants would have lunch in the nursery on two days in successive weeks.

> The kitchen staff helped me to lay on a really beautiful meal. The tables for four were set out attractively with cloths, a small pot of flowers, water jugs and coloured

paper napkins. There was comfortable space for everyone, no sense of hurry, no clatter. The food was well presented and attractive in appearance, ready waiting for us when we sat down, with the two nursery advisers and myself at different tables. Knowing there was a whole hour for lunch engendered a mood of relaxation, and conversation flowed. We almost forgot that we were on a training course!

After the meal was over the participants in pairs were asked to make a list of the good and enjoyable features of the meal that they had just finished. On the basis of these criteria they were asked to consider how the meals were run in their own nursery, taking point by point and deciding on a scale of 0–10 how the meals actually experienced by their staff and children measured up to the quality of the meal they had just had. It was made clear that this assessment was to remain a private matter between themselves and their own nursery staff. No one was asked to share their judgements with the other members of the course. The group then came together and I asked them during the following week to look at exactly what was going on in their own workplace and to consider how they could use the day's experience to initiate change.

The following week we spent the morning working on another theme unconnected with mealtimes. We were all engrossed, and at half past eleven we were startled by the noisy, bustling entrance of the two under-fives advisers (duly primed) who moved into our circle saying, 'Come along now, put your things away. We're a bit late, so don't bother to finish what you're doing.' Our group felt somewhat irritated but were compliant, and obeyed the instruction of the advisers to get along to the bathroom with the comment, 'Sorry there's only one available so you'd better stand in line and don't play about.' We duly followed each other and crowded into the bathroom to take our turn as directed, though everyone (except me of course) felt very puzzled and vaguely rebellious.

What happened next, quite spontaneously, was that in different ways, some more active than others, we all started to behave badly. One of the advisers corralled us into the dining room, insisting that we form a 'train' holding each other's waists. All twelve of us sat at one long table with no cloth, with chairs crowded up together, some too high and some too low for comfort. The advisers stood about telling us to be quiet and sit still, and a wait of 15 minutes began before the food came.

Everyone wriggled about and rocked their chairs. The advisers, exchanging looks of exasperation, gave us books to look at, but most of them were dropped on the floor. The noise level rose and only quietened after the arrival of the food trolley, which was greeted with clapping and banging on the table. The advisers standing by the trolley doled out the food rather slowly, heaping the same amount on every plate. One adviser insisted that each person said 'Thank you' before she would put down the plate. No choice or refusal was allowed. The food was good in quality but quite monotonous in appearance – steamed white fish, mashed potatoes and cauliflower.

The advisers sat either end of the long table, and talked to each other about their holidays. They did not address the participants except to tell them to sit still and eat up their dinners. The advisers had to get up three or four times to pick up a fork or spoon from the floor and wash it before giving it back because there was no extra cutlery on the trolley. It was evident from their faces and movements that they were not particularly enjoying their own meal.

The second course was served only when everyone had finished, and two 'slow ones' made everyone feel irritated. Again there was some delay as there were two plates short and one adviser had to go to the kitchen to get another. The pudding consisted of rice pudding with stewed pears. Somebody asked for water but was told they could only have a drink when they had finished what was on their plate. There was a jug of water on the trolley but the glasses had been forgotten and an adviser had to get up again to get them.

As the meal went on everyone had seen the point of the exercise. We were all laughing and making suggestions as to how the meal could have been made even more awful! Direct experience focused attention on detail in a way that no amount of talking would have done. People noted with interest, and some surprise, the way in which they reacted to being ordered around even though they had obviously realised quite early on that it was a 'game'. We then went on to discuss some of the problems they had observed in their own nurseries during the previous week and they quickly began thinking of practical steps which could be taken to improve things.

Practical organisation and attention to detail

As Elinor's account of this training exercise demonstrates, it is the little things, the close attention to detail that matters when working with very young children. Without this, mealtimes can become something to get through as quickly as possible. Sometimes time constraints are imposed by other factors in the setting beyond the control of the nursery staff. However team discussions where the practitioners are able to share observations of mealtimes and the effects on children and staff are a starting point for making small but significant changes.

The transition time from playing to shared use of the bathroom to mealtime is a difficult period that can be made easier by careful planning. The description of the key person approach in Chapter 2 sets out how each staff member can act as the central focus for her own small group of children during the period from the end of play activities. This is the period which Elinor called the 'island of intimacy'. Further details about organisation and materials can be found in Chapter 6.

One of the underlying reasons for ensuring that washing and pre-dinner time are spent in a small group is to calm the atmosphere before the meal. This eliminates to a great extent noise and tension, and makes it possible to avoid the disastrous situation of children being expected to sit down at the table and wait before the dinner trolley is brought in. The training exercise described above highlights all the elements which go towards the successful conduct of a meal. There follow some points to consider when planning how to make mealtimes more enjoyable for children and staff alike.

Engaging the whole staff group

When catering and ancillary staff regard themselves as part of the nursery team, attending staff meetings and contributing to planning and policy development in the setting, they gain a better understanding of each other's roles and responsibilities and become committed to providing the best possible experience for the children and staff around food and healthy eating. It is important for the leader to explain fully the educational reasons behind any decisions which will involve more work. The cook needs to understand what the nursery practitioners are aiming for in the organisation of meals, just as the nursery staff need to understand the constraints that the kitchen staff work under. For instance, nursery staff should know that there are many legislative requirements for food storage and preparation in a childcare setting. On the other side it is important that catering staff know why it matters that they set up the trolleys with the right amount of cutlery (and extras in case they are needed at the table), water jugs, mugs, and so on.

In one nursery, where there was a harmful and disturbing sense that the meal had to be 'got over with', we traced it to the fact that the kitchen staff who did the washing up had a contract which meant they had to finish by 1 p.m. This deadline had a kind of 'ripple effect' right back to the moment when the children sat down at their tables. It was not possible to change this arrangement immediately, but at least we had identified one source of the problem of 'rush' and could look for ways to reduce its impact.

Creating a comfortable and peaceful atmosphere

An important objective in conducting the meal is to minimise clatter and movement. Uncertainty and confusion can be avoided if all the children know which is their table and their place at it. A separate table is needed for each key person and her small group, with chairs (not too close together) that are the right height so that children can rest their feet on the floor and their elbows are level with the table top. If a child's face is too near his plate, because his chair is the wrong height, he will have added difficulty in manipulating his spoon. He will have to raise his shoulder to bring the spoon to his mouth, since small children do not flex their wrists as we do when using a spoon or fork. Short-handled spoons and forks are best for small hands, as are bowls that have slanted sides, making it easier to push the food around to the side and get it onto the spoon.

The key person, once she is seated with her group, should be able to remain seated, with everything to hand. A member of the ancillary staff should bring in the food trolley so that no nursery practitioner is obliged to absent herself from her small group. Each key person should have, within easy arm's length, a side table, the top of a low piece of furniture or a shelf of the food trolley on which can be put both the food for her table and all the equipment she will need during the whole meal. The adult should avoid standing over or helping the children to eat from above or behind them. This gives them the feeling that your presence is temporary, and again creates a sense of uncertainty. It is also very uncomfortable for the practitioner and not good for their posture. Staff

Figure 9.1 Enjoying lunch with her key children (Photograph: Coram Early Childhood Centre)

should sit at the table with the children during the meal, ideally having their own lunch at the same time. They are much more likely to do this if the food is interesting and varied.

There should be individual containers for each table so that the key person can serve her own group whose appetites and likes and dislikes she will know. Second helpings can always be given to children who want them, and in this way waste is avoided. The separate containers will mean more washing up for the kitchen staff, so this needs to be negotiated if it has not been the practice in the past.

Another detail which can often create stress for a small child, seated expectantly at the table, is when a whole portion of something hot is put on a plate, and the hungry child, already coping with the complex manoeuvre of handling her spoon, is faced with yet another obstacle to eating. The solution is for the nursery worker to put a very small amount on the plate. The food will cool immediately because the plate is cold. When the child has finished she can have a second helping, by which time it will be at the right temperature for eating.

Water for drinking must always be available and actively offered, especially to the children who do not yet have language. Mugs should have a wide base. As soon as children can pour for themselves they should be encouraged to do so. Small jugs with a lid make it more manageable.

Feeding younger children

Feeding babies

Where meals and drinks for babies are prepared and provided, staff will have to ensure that they are following guidelines from the Department of Health, health visitors, and of course information from parents. Resources such as those from the Caroline Walker Trust – CHEW (children eating well) – are useful, and some of the documents available focus on the first year of life (Crawley 2006). Feeding babies, whether formula or breast milk, will naturally be dictated by the mother (usually), however it is important that settings have a policy and procedure for making up and storage. Many areas have a breastfeeding policy as part of their wider health promotion programme. The key person will discuss with parents as a matter of course whether the baby has formula or breast milk and ensure that the home routine is followed as closely as possible. As discussed in Chapter 4, breastfeeding mothers who are able to come into the nursery should be encouraged to do so and a comfortable space found for them.

Helping younger children to eat

If the key person has a group of mixed ages she will generally have near her any younger ones who need help with eating. Luckily today it is understood that fingers came before forks and that, in the first stages of independence in feeding, a child should feel quite free to eat with his fingers everything that can conveniently be picked up. When a child

Figure 9.2 At 15 months fingers are still the main tool

can accept help as he learns to use a spoon, it is important for the adult to have an extra spoon so that there is no need to take the child's own spoon from his hand.

A real trap for the adult is the temptation, when a baby is in the process of eating a mouthful, to put a loaded spoon again to his lips. This can be a harmful practice because it means that we are pressuring the child to gulp down what he already has in his mouth in response to the waiting spoon. Older children are always being told off for eating too fast and not chewing their food properly. Perhaps the roots of such behaviour lie in earlier adult impatience.

Some children, particularly the younger ones, may not be accustomed to sitting down at a table. It is especially important for them that we organise carefully to maintain an atmosphere of tranquil efficiency, and make mealtimes, which inevitably involve some restraint on their activity, an enjoyable time for them.

Sitting with children who eat slowly can impose a quite stern discipline upon us not to let 'institutional rush' take over the meal. There is a temptation to hurry children along by feeding them instead of letting them discover their independence. On the other hand, excessive playing with the food as opposed to getting any into the mouth indicates that the child is not hungry or has had enough and is ready to move on. As noted above, keeping everyone waiting at the table until all have finished creates frustration both for children and staff.

It is now fully recognised that, however much the adult feels that a child ought and needs to eat, there must never in any circumstances be pressure. Adults have learned to disregard the messages they receive from their bodies and eat, probably more than they need, when it is socially expected rather than only when they feel hungry. Children in group care usually learn to conform to adult expectations, especially when they see other children eating with enjoyment. But sometimes they may just not feel like food at the time it is offered, and that should be respected. Also, in their anxiety that children should eat well, nursery workers (and parents) may give overlarge helpings which can be very off-putting. It is worth remembering that obesity is a much more serious problem in this country than undernourishment (National Audit Office 2012), and that trying to persuade children to eat when they don't want to is always counterproductive (Douglas 2002). Staff should reassure parents that especially during the settling-in period and other key transition points, eating is not always a priority for the child, but it is unlikely that any child will go hungry provided that appropriate and sufficient food is offered during the day.

Learning through play

Making 'tea' and pretend play feeding dolls, teddies and each other is an important part of toddlers' play. Tea parties, feeding dolls in high chairs, shopping and 'cooking' dinner will be observed daily in the nursery or home. These are all important elements of a toddler's life – their experiences of the local supermarket, their parents in the kitchen at home and family meals will all be played out. We see and hear toddlers mirroring the adults around them as they play – 'eat it all up baby or you won't go out to play' or 'no pudding then if you don't finish' or 'what can I get you today?' as they play out a café experience – will have all been heard by practitioners and parents alike.

Toddlers will 'cook' dried pasta, corks and any other play materials. They will also enjoy making real sandwiches to be eaten at teatime or cooking simple cakes and biscuits. In this way mealtimes in the nursery or with their childminder are not only a pleasurable and healthy experience but also an important part of the curriculum for these youngest people under three.

Maintaining the key person approach

When the staff in a group room have decided to set out (say) three tables for five or six children and three staff, it can happen that at one table three children are absent. There is then a tendency to put the two tables together – one practitioner told us she felt guilty if she had only two children while her colleague had the usual number of five. But we could say that the nursery worker with the fewer children has more cause to feel guilty if she passes by a rare opportunity to give close attention to two children for whom she has special responsibility. This is a good discussion point for a staff meeting.

Figure 9.3 Tea time with teddy

Using mealtimes for observation

A useful exercise is to arrange from time to time for each member of staff in turn to be freed from responsibility for her table and to sit apart as an observer during one meal-time, making detailed notes of all that happens. Comparing these observations at a group room meeting will highlight problems that otherwise can remain unnoticed. As a result of one such exercise a staff member commented that when Peter, a child who was partly feeding himself with his fingers and partly being fed, had food around his mouth, the adult scraped it off with the spoon. This was repeated many times, and the observer noted that each time the child winced slightly. In the group room meeting, staff tried doing it to each other to see how it felt. As a result they vowed never to do it to a child again.

Eating outside

Most of us enjoy the occasional picnic, and there is no reason why meals should not sometimes be taken outside, a practice much more common in other countries, not necessarily hot ones. This brings another dimension again to eating, emphasising the social aspect, appreciating the garden or covered patio area, talking about the garden, and about plants grown for eating. As discussed in Chapters 8 and 10, many centres like to involve children in the whole process of 'plant it, grow it, cook it, and eat it', encouraging children, staff and families to play a part in looking after the garden. Starting with containers of salad leaves, herbs and tomatoes will encourage even the fussiest eater to try something they have watered and nurtured themselves.

Café-style snack time – encouraging choices and decision-making

At times of the day other than the midday meal – breakfast, mid-morning juice or fruit and at teatime – it is easier to be more relaxed, and for children to mix with the wider group of staff and children, though it is still essential to plan in detail if these moments are to be enjoyable breaks in the long day. Being informal does not mean being disorganised. For example, at breakfast and teatime there may be parents present so that attention needs to be given to their comfort, particularly in seeing that there are adult-sized chairs for them to sit on. In one centre, we observed the undesirable practice of insisting that every child was sitting quiet and still at table before any were allowed their drink. The children obviously found this very frustrating and boring. It was also extremely trying for the staff who were continually having to restrain children who wanted to move about or talk.

Many settings now take a different approach. The food and drink are set out on a table or trolley near the 'café' area and the children are encouraged to sit at the table and help themselves when they want to. It is important that there is an adult assigned to the 'café' to encourage conversation and support children who find it more difficult to eat. Tablecloths, and flowers on the table, as in Elinor's training exercise, all help to make this a pleasurable experience. Two baskets, one with photographs of all the children in the room and an empty one, enable children to 'register' that they have visited the café. It takes a little time for everyone to learn the system. In one centre that we know, when they first introduced it, portions of fruit and cheese disappeared much faster than anticipated as the same children visited the café several times.

However with careful explanation and commitment from all staff, initial problems were soon ironed out. It was observed that children were spending longer engrossed in their play activities, but also took pleasure in having time to sit and enjoy their snack next to a friend or to meet up with someone they hadn't played alongside that morning. There was no interruption of conversations by a call for 'tidy-up time' and children knew that the train set or the building blocks would still be out if they wanted to return to them. Staff reported that the morning 'flowed better' without the need for clearing up and setting up tables for a whole group snack time.

This café system works well for children aged two and over. It encourages them to make decisions for themselves about when they feel hungry and what they want to eat. Children attending for morning sessions might have had a hearty breakfast and not want anything more than a drink mid-morning. And of course we do not always feel like eating at the same time every day, so a café system enables those who have come without breakfast to eat earlier and those who prefer to wait until later to do so.

Careful observation of any change like the introduction of the café is essential, so that staff can identify and iron out any difficulties as well as noting the reaction of the children (and asking those old enough what they think about it). A few questions that arise:

- The child who is eating everything in sight – is it just easier access or is he very hungry all the time? Should we be concerned about him and enquire more closely what goes on at home? (See Chapter 14.)
- The child who remains engrossed in activities all morning and forgets to stop for a snack – a gentle invitation from a staff member to join her at the table would be a good idea.
- How does the café system fit in with the kitchen routine? For example, one centre had to order extra cups for drinks as the later running time of the café meant that kitchen staff were not able to wash up in time for lunch.

Healthy eating

Attitudes to food and eating

As already noted, parents can become very anxious if they feel a child is not eating enough at nursery. If this is about the child not liking a particular food, the practitioner should reassure the parent that rejection of food is always noted and that this item could be reintroduced a week or two later. If it persists, on the other hand, the child's dislike should be accepted. The other thing that causes anxiety to some parents (and staff) is children playing with their food and utensils. At this age it is natural to mix, pour, stir, drop spoons and forks and sometimes turn a bowl full of food upside down. Dropping things and looking with interest to see where they have gone is part of learning about the properties of objects. As Manning-Morton and Thorp (2003) observe, some practitioners may have to rethink messages from their own upbringing on how free the younger children should be to explore in their own way and how much mess to tolerate. The complex issues around food and eating need discussion in staff training or meetings – for example, sharing feelings about wasting food, trying new foods, playing with food, food as punishment/reward, concerns about eating disorders and the effects of food on our emotions.

Food and nutrition

So far we have said nothing about the food that is provided for children and staff to eat, and often surprisingly little thought seems to be given to this, although if the food is not good, nobody will enjoy the meal, however well organised it may be. As we showed earlier, it is also important to present the food in an attractive way and to think about its appearance, colour and texture. Children are very sensitive to these aspects of food even though they may be too young to find words to express their opinion.

The food provided for children in early years settings is significant, not only for its immediate impact on their health and development but because it lays the foundation for future eating habits. The Health Survey for England 2010 figures for childhood obesity show that almost a quarter of children are either overweight or obese on entry to primary school reception classes (National Audit Office 2012). Practitioners in early years settings, Children's Centres and childminders should be aware of this and work to promote healthier lifestyles and eating habits, both for themselves and the children they look after.

In schools, regulations introduced in September 2006 mean that deep-fried products can only be on the menu twice a week, and chocolate, crisps and fizzy drinks are no longer part of school lunch (National Audit Office 2012). The Schools Food Trust was commissioned by the Department for Education to develop the 'Eat Better Start Better' programme aimed at pre-school children. In response to concerns that food offered in many private and voluntary settings for children under five was of poor nutritional value, a consortium of early years providers compiled a set of 'Voluntary Food and Drink Guidelines for early years settings in England' designed to lead to a 'healthy, balanced and nutritious' diet for children in day care (School Food Trust 2012). This is a practical document which should help childcare centres to evaluate their approach to food and drink. It includes menu-planning checklists, a template code of practice and sample menus and recipes, with advice on portion sizes and the nutrients needed for growing children.

Involving parents and families

When a setting decides to review its food policy and provision this offers a perfect opportunity to work with parents and find out their views on the quality and variety of the food offered to their children. Some settings already do this on a regular basis. Parents will know their child's likes and dislikes, but it is not difficult to encourage children to give direct feedback by offering photographs of different foods and asking them to pick out their favourites and the ones they like the least. Staff observations will also feed into any evaluation of the meals provided. A necessary first step is to create the motivation for change, which means ensuring that all staff understand the principles involved, and then engaging everybody in a critical examination of current practice. How does the food served in the nursery over the past month match up to criteria for a healthy diet? How much waste is there? This could be carefully monitored over a one-week period. If a lot of food is left on plates or regularly gets thrown away, this obviously raises questions.

Having assessed the quality of the diet currently offered and decided that change is necessary, the next question is what can be done immediately, and how far is more fundamental rethinking required? Of course it goes without saying that the cook and kitchen staff must be fully involved in this discussion. Substantial improvements can often be made very quickly: for example, the substitution of wholemeal bread for white, fresh fruit for sweet puddings, carrot sticks or unsweetened rusks for biscuits, avoiding foods with artificial colouring or preservatives. It is also important not to give children the idea that sugar or salt should be routinely added to food, which may require staff to change their eating habits too. For example, they should not be seen by children adding salt and sugar to their plate.

Introducing new kinds of food

Many nurseries ensure parents have copies of the weekly menu, keeping them informed and helping them to plan meals at home. Many parents in settings we know, both mothers and fathers, ask for recipes from the kitchen as their children become more adventurous in trying new foods. Creative cooks and nursery staff will work together. One nursery bought a salmon for a special celebration day. The cook showed the children the whole fish first and then each stage of boning, cooking and setting it out on a platter. Later many of the children tasted salmon for the first time, with evident enjoyment.

Some children come into the nursery having been used to a very bland and restricted diet. It may be difficult at first to persuade them to try new foods, even such a minor change as wholemeal instead of white bread. However, they will gradually accept unfamiliar tastes and textures if these are first offered in very small quantities and they see other children eating with enjoyment. Of course, parents need to be involved in this process (which most will welcome) and great care should be taken that any dietary restrictions, whether for religious or health reasons, are thoroughly understood and respected by all staff.

Figure 9.4 What's this? Looking to her key person for reassurance

Food from different cultures

Every country has its distinctive style of eating, and the food offered in early years settings is often a scaled-down version of the typical adult meal. This is immediately obvious if we look at nursery menus from another country. In Italy, instead of 'meat and two veg' and pudding, Italian infants are offered a first course (*primo piatto*) of pasta, thick vegetable soup or rice, followed by a second course (*secondo piatto*) of a small piece of meat or fish, followed by salad or a vegetable, usually ending with a piece of fruit.

Our eating habits are a very basic expression of our cultural identity, and nursery meals ought therefore to reflect the backgrounds of the children in the nursery. All should have the experience of eating some food which is familiar from home and some that is new to them. This needs to go much beyond the occasional 'multicultural' event when a special meal is provided, though these also have their place. Food is an important element in all the feasts and festivals that will be celebrated as part of the nursery's commitment to multicultural practice. However, food from many different cultures and national cuisines can be introduced as a normal part of nursery meals and will greatly increase their interest and variety. Chapatis, wholemeal pitta bread, unsweetened yoghurt, brown rice, yam and plantain, can become regular components of menus. Although some kinds of food may need adapting to suit children's more delicate tastes, it is best to have the real thing and not an anglicised version of it.

Where many different ethnic groups are represented in the nursery, the best resource is the parents (usually, but not always, mothers). They might be asked to suggest some dishes that they serve to the family at home which would be suitable for nursery meals and to come in to show the cook how to prepare them.

Sometimes adults from different ethnic backgrounds continue to eat in their accustomed way but give their children 'English' food because 'they like it better'. This is unfortunate for two reasons: first because it is likely to lead to the children having a less healthy diet, but also because it suggests that the nursery has failed to convey respect and appreciation for different lifestyles, of which food is so important a part, and this may in turn lead to children devaluing aspects of their own culture (Siraj-Blatchford and Clarke 2000).

Special diets and allergies

Before a child starts at a nursery or childcare centre parents will be asked to complete a form detailing the child's medical history. This will include any known allergies or special diets that he may have been prescribed. Food allergies affect an estimated 5–8 per cent of children in the UK. The most common foods that can cause an allergic reaction in susceptible children are eggs, milk, soya, wheat, gluten and peanuts (Schools Food Trust 2012, p. 48). Some settings use different coloured plates for children with special diets. Displaying information about special diets and allergies somewhere accessible to all staff is crucial, especially for those who work on a rota basis and not always with the same group of children. Regular discussion with parents will ensure that the nursery is kept up to date on any changes in a child's dietary needs and this must be carefully recorded and shared with the cook. Vegetarian diets should contain meat alternatives such as soya or tofu, eggs, and pulses. Most important, all staff must know how to recognise and respond to an allergic reaction, which in a very few cases may be life-threatening.

Summary

The content and conduct of meals have a very significant influence on staff well-being and job satisfaction. The importance of food and mealtimes in full day care cannot be overstated. Being fed is a key time in a very young child's day, an intimate and special time of the day, a time for talk and sharing experiences. It is an area which needs much more attention than it has received in the past. Close attention to detail is the key to making mealtimes an enjoyable and educational experience for children and staff alike, introducing more interesting and varied food which reflects cultural diversity and offers a valuable opportunity for staff and parents to collaborate. Since it will often be the staff who are learning from the parents, it can also help to create a more equal relationship.

<table>
<tr><td>

10

</td><td>

Out of doors

</td></tr>
</table>

Thrice happy he who, not mistook,
Hath read in nature's mystic book
(Andrew Marvell)

In this chapter we will consider:

- How practitioners, together with the children in their setting, parents and the local community, can use the outside space and explore the different opportunities for play and learning beyond the nursery building;
- Making the best use of the garden;
- The outdoor space as an inclusive learning area;
- Growing and discovering;
- Creating an environment that works for all children and adults;
- Using the resources of the neighbourhood.

Seeing through the child's eyes

Ask anyone for recollections of their primary school playground and their answer will fall into one of two categories: either they remember the blessed release from the confinement of the classroom, the chance to run and jump, fight, shout and play games, or they had the very different experience of being the odd one out, hanging about by the railings with nobody to talk to. In the midst of all the activity, there was the teacher in charge, visibly bored and having little communication with the children. Invariably, the whole class – often the whole school – went out and came in together, so that for much of the day the playground was unused space. Echoes of this model persist in the practice of some childcare settings and need to be re-examined. Once nursery workers rethink the idea of the outdoor area as a place for learning, they will want to go out with their own small group and act in a facilitating rather than a supervisory role.

When the idea is first suggested, however, it may not be greeted with universal approval. Staff may have been used to the welcome respite offered by all the children going out together, with one or two colleagues looking after them, while they used the time to clear up or take a break. They need to have some good experiences of working actively with the children outside before they can appreciate the value of a different arrangement.

A nursery garden can be a wonderful resource as an enabling environment, where young children's physical development is supported, and where their interests and innate curiosity are nurtured. There might be places to dig and mix magic potions, quiet corners to watch other children, or to daydream, spaces large enough to push a trolley full of stones or to carry a 'heavy' can with a friend to water the plants. But however well designed, the outside space will only be as good as the use the adults make of it. A serious deterrent to some practitioners in this country is the absence of any dependable period of fine weather and the long winter months when it never seems to stop raining.

This is where nursery workers should try to put themselves in the place of a child, who is not only indifferent to rain but often positively enjoys it until he takes on the

Figure 10.1 Snow: a rare opportunity

negative attitudes of adults. The rare snowfall, which may occur only once in two or three years, is a wonderful bonus which provides immense enjoyment and should be fully exploited.

Some of us may have childhood memories of dandelion clocks, hoar frost suspended in a spider's web, frozen puddles, or grass wet with morning dew. Children living in cities are often deprived of such simple experiences, spending a large part of their early years indoors or in uninspired man-made environments. Carefully planned outdoor space can provide countless opportunities, not only for play and social experience but for first-hand learning about living things that no book can teach. There is nothing new about this. Margaret McMillan in her classic book, *The Nursery School*, first published in 1919, thought the garden should be 'enticing' with trees, herbs and scented flowers, as well as having exciting apparatus made out of natural materials (in contrast to the playground equipment of the time).

As in many other aspects of early years work, we have much to learn from practice in other countries. Over the past twenty years, leading early years settings such as, among others, the Pen Green Centre in Corby and the Coram Early Childhood Centre in London have welcomed visitors from Australia, New Zealand, Portugal, Italy and a host of other countries. The knowledge gained across a range of early years disciplines has been shared through conferences and seminars where practitioners debate and shape both the practical and theoretical aspects of early years pedagogy. The creative use of outdoor space is one of these.

Italian nursery gardens are often miniature versions of those in the villas visited by tourists, with rockeries, waterfalls and statuary. In Australia the garden of a childcare centre has long been known as the 'outdoor teaching area' and much thought and care goes into its planning and organisation. As we have already said, this is much more a matter of attitude than of climate. Children in Sweden and Denmark spend up to half the day in the open air. The outdoor space for kindergartens in Bodo, Norway has to be six times the size of the indoor activity area (Krog 2010). In this country the potential for children's learning and enjoyment offered by outdoor space tends to be overlooked. Too many early years settings are surrounded by featureless rectangular patches of grass and asphalt or have become 'victims of commercial companies selling plastic landscapes, like man-made fibre grass or other very brightly coloured ground coverings with equipment that is not moveable' (Carruthers 2007, p. 178).

Forest schools

In the last ten years there has been an upsurge in the importance placed on outdoor play and the outdoors as an essential part of the learning environment. Many settings now have staff trained in 'forest skills', many nurseries work on the forest skills principles, and organisations such as Learning through Landscapes promote and support practitioners and settings.

Forest schools originated in Denmark, their aim being to help children develop an appreciation of the natural world and learn through outdoor play. Training for UK practitioners started at Bridgwater College, Somerset, and is now delivered across the

Figure 10.2 Working in the Children's Centre garden

country (Holmes 2008; Carruthers 2007). There is no need for a forest or wooded area as part of the nursery, although this is a bonus. Settings can make links with the Forestry Commission or Woodland Trust, or local colleges, schools or universities where there might be a suitable woodland area. Observations from staff involved in planning and leading forest school sessions conclude that they promote self-esteem, risk-taking, independence and respect for nature (Bromley 2010; Holmes 2008).

The Statutory Framework for the EYFS Foundation Stage (DfE 2012b, p. 5) states that 'children [should] have opportunities to be outside on a daily basis all year round'. Outdoor activity at nursery or pre-school may be a child's only access to real physical activity – climbing, running, jumping. Being out of doors is known to be beneficial for the emotional, physical and mental health of adults as well as children. The rising figures for childhood obesity (see Chapter 9) provide an additional incentive to see that young children spend as much time as possible out of doors.

Planning outdoor space as a learning area

Three important considerations in planning the use of outdoor space are: access from the main building, storage, and inspiring practitioners to use the garden creatively.

Access

It should be as easy as possible for children to move between the inside and outside spaces. When this is difficult there is a strong tendency to save trouble by staying indoors. Depending on the design of the building, it is often something we can do very little about. But if we can link the indoor and outdoor area with covered play spaces which can be used whatever the weather, we offer children an easier transition to the larger outside area. This is especially useful if the younger children have to share the garden. It offers a safe place to access familiar resources such as a sand or water tray or easel, while at the same time being able to watch what is going on outside until they feel confident enough to venture there themselves. Some settings are fortunate enough to have a conservatory or covered pergola area, perhaps with weather-protective sides, which can act as transition points to the 'proper' outdoors. The space should be designed to be accessible to all children, including those with disabilities.

Storage

The importance of well-designed storage facilities is often underestimated. It is not just a matter of somewhere to put things away, like a garden shed, but how to use the storage space to enable young children to access, choose and return items. So we need to consider trolleys to move equipment, places to stack a variety of playthings, boxes with picture labels and hooks to hang gardening tools. If we really want to enable children to make their own selections and provide opportunities for child-led play, then the organisation of the storage is as important as the storage itself. If the shed simply becomes a dumping zone, then equipment will break, there will be no rotation of toys and little respect or care for the contents, either from children or staff.

Inspiration for practitioners

The third element is to establish an expectation that staff will want to work in the outdoor space, to be inventive and flexible about its use. It is good for them to visit other settings or play parks to see what can be done. Looking at resources from and working directly with people from organisations such as Learning through Landscapes, the Wildlife Trust and the Royal Society for the Protection of Birds gives practitioners access to a wealth of materials. It is the job of the nursery leader or organiser to make sure that all staff understand that the outside learning area is as important as the indoors. To achieve this may require much discussion and perhaps formal training with an outside facilitator. Although there are often practical obstacles, for instance an upstairs group room with no direct access to the garden, we are convinced that attitudes, sometimes unconscious, are an equally important barrier.

A point to consider is how far children can be enabled to flow freely between inside and outside and how far outdoor time needs to be timetabled – when mixed age groups are using the space, for instance. In that case it is important to allow long enough time-slots for the play to develop and children to become fully involved.

Playing and learning out of doors

Observing children

One way of creating a hospitable climate for change is to look in detail at how the space is used at present and how the children behave in the freer context that the garden offers. A staff meeting discussion could focus on how everyone sees the value of the garden area and their own role during outdoor play. This discussion is almost certain to throw up a number of frustrations and negative feelings which should be noted as problems to be solved rather than excuses for inaction.

Close observation of individual children can be particularly revealing in undertaking an assessment of the use of outdoor space. Children should be asked about what they like in the garden and what they might want to be different. Parents, too, should be asked for their observations. A study of the garden could be a useful project for a student. Putting these observations together should provide a good idea of the quality and variety of experience that the outside area already offers, and where it falls short.

Some questions that the observers might have in mind are: What do equal opportunities mean for boys and girls, older and younger children, the outgoing and the

Figure 10.3 Part of the outdoor learning area in Coram Early Childhood Centre

timid? How do the social strains of being in a group outside differ from being indoors? Do some children always dominate the equipment, such as swings or climbing frames, while others seem unable to assert themselves? How do the children learn to negotiate and take turns, and what is the adult's role in this? Are there opportunities for the children to experiment and take small risks to test and extend their abilities? Which children take advantage of them? These would be useful questions to begin discussions amongst the staff team, reflecting on the observations of what the children are doing and talking about in the garden, in preparation for any changes to be made to the outside area.

Safety, accessibility and inclusion

In the risk-averse twenty-first century, we need to give children, including the youngest, the chance to use their physical selves fully, to crawl, walk, run, climb, roll and slide. Watch a group of children playing freely in a grassed area, making their own games, and see how they use every part of their body during their play. We should ensure that our outside space gives children opportunities to make choices and decisions, climbing the steps to the slide alone or wanting at first to hold on to an adult hand, clambering over the large wooden blocks, rolling down a grassy slope, jumping off a log or balancing precariously along a plank.

Risk assessments are carried out as a matter of course in most settings, and staff will need to discuss these as a team, so that children are enabled rather than restricted (Richardson 2007). The view of the Royal Society for the Prevention of Accidents is that we should aim to provide a play environment that is 'as safe as necessary but not as safe as possible' (ROSPA 2013, electronic source). Practitioners' attitudes and modelling are

Figure 10.4 Concentrating on the challenge ahead

Figure 10.5 Children use their own ideas to make the outdoor space more exciting

crucial, fully involving the children. For example, we might discuss why it is important to wash all the pots and pans used in the outside kitchen area or sandpit, or why there is a limit to the number of children on the climbing frame at any one time.

Practitioners should use positive language to reinforce important messages, so when a toddler is just about to sample a caterpillar, rather than shouting 'Don't! it's dirty and you'll be sick' we try something like 'Don't lick the caterpillar, Sam, he doesn't taste nice and will be very frightened'. In this case the caterpillar was returned to the plant and examined through a magnifying glass with adult support.

Thoughtful planning of the outside area can ensure that it is an inclusive space, as discussed in the section below on creating a new garden. Carruthers (2007, p. 180) suggests that 'the outdoors can provide a child with special needs access to risk-taking and adventure'. If the garden really does respond to all the senses, for example, visually impaired children can enjoy the scents of flowers and earth, the sound of birdsong and wind chimes, and then all the children will benefit.

Outdoor experiences for very young children

While some suggestions for activities can be helpful for practitioners, we would emphasise that they should always be based on observations of individual children or small groups and be guided by what they are interested in, trying to do, or can nearly do. Then we should 'match' the provision to the child, and support and extend their play (Bruce 1991). Rather than plan adult-directed activities, it is better to have areas of the garden geared to those growing and developing needs and interests, and offer spaces and equipment that provoke curiosity and enjoyment – things to climb over, crawl through, vehicles to push or ride, places to dig, bury and find treasure, and crates, bricks, blocks and blankets to create tunnels, towers and dens.

Quiet spaces for conversation should not be forgotten. Bromley (2010, p. 5) observes that children who can be reluctant to speak indoors can be 'transformed when they step outside into confident talkers and thinkers'.

For non-mobile babies, and those just beginning to roll, stretch, crawl and pull themselves up, the outside environment is just as important as for the busy two- and three-year-olds, bustling about watering plants and making dens. Of course their key person will ensure that they are warm enough in winter and shaded from the sun in hot weather. Then there need to be things to tempt the senses of the youngest children. Most babies love to see leaves and branches moving in the wind but creative practitioners will find other things of interest to hang above them. CDs twist and turn, lengths of ribbon flutter in the wind, and shells strung on garden twine make intriguing sounds. A parachute was hung across the fence to the side of the building outside one baby room we know. It waved gently in the breeze above the babies and toddlers, to their obvious enjoyment. Musical chimes to hang in the garden can be bought or made; scented plants can be grown in pots near where the babies lie on blankets or mattresses.

Art, story, music and dance

Dorothy Selleck (1997) tells of a group of toddlers observed in Reggio Emilia after a rain shower playing at trail-making in the puddles with long lengths of ribbon. The children strutted and cooed and hooted with excitement as they wore the ribbons tucked into their clothes and watched the intriguing patterns being created on the paving as it dried. This is a cautionary tale for practitioners intent on 'art activities' for young children, for what was this trail-making if not a combination of art and movement? We should be looking to the environment for natural art, using sticks in wet leaves, squeezing mud between fingers and toes, mark-making in sand and earth in place of paper (Forbes 2004). Home-made rattles using pebbles and seeds can encourage outdoor movement games accompanied by special outdoor songs, using new words to known tunes. Outdoors lends itself to storytelling; for the little ones the chance to have a one-to-one story time sitting in the willow tunnel or other private space in the garden is not to be missed.

Collections of objects

We know from our observations of the Treasure Basket and heuristic play that collections are fascinating, both to children and adults. In the outdoor environment, baskets or containers of interesting objects from the real world can be put together for exploration with an adult sitting close by, supporting the learning by offering unobtrusive comments and responding to the child's investigations rather than asking questions. Sensitive practitioners will know when to hold back and allow the children to immerse themselves in their exploration. Collections might include baskets of pinecones of

assorted sizes, large pebbles, shells, leaves, seed and flower heads, lavender and nas-
turtium (both edible), shiny conkers, some still in their prickly cases for children to
handle with care and supervision.

Transporting things from one place to another seems to form an important part of
toddlers' schematic development. They need transporters like wheelbarrows, trolleys,
buckets, baskets, anything they can carry or push – and things to put in them.

Sand, soil and mud

Babies and toddlers generally need little encouragement to explore sand, soil or mud,
but there are some practical points to ensure that they can do so safely. It is best to use
topsoil bought from a garden centre or plant nursery that has been sterilised rather than
compost. Practitioners will still need to be observant as babies will put the soil in their
mouths. Offer mud or sand in large, flat builders' trays for the youngest children. Just
let them explore it with their hands, patting, poking and squeezing. Later, when they
are ready for tools, find ones with short handles, large measuring spoons or small
shovels that can be found in kitchen shops for use with cereals and flour. With the soil
you can add more or less water to vary the consistency. The babies may want to walk
through it, stand or sit in it, make marks with their feet and hands. You can add objects
from the natural world, such as sticks, pinecones and small washable toys. As the
children's fine motor skills develop you can provide moulds, cake tins and spoons for
mixing and 'cooking'. Jan White's delightful book, *Making a Mud Kitchen*, is full of
beautiful photographs and useful advice for practitioners on the possibilities of using
mud with slightly older children, incorporating elements of the home corner and pretend cookery (White 2012b).

Growing and tending plants

Many nurseries grow beans, carrot tops or cress on indoor plant tables but make less
use of the outdoor area. Children can join in planting bulbs and bedding plants to
enhance the general appearance of the garden, but if there is space it is good to create
individual gardens for children.

A good way of defining the space is to use small car tyres (easily obtainable from
garages specialising in changing and supplying tyres), half-embedded in the earth. This
kind of individual plot is manageable both for the child and the nursery worker – rather
in the way some people will happily tend a hanging basket but feel overwhelmed by a
whole garden. The children can be helped to sow different types of flower and vegetable
seeds, to water their own tiny plots and watch the results. When the plants come up they
can be compared with the pictures on the packets or in flower books or on postcards.

In using recycled tyres for this purpose or to create play structures, there are some
safety points to be noted. Steel belt tyres should be avoided as they may eventually wear,
exposing steel bands. Tyres should be checked for broken rims before use and when
filling them with soil.

Figure 10.6
Music in the garden

Tools not toys

Small groups of two-year-olds will enjoy beginning to plant and take responsibility for growing things, especially if they can be harvested and eaten during the nursery day. Basic requirements are an adult-sized rake and broom, small rakes with short handles, small brooms (real ones, not toys), wheelbarrows, watering cans, trowels and small forks. Metal tools are more effective and easier to use than plastic. Wheelbarrows are essential as this age group will enjoy moving 'stuff' around the garden. Also needed are baskets with handles for carrying weeds or produce, pots and seed trays, easily obtained from parents or garden centres. Having a range of sizes, shapes and materials gives an opportunity for the beginnings of mathematical language. Children can be encouraged to find a bigger or smaller bucket, or 'one more pot and then we will all have one' or to divide a packet of seeds into three heaps before planting. By working alongside the children in small groups and showing them how to hold and use proper tools, like trowels or forks, the key person is laying the foundation for much future enjoyable gardening activity.

Access to water is important. Ideally there should be an outside tap, but one setting where this was not possible used large jerry cans placed at strategic points in the garden where children could fill up containers independently.

Care and maintenance

As with the group room, children can make a real contribution to keeping the garden looking well-cared-for and attractive, at the same time as enjoying themselves. Even small children can join in by picking up waste paper, raking and sweeping up leaves and piling them into a wheelbarrow with hands and trowels.

Learning about living things

Long before they reach their third year, many children will already have learned to dislike and fear crawling and flying insects. Their immediate response to an insect seen in the garden may be to stamp on it. By expressing our own interest in and respect for 'mini-beasts' we can play a significant part in re-education, and the children will soon pick up our very different attitude.

Bees, wasps, ants, beetles, spiders, earwigs, ladybirds, woodlice, centipedes, snails, caterpillars, worms and butterflies, all offer scope for conversation, and some for close examination.

Figure 10.7
Transporting and watering at the same time!

Figure 10.8 Learning to use real tools (adults out of shot)

Each child in the small group needs a plastic magnifying glass, and the older ones will like to identify the insects they have seen in a well-illustrated book. Of course this activity takes place under close supervision, and children quickly learn to distinguish between insects which must on no account be touched, such as wasps and bees, and those that can safely be picked up (gently) and inspected at close quarters.

Children old enough to appreciate the need for quiet and stillness will enjoy observing birds if the garden is provided with a feeding tray and birdbath out of reach of local cats. The children can help to put out different types of food to attract a range of different birds. Describing them helps to develop vocabulary – what colour are their heads, beaks, wings? Do they run or hop? What sound do they make? Which bird in the book looks most like the one seen in the garden and what is its name?

Pets such as rabbits, hamsters and guinea pigs can be an asset in a nursery setting, provided that the children are involved in their care and feeding and at least one staff member is prepared to take responsibility for their well-being, especially for care at weekends and holidays. This needs to be someone who really loves animals and does not have to be persuaded to do the job as a tiresome obligation. If there is no such person on the staff, it is better to do without pets altogether. An adequate-sized cage and run are needed, so space is another consideration.

Figure 10.9 Learning about living things (Photograph: Shutterstock)

Creating or redesigning the outside area

If a new nursery is being set up from scratch, the outdoor area needs to be planned with as much care as the interior. Occasionally the chance may arise for the redesign or restructuring of an existing outdoor space, so we suggest below some of the aspects that need to be considered in that case.[1] The first point is that, even though the decision is likely to be taken at management level and it will be necessary to seek expert help from a landscaping expert or garden designer, it is essential for ideas to be evolved in close collaboration with nursery staff and those who will be responsible for future maintenance. This is to ensure that the design responds to the needs of everyone who will be running and using the centre.

There may be parents in the nursery who have the skills, knowledge and enthusiasm to contribute to a garden project. Also, more and more communities are getting involved in the regeneration of gardens and public spaces, both to enhance the appearance of the environment and to grow food. Charities such as the Prince's Trust will work with early years centres on garden projects, and we know of a Children's Centre garden area that was transformed with the help of a group of hard-working young volunteers.

Aims and priorities

These will differ to some extent with the size of the area available and the numbers and age of the children using the setting. For example, is there space for a separate outdoor area for under-twos, or must the garden serve the needs of a wider age group? Ideally, the garden might be designed to meet all the following requirements:

- Provide a range of stimulating play and learning opportunities for children of different ages and abilities;
- Allow freedom for boisterous and energetic play as well as areas where children can be quiet and private;
- Accommodate group and individual play, and occasional larger events, such as a parents' or community picnic;
- Offer sensory experiences, enabling children to explore scale, space, light, shade, colour, sound, shape and scent;
- Produce some material that can be brought and used indoors, such as flowers, leaves, seed heads and fruit.

Generally practitioners will have limited opportunities either to plan an outside learning area from scratch or to institute a radical transformation of the existing garden or external space. However, even with a limited budget, there is much that can be done to make better use of the outside area. Many of the points made earlier about the arrangement and use of the garden should be borne in mind. For example, equipment for large-scale physical activity will always be a key element. Natural materials with natural finishes – wood, bark, stone and metal – weather gracefully and look good far longer than the plastic creations in garish colours to be seen in some playgrounds, which quickly start to look grubby and stained. Mosaics are a better way of providing colour, and can be used to good effect on animal shapes or structures that the children can ride or climb over. Lengths of tree trunk are infinitely versatile and can often be obtained from parks departments or tree-felling businesses, which may be willing to cut them into specified lengths. These can be laid horizontally or on end as steps or stepping stones. They can be used for climbing, balancing, jumping off and imaginative play. A useful idea is to set an old car steering wheel into one end of a length of tree trunk. Branches can make a catwalk in a grassed area.

It is better to have two smaller sandpits rather than one large one so as to reduce crowding and occasions for conflict between the children. Smaller ones are also more easily protected from cats as the covers will be more manageable to take off and replace. Sand needs maintenance, and this makes a useful outdoor activity for a worker with a small group. Raking and sieving will be enjoyed, and the sand can be disinfected and kept damp using small watering cans – water play with a purpose. As with the indoor sand tray, there must be plenty of sand and not too much equipment, and this should be checked regularly and stored, not left cluttering up the pit, which can quickly develop a neglected and uninviting aspect.

Space and layout

Every outside area has its unique opportunities and constraints, and it is necessary to identify these right from the start. If the area is cold and windy it will not be an attractive place to play and learn. Shelter and enclosure are extremely important. A covered area is essential for use in wet weather and for shade when it is hot. Are there any existing trees or hedges? Are there views into and out of the play space which you might want to enhance or screen? How will the garden be maintained? Will outside assistance be available or will maintenance fall almost entirely on the nursery staff, children and volunteers?

The size of the space should be assessed in relation to numbers of children and the need for nearby seating for adult carers. Small children need the reassurance of a close adult presence, so sitting places for practitioners are essential. If possible, the quiet corner should be situated on a slight rise, so as to give the adult a view of the whole play area, but be given a limited sense of enclosure by a low curved hedge or wall. Accessibility for disabled children and adults and children with additional needs should be considered. Ideas incorporated at the planning stage for the benefit of disabled children can be valuable for all children, for example enhancing the sensory impact of the environment. Smooth-faced, wide pathways for wheelchair access and ramps instead of steps will also be good for play with wheeled toys. Raised sand-play trays or water containers, walkways or mazes with kerbs and handrails, designed for children with visual problems, will be fun for others as well.

Ideally, the smallest children should have their own outside space, opening out of their group room with a covered terrace area. It is best situated next to the older children's garden with a low fence or hedge and a connecting gate so that the children can see each other and sometimes play together. Unlike the older children, they do not need a large active area or fixed equipment, but they do need space because they are constantly on the move, walking unsteadily, tumbling over and bumping into things. This means eliminating unnecessary hazards, sharp edges and protrusions.

Levels and contours

A small space need not be a disadvantage. The most modest contouring will increase play value and give variety to movement patterns, which makes it all the more surprising that so many nursery gardens are relentlessly flat. Children love abandoning themselves to the force of gravity, and a grassy slope will encourage many activities such as rolling, balancing, swinging and jumping. The smallest bumps and wrinkles will become hills, valleys, mountain ranges or river canyons. What better than a grassy hollow, perhaps combined with shrub planting for a secret hiding place or den? Mounds can be used to create enclosure, provide shelter or separate different play activities.

Planting schemes

Children's gardens should be full of eye-catching and interesting plants, designed to stimulate curiosity both in the plants themselves and in the wildlife that visits them. Areas for energetic activities should be planted with robust shrubs or trees which can survive the impact of play, while other areas should aim for visual interest, fun and sensory stimulus throughout the year. Powell (2001) points out the potential of planting to produce a range of different sounds, for example plants with large leaves on which the rain plays like a drum, bamboos and grasses which rustle, plants with exploding seed pods, shrubs and bushes such as corus, hazel and willow, close to fences so that they rattle against them. Obviously great care should be taken to ensure that none of the selected plants produce poisonous berries.

Working out a planting scheme is a job for someone who has a real inclination and feel for horticulture, or an interest in learning about it. There might be someone like this on the nursery staff who can work closely with a landscape consultant. Another possibility is to involve a volunteer, either by a general appeal or through a gardening club. A local newspaper will probably be willing to publish an article on the subject, and local nurseries or garden centres may become involved by donating or sponsoring with plants or other outdoor resources.

Some general points about planting are:

- Planting should be dense and massed.
- Where active play is envisaged, robust material should be used – vigorous, fast-growing trees and shrubs.
- Paths or steps should be incorporated within grassed slopes where heavy use is expected (for example, for access to a built-in slide).
- Prickly species should be incorporated on boundaries to deter access and reinforce site security.
- Small-scale planting or herbaceous species should be incorporated in raised beds or clearly defined by kerbs as non-play areas.
- Care should be taken to ensure that all poisonous plants are eliminated. Lists are available from local authority early years teams and Ofsted.

Wildlife

A variety of trees, shrubs and flowers will attract many birds and insects, and this can help children to overcome their prejudices about creepy-crawlies. If space is limited, climbing shrubs grown on walls or fences can substitute for trees. Flowers should be chosen with strong scents and single (rather than double) blooms to attract butterflies and bees. A small rotting log or tree stump in a shady spot will soon harbour colonies of mini-beasts.

Water

Children love water, but obviously safety must be taken carefully into account. An asset for any play space is an outdoor tap fitted with a hose and a selection of spray attachment which can be used for special fun events in the summer, as well as for garden maintenance. Outdoor paving could feature drainage channels which a child can fill with water to create a stream. Other play use of water might include scope for damming, diverting the flow, creating waterfalls, or sailing toy boats. It is interesting to note that playing with water was the focus of one of Elinor Goldschmied's early films (Froebel Trust 2013).

A nature pond for fish, frogs, snails, water beetles and plants can be a valuable educational resource that will capture children's imagination and promote much enquiry and conversation. To reduce the likelihood of a child falling or stepping into it, the pond can be constructed above ground level, and as an additional safeguard a wire mesh can be fixed just below the water level. In principle no pool should exceed 20 cm in depth.

Surfaces

Paths and paved areas should be spaced throughout to enable access at all times of the year, and these need to be durable, nonslip and wide enough to manoeuvre prams, pedal cars, tricycles and wheelchairs. Children love to follow tracks and trails, and the more interesting these can be the better. There could be a path which vanishes through a planted area or follows the gradient of a slope. Stepping stones could lead into a secret corner or be laid in grass between trees. Recommended surfaces are paving slabs, bricks (not the slippery engineering bricks), tarmac, asphalt, brushed concrete, but not loose gravel or reinforced 'Grasscrete'.

Beneath and around play equipment there should be all-purpose, all-weather surfaces. The main suitable safety surfaces are 'loose fill' (tree bark, sand or pea-gravel), rubber crumb or rubber sheet or tiles. All have their assets and drawbacks which need to be considered in relation to their situation and expected use. For example, loose fill surfaces are more difficult to maintain and are not suitable for scuff points, such as under swings and at the ends of slides. Rubber surfaces become less impact-absorbent as they compress and wear out. Moulded rubber is non-porous and puddles can collect unless the ground is flat and well drained. Professional advice will be needed to decide on the best combination of surfaces for the intended use of the space.

Using the resources of the neighbourhood and community

Here we are less concerned with major outings than with small-scale expeditions, usually at a short distance from the nursery or at least no further than the town centre. There are both negative and positive reasons for building these into the centre programme. On the negative side there is the fact that many children in childcare spend most of their waking lives in one room. If parents are working full-time they may be too occupied with domestic tasks at weekends to take the children out on leisurely shopping trips or child-paced walks. They may not have the energy or the money to take children out when they are not at the nursery. The result is that children can miss out on quite ordinary experiences and live in a world limited by the walls of the nursery and their own home.

There are also positive reasons: first, the opportunities that even the most ordinary neighbourhood offers for interest, learning and conversation, and second, the advantages to the nursery or centre in getting to know the local community and making friends. This is especially important if most of the staff do not live in the district where the nursery is situated.

Visits and outings

Successful outings depend on good organisation and preparation, a small group of children, and enough adults to ensure safe supervision – at least one to every two children, which will probably mean involving parents, volunteers or students. Every neighbourhood has its own particular features: parks, markets, fire station, railway station or bridges, museums, libraries, swimming pools. What seems quite unremarkable to an adult – builders at work with a cement mixer or mechanical digger, a crane, traffic lights or the different types of fruit and vegetables on display outside a greengrocer's – can all provide a focus of interest – think of that favourite children's book, *Harry the Dirty Dog*.

It is important that all the adults involved are in clear agreement about the purpose of the outing, which is to provide enjoyment and learning opportunities for the children, not to achieve some adult objective which has little meaning for the child. The going matters as much as the arriving (which can if necessary be postponed for another occasion). Thus, the nursery worker's intention may be to visit a particular place, and she should build in plenty of time to get there without hustling the children. But, if on the way they become engrossed in something else – a tree just shedding its shining chestnuts, for instance – she should be flexible enough to negotiate a change of plan with the children and her colleagues.

If one of the adults has a camera, he or she can take the occasional photograph, which can be used later by the key worker as a way of reviewing the experience with her small group and as a focus for conversation. A group photograph album is also useful for keeping parents informed and sharing nursery experiences with them, but photographs of individual children for display or to go in their own books are also needed.

When planning an outing, it is a good idea for the practitioner to do a dummy run and talk to any outside people she plans to involve. For example, if she intends to take the children to visit shops of various kinds, they are likely to get a much better reception if they go at a time of day when business is slack rather than at a peak period, and she can also find out which shopkeepers are prepared to be friendly and helpful.

Trips to the local children's library can start very early in a child's life, whenever possible involving a parent too, reinforcing the interest and pleasure in books for which the nursery has laid the foundation. As mentioned in Chapter 8, the nursery will probably already have a good relationship with the children's librarian and may have an arrangement for a stock of books changed periodically.

Museums and art galleries are not often thought of as places to take young children, but are full of objects and pictures that can hold great interest for them. Obviously the visit should be scaled to the attention span of the child. The nursery worker leading the outing should discuss with the person responsible for the educational work of the museum or gallery what is likely to appeal to small children and ask if possible for a guided tour. She can then make her own selection from her knowledge of the children and compile a list of exhibits to last over several visits, taking the children to look at no more than two or three different things on each occasion. This, of course, is entirely different from most people's past experience of visiting museums, either in school parties or as tourists, when we tend to rush round the whole place, ending up exhausted and with no clear impression of what we have seen.

Swimming

Another possibility worth consideration, though it may take some effort to set up, is swimming. Children can learn to swim from a few months old and get great pleasure from it. This is commonplace in California and Australia, where the ubiquity of private pools makes it necessary for children to be 'watersafe' from an early age. Baby swimming classes are becoming increasingly popular in this country as well, and conventionally taught adults may find it surprising that they learn first to swim under water. Some organisations are teaching up to 10,000 babies a week, with their parents (Waterbabies 2013).

One difficulty is that public pools are often kept at too low a temperature for small children, but where there is a separate learners' pool it is sometimes possible to negotiate warmer water for particular sessions. Another possibility is to use a hydrotherapy pool attached to a medical or disability centre. Schools or centres for disabled children sometimes have a purpose-built pool suitable for use by young children. The need for an adult with each child can be a difficulty if most parents are working full-time, unless the nursery is supported by a very strong group of voluntary and occasional helpers willing to go in the water with the children. The setting could support the volunteers to gain lifeguard qualifications as part of their commitment and community outreach.

Unless swimming can happen at least once a week, it is unrealistic to hope that many of the children will learn to swim independently unless they are also taken regularly by their parents at weekends. However, they can learn to feel happy and confident in the pool, to propel themselves using 'dog paddle', and become used to putting their faces in the water, so that they will learn to swim more easily when they are older. If the local pool has an instructor with a special interest in young children and if one of the nursery staff is a keen swimmer, a more ambitious programme may be possible.

Transport and outings

Many nurseries have their own minibuses, especially if they have an after-school club or a breakfast club when these vehicles are used to pick up and drop children off at school. The use of a minibus, perhaps shared with another centre, greatly widens the scope of possible outings, providing much pleasure and stimulus to the children. Many Children's Centres have transport, and there may be local arrangements to enable other early years settings to use it. Staff members with their own cars may also be willing to use them, provided the necessary insurance arrangements are made. Outings have a useful function in introducing parents to the resources of the neighbourhood and to activities they might undertake with their children that will also be enjoyable for themselves. The end-of-term trip may encourage parents to join staff on a day out to a farm or country park. A risk assessment by the nursery is essential prior to a visit. Obviously it is important to ensure that all the necessary hygiene principles are observed, to reduce any possibility of infection from sheep, goats, chickens, rabbits and any other animals the children may encounter.

Summary

Outdoor space is often an underused asset. This chapter shows how it can become as important a resource as the indoor provision. Given positive staff attitudes, the garden can become a genuine 'outside learning area'. We suggest some ways in which a garden can be used to best advantage, or even be transformed by well-planned contouring and planting into a place with infinite possibilities for play and enjoyment, both for the children and those who look after them. Finally we explore the possibilities offered by the surrounding neighbourhood for visits and small-scale outings to provide new experiences and stimulate interesting conversation and activities for both children and adults.

Note

1. The first and second editions of this book included an extended section, contributed by Judy Hackett, on creating a new garden or redesigning an existing one completely. As that will seldom be possible, in this edition we have limited ourselves to basic guidelines.

<table>
<tr><td>

11

</td><td>

Leading and managing in the early years

</td></tr>
</table>

That the birds of worry and care fly above your head, this you cannot change. But that they build nests in your hair, this you can prevent.

(Chinese proverb)

In this chapter we will consider:

- The role of the leader or manager;
- Developing a vision and establishing a common purpose;
- Systems to aid communication and decision-making;
- Planning and organising meetings;
- Relationships with parents;
- Multi-agency working.

With few exceptions, people choose to work with young children because they like them, enjoy their company and are interested in seeing them grow and develop. Children are a delight, and yet they make heavy demands on those who look after them.

We have generally used the term 'leader' to describe the person who heads up the setting and is responsible for its day-to-day running (Moyles 2006). Some European countries favour a collegiate style of management in which a group or pair of equal professionals, usually teachers, take on the leadership role in rotation. By contrast, the traditional style of management in the UK is very hierarchical, partly because of the range of qualifications at different levels discussed in Chapter 1. However, the value of teamwork and a democratic style of organisation is increasingly accepted across a range of provision.

The manager or leader of a childcare centre has a task which has become increasingly exacting over recent years (Beaty 2011; Moyles 2006). Expectations about the quality of education and care offered to children under three have risen but training and resources have not kept pace with them (see Chapter 1). The many changes to legislation, inspection and registration requirements alone, plus repeated revisions of the early years curriculum, have produced a massive increase in the reading and reflection time required for managers to keep up to date (Rodd 2006; Whitaker and Whalley 2003). There is also increasing recognition that the challenges and tasks of nurseries and early years settings and the rapid growth of the sector make them amongst the most difficult and demanding organisations in society to manage, demanding a high order of skill, ingenuity and commitment (Whitaker 2001). All this can put a heavy load on the leader, and she needs to empower her staff group to work as effectively and efficiently as possible and to feel valued and able to contribute to the organisation of the setting.

Research has brought enormous advances over the last two decades in our understanding of young children's learning and development, research that now informs practice and closer thinking between neuroscientists and educationalists. When we add to this the range of relationships involved and the statutory and legal responsibilities, the complexities of leading and managing an early childhood setting become evident. Leadership learning and management qualifications are becoming more available: training providers have risen to the necessity for highly qualified and skilled leaders of early years settings. But there are still many managers who have not had the opportunity to debate the theories and knowledge related to early years leadership through a formal study programme.

Much of the atmosphere and ethos in a childcare setting depends on the way staff work together, especially whether there is a clearly expressed understanding of the aims of the service offered to the children and their parents. Lying behind the day-to-day operation of the setting there is the broad policy of the responsible local authority or other administrative body to which the institution is accountable, whether this is a voluntary organisation, private enterprise or workplace employer. Unless an organisation develops coherent policies, which are understood, agreed and used by all staff, problems tend to be resolved on an ad hoc basis and serious issues are never properly addressed. Where conflicts arise it is essential that they are discussed in terms of the policies involved rather than the personalities who carry them out.

Leadership and management

The role and style of leadership in day care settings has previously had rather little discussion although it is a crucial element in the way that they function.

Leadership could be described as the driving force that motivates and provides a vision for staff, colleagues, partners and stakeholders to aspire to: it is about the development of people, and services, involving others in an environment of collaboration and trust. Managing can be seen as more about the moment, focusing on purpose, policy, practice and product.

Leadership and management are often considered to be different, but we think that they go hand in hand, and complement each other. A leader and manager must be able to plan, organise, establish systems and procedures, check and control – the 'doing' of essential administrative tasks – recording staff attendances, absences, managing sick pay, holiday requests, planning meetings, organising open days. All this planning and organising is essential to ensure the vision becomes a reality. Some settings will be fortunate enough to have staff with designated responsibility for administration, finance or reception duties, giving the centre leader freedom to focus on the staff team, parents, children and wider partners.

What does a manager do?

In addition to the previously mentioned tasks, a manager will be responsible for ensuring that the objectives of the organisation or setting are met, and that all the resources available – human, financial, material – are used efficiently and effectively. If she is responsible for budget setting and overall finances as well as curriculum, she will need to formulate a business plan. Training plans for the staff team are an essential tool for staff development, so a 'training needs analysis' should be carried out. Leading the setting may well include responsibility for developing marketing strategies and promotions now that local authority provision of childcare is disappearing and the sector is dominated by for-profit providers. Budgets and staffing, developing policies and procedures in line with government requirements, complying with health and safety regulations, and maintaining an ethos and culture of working closely with parents are just some of the extraordinary range of tasks leaders in early childhood settings have to take on.

Developing a vision

Most early years settings have a statement of intent or 'vision', something that tells their customers and service users (parents and children) the purpose, beliefs and aspirations of the setting. In the case of larger corporate childcare providers there will be a company vision, to which all staff may be expected to sign up. This is quite likely to be couched in such general terms that it will have little impact on practice and, being imposed from outside, may not really be 'owned' by the staff.

Smaller settings and providers will need to create or revisit the vision as an essential part of a teambuilding exercise, exploring such basic questions as 'Why are we here?' and 'What do we want to provide for our children and families?' and then put together a strategy for achieving long-term plans, not only for the children's learning and development, but for the staff and the working environment.

According to Smith and Langston (1999, p. 28, cited in Moyles 2006), 'Having a vision means being able to articulate your own philosophy to a range of people.' Moyles (2006) adds to this, 'having the confidence to do so and respecting other people's views'. Although confidence is an important attribute for a leader, we would suggest that the leader must have a sound theoretical and knowledge base, and this is where the combination of pedagogy and practice come together. If the leader is to bring her staff team and colleagues from other agencies on board, she needs to be able to articulate how children learn and develop, and also have an understanding of how adults learn.

From the vision come the 'values', which are easy to talk about, but often harder to define. Values are about principles and standards – for example, how you will address issues such as equality, inclusion, improvement, respect, professionalism and variations in children's development in your setting. Do you aspire to be an ethical organisation and how is this reflected in your practice? Do all staff have a deep commitment to children's well-being and learning? Articulating and publicly acknowledging your vision and values carries an element of risk because other people then have the chance to measure you against them.

Working alongside the team

Nurseries and childcare centres often have a high turnover of staff, which makes it very important for the leader to be committed to the setting over a number of years, and to developing a community profile.

The leader in a small day care centre can find herself in the position of taking administrative and financial responsibility for the setting, managing most of the day-to-day tasks involved in running a nursery, and also being one of the staff in a group room, directly responsible for the care of children. This can be problematic for nursery staff. They may be unsure how to work alongside their leader, when she is operating as a member of the team. If this only happens in emergencies or to cover planned in-room meetings, it is not too difficult, but if the leader's working time is regularly divided between working directly with children and managing the administrative side of the nursery then it needs to be managed carefully. It can be very positive for the leader to be part of the team some of the time. It gives her the opportunity to observe daily practice on a regular basis and to lead by example.

An effective team leader will encourage and promote self-esteem and confidence in her staff, be a good listener, and an objective observer, be able to give feedback to staff appropriately and objectively, and support the improvement of performance. The leader will act as a model to her staff team, demonstrating through her actions a range of behaviours, attitudes and skills across a raft of daily occurrences – from talking to and managing difficult situations with parents, making decisions about referrals to Children's Social Care, to talking about the giant snails with a small child, and discussing curriculum delivery with staff. She needs to be in tune with her own leadership styles and behaviours, adapting and changing to the person, their mood, the situation and complexity of the task in hand.

Planning, reflection and discussion

From talking to leaders and managers, it appears that the organisation of most settings does not allow nearly enough time for reflection and discussion or for professional dialogue and development. Practitioners will not read or think in a systematic way about their work unless this is built into their day and valued as an essential part of their work with children. Nutbrown and Abbott (2001) note that educators in Reggio Emilia pre-schools and childcare centres spend 6 of their 36 working hours every week without children – participating in professional development, planning, preparation, meetings with families and thinking together about children.

By careful organisation of staff time it should be possible to build in regular planning and discussion time for all workers. One centre arranges for two members of staff to look after two groups of children for half an hour on alternate days so that the other two can have planning time. On one day a week there is a whole centre meeting with a rota for one teacher, with a nursery support assistant, to look after the children. Building in non-contact time is essential for staff to develop their skills as reflective practitioners (Whalley 2007).

This can be a challenge for many settings, especially where the majority of parents are working. If a new provision is opening, then information about the plans to ensure non-contact time for staff and the reasons for it could be part of the marketing and information package provided to parents. It is more difficult when an established setting decides to make changes to opening hours for this purpose. However, if the rationale is discussed with parents, enough notice given for implementation of the change and the setting is able to support parents with options such as early closure or late opening, meetings within working hours can work. Using attendance registers is a good way to find out which is the best day of the week to close earlier or start later while causing the least inconvenience to parents. We have in our experience found parents to be understanding and supportive. It is not an entirely strange idea after all. Many businesses open later one morning or close earlier to make time for staff training. Early years settings need to consider implementing non-contact time as an essential part of continuing professional development.

Delegation

Daily life in any early years setting, but particularly in one providing full day care, is very busy. Frequently, the leader has to draw on the capacity to respond to demands from several different directions at once, but at the same time she needs to maintain an overview of the whole working of the nursery. A personal style which gives true value to negotiating, empathising and attending to detail also requires built-in time for reflection. A leader has to protect her own breathing space to enable her staff members to do the same. She has also to see that she is available to deal with the many unpredictable emergencies that may confront her.

Delegation is not just a matter of convenience and reducing the workload on the leader, it also promotes the professional growth of other nursery workers. It is important that the leader consistently delegates a full range of tasks and responsibilities. Staff motivation, commitment and development suffer if only unpleasant or routine tasks are delegated, and staff may see this as an abuse of power. On the other hand, the 'quicker to do it myself' style, just as in the education of young children, does not produce maturation in others. For example, we know that it takes more effort, especially if we are in a hurry, to encourage a child to fasten her own shoes. But the time and patience spent will pay off later because the child will have gained a skill. She is being empowered by us, reducing her dependency on adults and feeling a sense of achievement.

The principle applies equally to adults. The leader needs to consider each demand on its merits and to consider 'Who else can do this, or learn to do it?' Delegating, in other words, can be seen as transferring power and skill to another person. Selecting the right person for the task is key to effective delegation – knowing your team and knowing who is ready for further responsibilities. Handing over authority relevant to the task will ensure the task can be completed; withholding this can slow or even stop the process.

An example of the transfer of power is seen where the leader, changing the practice of her predecessor, delegates to the cook the task of drawing up menus and ordering food and domestic cleaning materials. She may need to arrange training opportunities and offer close supervision at first, probably helping the cook to work out menus for the first week or two, or ensuring someone with those skills is available for support until the cook feels confident about applying what she has learned. The cook in turn is encouraged to delegate to her kitchen assistant so that the work of the kitchen can go on smoothly if the cook is away. Similarly, the junior nursery worker who is given responsibility for day-to-day decisions will give appropriate responsibilities to the children, for example, involving them in clearing up and the maintenance of the group room. Thus, delegation is not only an effective management technique but a model of good practice.

When the leader has decided on a task and selected a suitable member of staff (our cook in the scenario above) she then needs to invite the staff member to undertake the work. Delegation by definition assumes that the leader will be available for support and consultation, rather than supervision, and this is often where some managers get it wrong. They either seem unable to step aside and let the job be completed, maybe in a way different from how they would have done it themselves, but still to the agreed outcome, or they simply 'dump' a task with little or no explanation of the required outcome and boundaries. This is not helpful. It is important for the leader to let the person to whom the task has been delegated make the day-to-day decisions, do the worrying, solve the problems and sometimes make mistakes. If the leader spends her time checking to eliminate mistakes then delegation hasn't really happened at all. Rodd (2006) provides some helpful guidelines on delegation. It is important that the leader explains:

- The nature of the task to be undertaken;
- The deadline by which the task must be completed;
- The level of authority and accountability that will be assigned to the member of staff who undertakes the task;
- The reasons why the staff member is considered to be the best person for the job.

Clear communication is essential, and the staff member should be asked for feedback at agreed time points so that the leader can identify possible obstacles to completion, and offer support.

Failure to delegate and its symptoms – slow decision-making and detailed planning done at too high a level – can have a very negative impact on the team and the culture of the setting.

Some managers and leaders lack confidence in the staff team's ability to accept and deliver delegated tasks thus depriving practitioners of the opportunity to develop and try out new skills. Without necessarily being aware of it, some leaders withhold knowledge and skills from their staff team as a way of underlining their own power and authority. This doesn't only apply to leaders. Experienced and long-serving staff may also raise barriers to junior workers taking on greater responsibility. The leader needs to have a clear picture of what is appropriate at different levels and how to ensure progression – for example, from the day-to-day stocktaking of consumable resources such as paint, paper, play-dough ingredients and crayons and keeping the art and craft storage area tidy, to costing and ordering those resources. The settings leader will always be responsible for monitoring and quality, evaluation, policy development, setting budgets and managing income, but this could also involve deputies or senior members of the team as part of their continuing professional development.

Communication in nurseries and childcare centres

Good communication is essential in a busy day care setting and systems need to be constantly reviewed if they are to be maintained and developed. Alongside an ongoing programme of appropriate delegation, seen as part of staff development, the leader has the task of ensuring that daily communication arrangements within the nursery work effectively.

Today most nurseries are using a range of media to enable communication, both within the staff team and with parents and outside professionals. The use of the internet has revolutionised childcare: this is where many parents have their first contact with a setting. Most childcare and Children's Centres now have their own websites where parents can find up-to-the-minute information. Settings will be using a range of paper and electronic methods to inform through newsletters, blogs, text messages and email as well as social networking sites. These will need to be managed around legal and guidance frameworks to ensure that data is kept secure and permissions have been sought and agreed for the sharing of photographs and storage and use of data. In some settings there may be webcams linked to the group rooms, so that parents can see their children and watch some of their activities during the day.

Essential to any leader's or manager's desk will be the nursery diary, where everything that is happening is recorded, either on paper or in electronic form: children starting or leaving, appointments, visits and visitors, events and outings, meetings and closure days. How the information is recorded is immaterial and will depend on the resources available and the preference of the nursery leader: what matters is ensuring that all staff are informed and prepared for what is going to happen each day. It is important that the appointments system is not too rigid and that parents can call in if necessary on an open-door policy, even though they may have to wait until a staff member is free to give them attention.

Much of the contact with outside people will be done by telephone, and efficient ways must be found to ensure that messages, often from parents, are noted correctly and passed to the staff member concerned. The leader needs to give special attention to this, otherwise conflicts and anxieties can easily arise. It is very difficult for a staff member fully occupied with the children to break off to take a verbal message, and often preferable for her not to be disturbed. One setting we know uses self-adhesive message slips on a clearly designated noticeboard to relay messages accurately to group room staff. Colour-coordinating the slips can help, so that the appropriate practitioner looks at the message.

Internal communication is a topic that can be usefully introduced at a staff meeting so that everyone grasps the problem and becomes part of the solution. The leader has a more difficult task in keeping communication flowing between staff when the nursery building is inconvenient, for instance when a converted house is used and there are stairs and passages to be negotiated. Nursery workers in this kind of building may feel isolated in their group rooms, and the leader should be aware of this and give thought to how she can minimise the problem – by regular visiting of all the group rooms, for example.

Building in time for meetings

The feeling that some meetings just take up time which would be better used getting on with the work is often quite justified. If meetings are not felt to be getting anywhere, a mood of cynicism and impatience is likely to develop. However, staff meetings are absolutely vital to the effective running of a nursery, like any other collaborative enterprise, and they need to form a regular part of the centre's routine.

Some centres recognise the importance of meetings by closing one afternoon or even a whole day a week, and using the time for purposes that require freedom from responsibility for childcare. Others have to add staff meetings on to the end of a tiring working day, which has serious drawbacks. An intermediate solution is early closure on, say, one day every two weeks. Even this is likely to exclude the ancillary staff, whose involvement can be very valuable.

The organiser should be clear about the purpose and conduct of staff meetings so that she can argue the case with her management to enable them to happen more easily, either by adjusting opening hours or by provision of relief staff. The staff meeting has to be given priority and be protected from interruption.

The purpose of the meeting should be understood and shared with all who come to it. If support staff, outside people or volunteers are included, special care needs to be taken to see that they are fully integrated into the discussion. The staff meeting can be a very important element in communication within the nursery and also a way of enhancing the skill and understanding of staff members in their daily work with children. If the leader feels dissatisfied with the quality and outcome of staff meetings in her setting, she will need to seek information and advice from her own management, from colleagues in charge of other units, or ask her organisation to set up a training day on the topic.

Planning and organisation of meetings

To be worthwhile a meeting needs to have a focus of interest planned beforehand. When this concerns an important policy issue (examples might be a proposal for a major fundraising effort, setting up a volunteer scheme, remodelling the outdoor area), the topic may need to feature on the agenda of several meetings, starting with a general discussion to explore the idea, a 'brainstorming' session at a later meeting and eventually the formulation of an agreed plan. Specific matters to do with the day-to-day running of the nursery need to be clearly presented, perhaps by a staff member who takes responsibility for setting out the problem or proposal and suggesting possible ways forward. It is often more effective for the leader to work with one of her staff to do this rather than always taking the lead herself.

In deciding on the format for the meeting, the question is how to achieve efficiency without bureaucracy. Discussion at nursery meetings may be informal and can be unfocused, which can produce a feeling of frustration at the end that nothing has been achieved. The key to effective meetings is careful preparation and follow-up, which does require a certain degree of formality and a greater willingness to put things on paper than may have been the custom in the past. However, with a greater emphasis on recording and using discussions to inform Nursery Development Plans, Self-Evaluation Forms (SEF), and Room Plans, recording is a necessity not an option.

Our experience of staff meetings is that they work best when considerable trouble is taken with both practical and organisational arrangements. The following guidelines may be helpful:

- The agenda for the meeting should be agreed at least a week in advance and distributed.
- Allocate timed sessions for each topic and ensure the meeting is effectively chaired to allow everyone to participate and for the discussion to remain focused.
- The time of the start and the end of the meeting should be agreed.
- The room should have seats placed in such a way that everyone can have direct eye contact with everyone else.
- Vacant seats near the door should be left ready for latecomers (for example, in an after-work meeting some staff may have to wait until the last parents have collected their children).
- If students are part of the meeting, it is imperative that they have signed the nursery's confidentiality contract.
- Every meeting should start with a check on action arising from the previous one (not a review of minutes, which can be time-consuming and invite a rerun of previous discussions).
- Information should be shared as clearly and concisely as possible. Where appropriate it should be reinforced by a paper copy.
- If possible have an administrator to take notes, clearly indicating who is to take action and by when. These notes should be posted or circulated as soon as possible after the meeting. In addition, those attending the meeting should make notes for their personal use.

- If ancillary staff are included at meetings – and they should be – plan for the topics relevant to them to be the first for discussion.
- Provide refreshments. It is a false economy to dispense with these on grounds of cost, especially for meetings that take place after work.

It is easy for staff to become preoccupied with questions relating to their own working conditions. One way of keeping the children and families in view is to set aside part of each or alternate meetings for a staff member to 'present' a child for whom she is a key person and invite discussion. It is important that this should not always have a problem focus but also celebrate achievement and enjoyable experiences.

When individual children or their parents are discussed, there must always be a careful reminder about confidentiality; it is a fine line which divides information from gossip and prejudiced comments. There may be aspects of family information that are only known to the leader and the key person, so it should be made clear that information is shared only on a need-to-know basis.

Room meetings

In addition to full staff meetings, it is good to establish a practice of regular group room meetings, even when these only involve two people (though they are also a sensible level at which to include volunteers). Staff might say, 'But we are talking to each other all the time, there's no point in anything as formal as a fixed meeting.' However, even 20 minutes of discussion about the more general issues of running the room can be a useful habit to develop. Senior staff can stand in for a short while to make this possible. Such meetings provide an opportunity for nursery workers to plan new activities which require preparation or to examine together in detail which are the moments of the day when they experience most stress and fatigue and how this can be reduced.

Encouraging productive participation

Some problems which may confront the nursery leader or manager in staff meetings are how to deal with staff members who never speak, what to say to the person who is always criticising and what to do when the staff group comes to a collective decision which is contrary to her own view.

Silent members can sometimes be persuaded to contribute by an encouraging word during the meeting, but an indirect approach may be better. The leader might find some point of friction in the working day which affects this worker. It can be suggested that she, together with a colleague, prepares a contribution based on her view of the problem and ideas for improving things and brings this to the next meeting. In her supervision session the worker can be helped to find the best way to articulate her point of view, so that her intervention is clear and persuasive to the rest of the staff.

It is essential to give the critical staff member special attention and a full hearing. In making her complaint she may well be voicing the negative feelings that others share but are unwilling to express openly. Sometimes a difficulty seems to become associated with a particular staff member, and it is important to keep attention on the problem and not on the person.

The third situation, when the collective view differs from her own, can be hard for an organiser committed to a democratic style of decision-making. Sometimes she may have to accept that the time is not right for some change she wants to introduce and, at least temporarily, accept the majority decision. At other times this is impossible because of the policy of the local authority or corporate management, financial constraints or the requirements of the law. For example, in one nursery, staff felt exploited by the behaviour of a few parents who persisted in arriving late to collect their children and wanted to retaliate by withdrawing the children's nursery places. Having explained why this was not an acceptable solution, since several of the children were thought to be at risk and nursery attendance was part of the plan for their protection, the organiser exerted her authority to insist that some other way should be found to deal with the situation.

Tension between staff members

Nothing is more exhausting than an atmosphere of misunderstanding and conflict between fellow workers. Sometimes people working together are afraid to raise an issue because of what they fear might happen if they were really to speak their minds.

Silent disapproval and unspoken resentments are very corroding to personal relationships, and they can and do exist in any group. However, one of the differences between a personal or family group and a professional group is that the underlying aims of the work are explicitly agreed and accepted, so that differing personalities can find respect if not liking for each other. With a proper structure of communication and consultation through staff meetings and regular supervision, disagreements can be brought out into the open and dealt with before they undermine the working of the group. All staff have a responsibility to play their part in creating a good atmosphere, understanding that if they fail to do this they are certainly harming themselves.

Senior staff, of course, play a key role in keeping their ear to the ground, defusing potential conflict and mediating between opposing views when necessary. In her experience of both day care and Children's Centre teams, Ruth and her deputies called this being the 'jam in the sandwich', the Deputy knowing when to address issues or concerns with the team directly, without needing to bring them to the leader's attention, and when the matter was sufficiently serious to take to the senior management team meeting. With the increasingly common structure where the manager is responsible for two or more settings, senior staff often have a tricky role to play, being the listening ear on the ground, deputising for the leader, making decisions in her absence, and often having the main responsibility for the day-to-day running and organisation of a setting. Rodd (2006, p. 177) suggests that the tasks of the Deputy, supporting the leader and the team as well as maintaining her own well-being, can be 'mutually exclusive and contradictory, as well as impossible to achieve'.

Relations with parents

Fostering positive and professional relationships with parents is critical to the role of the setting leader and is discussed in more detail in Chapter 13. Choosing a nursery is often the first major decision parents will make on behalf of their child, especially if they are choosing full day care. The sensitive leader (and team) will know and understand this, and support mothers, who may find the whole process of handing over the care of their young baby or child to enable themselves to return to work, a difficult and an emotional time. This heightened emotional state may occasionally lead to misunderstandings or conflict with practitioners. Such tensions often have nothing to do with the setting but arise from difficulties in the family's home life, for instance anxiety about debt or having to live on an inadequate income in substandard accommodation.

Any serious complaints or expressions of dissatisfaction with nursery practice need to be referred immediately to the leader and taken seriously, which means they can often be defused without spreading anxiety through the staff group or involving other parents.

Multi-agency working

Day care provision that is linked to a Children's Centre may well have access to a multidisciplinary team, where there is a named health visitor and possibly a social worker. The Children's Centre family support worker or outreach worker may be a familiar face on the extended team. Most early years settings now will be more aware of the need to work across agencies and organisations, sharing information, assessment processes such as the Common Assessment Framework (CAF) and working together to support the development and needs of the child and their family.

All settings will need to know where to access support if there are children and families with multiple or complex needs. Providers of statutory, independent, voluntary or private provision will have access to social workers through the established channels in their local authority children's services and it is essential that all staff are aware of and understand their duties regarding safeguarding of children and adults and the function of the Local Safeguarding Children's Board (LSCB) (see Chapter 14). Provision linked to schools may well work closely with the nursery or reception teacher, supporting the children's learning and transition process.

Visiting specialists

The responsibility for managing the wide range of potential visitors to a nursery lies with the leader or manager. These might include early years consultants or advisers, specialist workers such as physiotherapists, Portage consultants, SENCOs, and speech and language therapists, as well as prospective parents. Parents will have been made aware of the setting's commitment to working alongside other professionals and will always be informed if someone is visiting to work directly with their child. The leader will sometimes need to be firm, not only in limiting the number of visits by people who want to observe children or work with the staff team, but in indicating the best way to be present in a group without causing distraction.

When building, maintenance and repairs need to be done during opening hours, the leader becomes responsible for the health and safety of all those in the setting and checking that the visiting plumber or carpenter signs in, is made aware of the policy in relation to contact with children, and carries out their work in a safe manner for all concerned.

Outside experts can provide support and valuable knowledge, but they can also create pressure unless their visits are carefully coordinated and the central role of the key person is fully recognised. Arrangements should never be left to chance – 'I'll pop in during the morning' is the death knell to any effective collaboration. Precise appointments should be made so that the key person is not put in the difficult situation of dividing her attention between the children and a visitor with whom she needs a period of calm and concentration to discuss a basis for their collaboration. The practical difficulties of time and space are very real. If by good planning these can be overcome, there is still much to be done in enabling nursery staff and visiting specialists to work out how they can complement each other's particular skills.

Specialists such as physiotherapists and speech therapists routinely involve parents of children whom they are treating. The key person who spends many hours with the child in the nursery needs to be involved in the same way so that she, too, can complement the therapist's work. For example, a community physiotherapist was able to engage both nursery staff and children in her work with Sarah, a little girl whose disability affected her walking. She wanted Sarah to practise particular movements and devised a game that encouraged her to do this, involving the whole group of children. In this way the child being treated did not feel isolated or stigmatised, the key person could learn by participating, and the problem of finding space and time for individual treatment was solved. This kind of imaginative approach offers many possibilities which can be developed between nursery staff and visiting specialists, provided an initial basis of trust has been created.

Extending staff resources

How often have we heard at the end of a training course the despondent reaction, 'Oh, we'd love to do that but we just haven't got the staff.' On closer enquiry what is really meant is that there are not enough adults in proportion to children. There are two ways of tackling this problem (apart from recruiting more staff): one is by employing people for specific purposes on a sessional basis, the other is by using volunteers.

Having a pool of volunteers who have been inducted into the setting's policies and procedures, checked through the Disclosure and Barring Scheme (DBS) and are available to work in the setting, is one very useful way of increasing the spectrum of opportunities for the children. Volunteers with knowledge and skills across a broad range of areas can enhance and enrich the curriculum: gardeners, musicians, artists, potters, craft workers, poets, actors, storytellers and people who will come in simply to sit amongst a comfortable pile of cushions with a book box, ready for a child who wants to hear a story at any given time. Encouraging adults from the community into the setting is a two-way process: the volunteers will have the opportunity to develop their skills and may look to retrain, or return to work, as early years practitioners, and it gives staff the opportunity to develop their mentoring and coaching skills, and to gain from the experience and talents of others.

A programme of training, induction and monitoring, especially in relation to child protection, should be provided for all volunteers, to ensure they are well supported and enabled to become a part of the wider staff team. The same should be in place for all external teachers who are employed on a sessional basis to ensure the ethos and culture of the setting is not compromised and that everyone is working to an agreed curriculum. All the setting's policies and procedures should be shared with, understood and signed by all volunteers and sessional staff.

Summary

Leading and managing an early childhood centre has become increasingly demanding as a result of the growth of knowledge about child development and much more stringent inspection requirements. Leaders need to seek out and take advantage of available training if they are to carry out their role successfully. Effective leaders enthuse and motivate their staff teams by sharing their vision and co-constructing the culture and ethos of the nursery. They need to understand the theory that underpins their everyday work in order to provide the best possible care and learning environment for all the children and adults in the setting.

An important part of the leader's role in an early childhood centre is to enhance the enjoyable aspects of caring for young children and help to minimise the inevitable strains. She needs to give careful thought to communication systems and the most productive way to organise staff meetings. Multi-agency working is now standard to ensure information and assessments are shared appropriately; professionals from health, education and social care can provide valuable support and work collaboratively with nurseries and early years settings for the benefit of both the child and the early years practitioner.

12 Building a staff team

Vision without action is day dreaming, but action without vision is just random activity.

(Joel Barker)

In this chapter we will consider:

- Selecting and building a staff team;
- The need for diversity and balance;
- Training and development;
- Teamwork;
- Supervision;
- Looking after staff.

Building a staff team is one of the most significant elements of a leader's role. It may be that a new leader inherits an established team, or her task may be to form a team for a new setting. We discussed in the previous chapter the influence and legacy a leader or manager can have on the staff team and individuals. We will all have memories of a leader or manager we would like to forget and others who are imprinted on our hearts and our own practice. Ofsted (2012) look for 'inspirational' leaders when judging settings to be outstanding; leadership and management is an element of the inspection for day care, early years settings and Children's Centres. To build an effective team a leader needs opportunities to consider a range of theories, and to be reflective of her own practice in order to support practitioners to become reflective thinkers in their turn.

The leader of an early years setting is critical in creating the vision and passion needed to motivate and engage a team. Moyles (2006, p. 12) describes an Effective Leadership and Management Scheme (ELMS), in which she uses the metaphor of a tree, with four branches – leadership qualities, management skills, professional skills and attributes, and personal characteristics and attitudes. It is a useful tool to help leaders or aspiring leaders of settings to do some self-evaluation and reflect on how well their own attributes match up to this scheme. Moyles acknowledges that many leaders of early years settings have had to find their own resources to develop their skills and knowledge and that many have no formal qualification or training. Currently, leaders of Children's Centres are able to enrol on the National Programme for Integrated Centre Leadership (NPQICL). This qualification is for senior practitioners in an early years centre, with some experience of leading and managing the setting, and successful participants have the opportunity to complete a Master's degree. It encourages participants to become reflective, analytical, and rigorous, able to consider different points of view and challenge established practice.

Recruiting the staff team

In relation to staff recruitment, three important issues that arise are the ratio of staff to children, the professional qualifications considered appropriate for the work and the balance of the staff team. Sometimes these matters may be decided centrally, leaving the leader with little room for manoeuvre, but if she and her existing staff are clear about the direction and quality they want for the service, they may be able to exert influence. First, on staff numbers, the essential point is that effective relationships with families cannot be achieved on a no-cost basis and that must be allowed for in staffing ratios. Second, having a well-qualified early years workforce matters, as is now generally acknowledged and supported by research. Third, it is important that the team includes people with different interests, skills and backgrounds, preferably men as well as women. Having staff with artistic or craft skills – being able to play a musical instrument, speak other languages or having a particular interest and expertise in growing plants or identifying birds – broadens the potential for opportunities offered to the children.

Qualifications

The issue of training and qualifications for working in early childhood settings was briefly discussed earlier. Kathy Nutbrown's (2012a) interim review of early education and childcare qualifications identified an astonishing number of early years qualifications: her report cited at least 445 different qualifications, of which 223 are seen as 'full and relevant' by Ofsted. Employers across the sector face problems when recruiting and appointing staff, as the level of competence represented by the qualifications is sometimes very uncertain. Those interviewing may have to probe deeply to gauge the level of experience and expertise of the interviewee, regardless of their formal qualifications, and in addition to checking the detail of the curriculum on the web. Nutbrown's final report contained some 19 recommendations including a new early years teaching qualification, minimum standards for maths and English at entry level, and clear job titles and roles for early years practitioners (Nutbrown 2012b). As we commented in Chapter 1, if fully implemented, her recommendations would have led to a coherent structure for continuing professional development in ECEC and made it an attractive career for academically able young people, but unfortunately, as Nutbrown herself observed in her angry response to the government policy statement 'More Great Childcare' (DfE 2013), this was not to be (Nutbrown 2013).

The 'Effective Provision of Pre-School Education' (EPPE) project demonstrated that the higher the qualifications of the staff, particularly the manager, the more progress the children made (Sylva *et al.* 2004). Later research confirms this (DfE 2011a, 2012a electronic source). Settings which included an Early Years Professional (EYP) in the staff group made significant improvements in quality compared to those without one. The EYP is seen as the leader of the learning in a setting, responsible for supporting and developing both staff and children. Some EYPs have told us that gaining the status, often after a long journey of learning and study, had given them the knowledge and confidence to begin to make significant improvements and changes in their settings.

Effective leaders will be identifying and developing those in the staff team who demonstrate the potential for leadership (Garvey and Lancaster 2010). One of the best ways of doing this, as already proposed in the previous chapter, is by well-planned and supported delegation.

Selection

Leaders of day nurseries and early years settings should be involved in the recruitment of staff, and will have to follow local protocols with support from their local Human Resources team or management committee. Interviews and selection of staff can be a way of including parents in the wider aspects of the provision. It is vital that all settings have a recruitment policy and clearly understood procedures in line with local and national safeguarding requirements. Leaders should ensure that they access training and keep up to date with changes in employment law and the Equality Act 2010 (this is relevant to all adults and children using the setting). The National Day Nurseries Association, PACEY, PSLA, and Daycare Trust offer members advice and support with templates, policies and procedures.

When recruiting or selecting staff to work specifically with the 0–2s, leaders have to be mindful of the requirements of the EYFS, to ensure that staff working with this age group have appropriate qualifications and experience. The interview process should include specific questions on experience of working with babies, knowledge of the key person approach, and attitudes towards individualised care. All members of the interview panel have to be reminded of their legal responsibilities in relation to equal opportunities. Most organisations and especially all the large corporate childcare providers will have their own Human Resources department to offer guidance on recruitment and selection. Local authority early years teams may offer advice and guidance to smaller settings in the private, voluntary and independent sector.

Training and development

There is now a requirement in the EYFS framework for all settings to ensure that staff development and supervision is a priority for leaders. We discuss supervision later in this chapter.

The continual care over years of successive groups of very young children does not conform to the normal lifecycle of adults. If nursery workers are to retain their motivation and responsiveness to changing needs and social conditions, they need a sense of going somewhere, a view of themselves and their future which allows for professional growth and increasing responsibility. Staff development thus has three aspects: learning to do the job better, continuing personal and professional education, and career planning. A small but important point is that the budget should allow for a staff library, regularly added to, and preferably accessible to parents as well as staff. It is also important to allow for subscriptions to relevant periodicals and a quality daily newspaper to be kept in the staff room.

Training days are invaluable to maintain and improve the quality of the setting. This is when the staff group comes together to work on organisational issues, perhaps with an outside adviser, or to explore and discuss early childhood theories and different approaches to practice. The inconvenience to parents can be minimised by plenty of advance notice and help with alternative arrangements if necessary. Many settings plan in closure days for staff training as part of their annual calendar, allowing the staff to be together for a full day, whilst attendance at other training events can be covered by supply staff or senior staff not normally included in the ratios. If dates for training are planned into the calendar, along with dates for other special events, parents can also begin to plan.

It is also important to provide time for reflection in the nursery environment on common aims, pinpointing causes of difficulty and ways to tackle problems in the working day. After identifying the problems these can be studied in three ways:

* How to eliminate them;
* How to modify them;
* How to agree to put up with them and stop complaining!

By this process much of the energy expended in irritation and conflict (often unexpressed) can be freed for use in more constructive and enjoyable ways.

Outside the nursery there are courses, conferences and workshops run by local authorities, training bodies, educational institutions and voluntary organisations. It will depend on the policy of the administration responsible for the nursery or day care facility what opportunities staff can expect. The leader needs to press strongly for staff to have time off and funding for professional development, which is as important for the staff group as a whole as it is for the individuals concerned. Local authorities may have some funding available to offer training to community, private and voluntary providers as well as settings for which they are directly responsible. The National Day Nursery Association, Daycare Trust, Pre-School Alliance, the British Association for Early Education (BAECE), and many other organisations run courses covering a huge range of topics, including leadership and management, and financial and business planning. Many of the corporate (large and small) nursery businesses offer teambuilding days, management training and staff development programmes.

A course outside the nursery has the great advantage of enabling staff to get to know other early years workers and have contact with practice and developments elsewhere. There is another approach though and that is to have an 'informal-formal' approach to staff development, as described by Siraj-Blatchford and Manni (in Stacey 2009). Observations and discussion with staff on an informal day-to-day basis take place, but are followed up at staff meetings – the formal element, where staff are encouraged to reflect on their observations and receive individual feedback.

There may be a tendency for practitioners to see attending training courses as the only means of 'development'. Introducing reflective sessions to discuss children's learning may encourage deeper thinking and discussion. MacNaughton (in Stacey 2009, p. 77) takes a sceptical view of the value of training days, suggesting that the impact of one-off workshops is minimal: only 16–20 per cent of participants will take up recommendations and 'those who do put them into practice could have learnt them by reading a book'. A good library in the setting or access to a range of texts and online resources (and encouraging practitioners to read them) may be more effective and much less costly than most workshops.

Often practitioners go to training looking for 'Ten quick tips' – templates for planning, observation formats, etc. Whilst these can be a helpful starting point, they do not encourage practitioners to think creatively. Asking staff to read an article in preparation for a team meeting where the discussion is around a specific subject, such as replanning the outside play space, or introducing schemas, will open them to other people's thinking as a starting point. Building this up to a chapter, and then a book may encourage those who do not read regularly to consider the theoretical and practical issues in advance of group discussion. Staff embarking on higher level qualifications will need to develop their reading habits, so making this part of the team approach to problem-solving will encourage them to become more enquiring and to seek out evidence of others' points of view.

When a staff member is released to attend a course, the leader should ensure that there will be opportunities for them on their return to share their training with the rest of the team and to apply what has been learnt or propose changes to existing practice or policy. In addition, the value of continuing personal education should not be overlooked. Encouragement to attend evening classes to extend their knowledge of literature, art, music, languages, sociology or psychology, or to study through the Open University, will not only extend their own horizons but feed back into their work in the nursery. As Siraj-Blatchford (2014) points out, children benefit not only from the knowledge of their carers that is specific to the early childhood field but from their general level of education and the different ideas they can bring into the setting.

Induction

Once a new member of staff has been appointed to the team, the next important step is planning their induction. It can be helpful to draw up a timetable, and many settings will have an induction plan as part of their policies and procedures. The EYFS Statutory Framework (DfE 2012b, p. 12) outlines the essential elements of induction that all staff should receive, mainly related to health and safety issues – emergency evacuation procedures, safeguarding, child protection – and equality policy. However we think it crucial to introduce new staff to the vision, the ethos and the culture of the setting more generally. This means ensuring that there is someone to welcome the new person on their first morning, to show them where to put their things, deal with lockers, cloakrooms and uniforms, and give them a conducted tour if it is some time since the recruitment process. Being prepared for them, just as you would be for a new child, sends out a strong message of commitment and the value placed on the staff team.

Learning about the culture of the setting is probably best done by observation over time: seeing how things are done, how practitioners relate to parents, how parents interact with staff, what professional and personal relationships are like in the staff group. It is essential that the leader (or deputy) spends time with the new person, outlining the expectations of the setting, discussing in detail their role and responsibilities. Meeting their key children and families is the most important job for the new staff member, perhaps carrying out a home visit with another person already known to the family. Time should be scheduled to help the parents get to know this person with whom they will be sharing the care of their child – for example a 15-minute welcome meeting after work, when the key person can be freely available in the nursery, with no responsibilities for any other children.

One of the leaders might tell parents a little about the qualities and skills this new person is bringing to the team. If the selection and appointment period allows, it is helpful to include a brief introductory article in the newsletter and on the webpage, or at least send out a note to the parents of children in the room where the new staff member will be based. As part of the induction programme the rest of the staff team should be introduced, perhaps as part of a team meeting where people are encouraged to share a little personal information (within agreed boundaries). Other key colleagues should be introduced where appropriate – for instance, if the person is going to have special responsibility for inclusion, meeting up with other SENCOs in the area, or the Area Inclusion Adviser. It is good practice for the leader or deputy to meet with the new person at the end of the first week, just to discuss how things have gone and ensure all the essential elements are understood. If there is a probationary period the dates for meeting and reviewing should be set, as should the date for the first supervision session so that any concerns, issues and questions can be raised and discussed.

Effective teamwork

As a staff team develops, there may well be individuals at different stages. A skilful leader needs to support the staff team to accomplish the demands of a particular stage and to enable the team to move forward. What needs to be remembered is that every time someone leaves or joins the team, the process has to start again; the status quo of the team will be disturbed, colleagues may 'grieve' for a colleague who has left, perhaps someone whose practice was respected, someone who spoke up for the team. Likewise, there may be a quiet sigh of relief when a staff member leaves who has not been pulling their weight or whose practice fell below the expected standard. Rodd (2006, p. 152) sees the main stages of team development as:

Connecting – Confronting conflict – Co-operation – Collaborating – Closure

'Closure' is important. If the team has been involved in a particular project or task, they need the opportunity to celebrate, unpick, learn and move on to the next challenge. If it has proved impossible to carry out a project, for whatever reason, or there have been poor relationships in the team, it is even more important, but often harder, for the leader to engage the team in a process of closure. This is when individual supervision sessions are useful and important, for people to reflect on their achievements or disappointments individually, and for the group to review the team's dynamics as a whole and identify what led to the team failing to operate effectively. This brings us back to vision: the team needs to have a clear understanding and agreement on their purpose and objectives. Some of the qualities of an effective team include:

- Having pride in themselves (and the setting);
- Being able to talk honestly and openly within the team;
- Having a balance of skills and abilities;
- Trusting each other;
- Being able to look after each other;
- Recognising the importance of continuing development, both collective and individual.

A useful exercise to enable the leader to find out how the team thinks they are performing is offered by Thornton and Brunton (2010 electronic source). They suggest a list of statements, such as: 'As a team we . . . share the same values; are happy to learn from one another; collaborate to find practical solutions to problems'. Staff are asked to respond to each statement individually, using a scale of 'Always', 'Usually', 'Sometimes' or 'Never'. The results are then aggregated and discussed by the team.

The need for a diverse and balanced team

Ideally the staff team should reflect the wider population in such characteristics as gender, age and ethnicity. However this is difficult to achieve. As noted previously, the early years workforce is overwhelmingly female and the majority of staff groups include no male members, except in non-caring roles, such as maintenance worker. There are still negative stereotypes of men who choose to work in childcare. The few men who come into the work do so at a later stage than the women, since few teenage boys see childcare as consistent with their masculinity (Frosh *et al.* 2001). Those who embark on training often drop out, feeling out of place among a predominantly female group of students. Men who work in nurseries have to contend with many difficulties, of which their female co-workers may be largely unaware. A study by Charlie Owen and colleagues concluded that 'men feel they are positioned and constrained by the women's – and children's – expectations of them' (Owen 2003, p. 112). Few of the men interviewed in his study intended to remain in the childcare field.

Paradoxically, research by MORI on behalf of the Daycare Trust found that:

- 77 per cent of the public are in favour of men working in the childcare profession.
- 84 per cent say that they are willing to place their children in a setting where a male childcare worker is employed.
- 42 per cent believed that more men would be encouraged to go into childcare if there were greater trust.
- 47 per cent stated that a further way of encouraging men would be a change in the public perception of childcare, i.e. that it was not just seen as women's work.

(Ipsos MORI 2013)

More recently *Nursery World* reported findings from the Major Providers Group, made up of 14 of the largest nursery chains in the UK. This research showed that 98 per cent of parents who use nurseries were in favour of men caring for their children. On the other hand, a poll of 113 male school-leavers aged 16–19 found that none were considering a career in childcare. Two of the reasons given were low rate of pay and the fear that they would be negatively perceived by others if they went into childcare (Morton 2011). In Scotland, the organisation Men in Childcare has obtained funding to provide men-only childcare courses and this has led to the doubling of men working in the sector from 2 to 4 per cent. Since its inception the organisation has recruited and supported 1600 men through the programmes (Rogers 2012). The recruitment of men in childcare was described as a 'particular issue' to be addressed by Nutbrown (2012a). However Men in Childcare reports that lack of trust is a continuing obstacle, with high-profile abuse cases undermining the move to get more men into childcare (Morton 2012 electronic source).

The result is that the vast majority of nurseries and childcare settings are staffed entirely by women and headed by a woman. But on the positive side, this gives the opportunity to women to exercise and demonstrate new and different ways of working together. There are useful models to be found – in fields as diverse as large corporate organisations, publishing, the arts and wholefood distribution – of management styles that make use of things at which women are notably good. These include willingness to negotiate, being able to listen to and empathise with another person and assess his or her state of mind, giving due attention to detail in work, and the capacity to do several things at once without getting flustered (Marshall 1994; Eisenstadt 2012). How we think about feminine and masculine traits in leadership is a huge area for debate but it is not accidental that the collegial style of leadership is prominent in early years settings. Women are also good at taking opportunities: many successful nursery businesses (large and small) have been started by mothers (usually), unable to find the quality of day care they wanted in their area.

Another point which needs emphasis is that the staff group should reflect the ethnic composition of the neighbourhood and the families who use the centre. In many urban centres, English may be a second language for a high proportion of the children. It is good to have staff members who can speak at least some of the children's home languages. Energetic and imaginative efforts may have to be made to recruit people from different ethnic and cultural backgrounds. If no qualified applicants are available it will be necessary to take on suitable people as trainees or as part of the Apprentice Programme. It is obviously important for black children to have role models from their own culture, but it is equally important for white children and families to see black people in positions of responsibility if stereotypes are to be dispelled. Gathering a well-balanced and diversified staff group is an essential first step towards creating an effective working team.

Supervision

Following the Plymouth Safeguarding Children's Board Serious Case Review (2010), supervision for all early years staff, including leaders and managers, has become a requirement of the EYFS.

> 3.19 Providers must put appropriate arrangements in place for the supervision of staff who have contact with children and families . . . Supervision should foster a culture of mutual support, teamwork and continuous improvement which encourages the confidential discussion of sensitive issues.
>
> (EYFS Statutory Framework, p. 17)

All settings should ensure that they plan and timetable regular supervision sessions for all members of staff as an essential part of staff development and the feeling of well-being and safety. Discussions around individual children, families, training and professional development opportunities, how the nursery rooms operate and colleagues work together, need to be aired in a professional and respectful manner.

The Plymouth serious case review identified the need for staff to have opportunities to 'openly discuss good and poor practice and facilitate constructive challenge of each other' and the need for all staff to understand the concept of 'whistle-blowing' and to know who and where to go to if they have concerns about any aspect of a colleague's behaviour or practice in a setting.

We need to think about how to use practitioners' skills and knowledge in the most effective way. It is important for the leader to ensure adequate support for herself, which might be provided by a colleague from another nursery unit, a line manager or the chairperson of her management committee. Unless there is someone with whom she can safely share and discuss issues and concerns at work, as well as how these impact on her personally, she can become very isolated.

Staff supervision

The value of supervision needs to be understood and agreed by the whole staff group, and the time set aside for it strongly protected. The principle which lies behind supervision is similar to that which underpins the key person approach for children; adults, too, need the assurance of some special individual attention.

Sometimes it may be hard to imagine finding time for regular supervision slots. This is often because an open-door policy is operated, leading to constant interruptions by requests for a 'quick word'. There has to be a balance between reasonable availability and a style of 'feeding on demand' that can make it impossible for the leader to do her job properly and is ultimately unhelpful to the staff.

Emergency 'drop everything' happenings are sometimes inevitable, but when the difficulty is a minor one, it may be more appropriate for the staff member to manage by herself and if necessary discuss the incident at a subsequent supervision session rather than seek immediate guidance. When a regular supervision system has been established, it is noticeable how time-consuming consultations about trivial matters are reduced. This can mean real progress for practitioners, who then develop confidence in their own judgement and ability to make decisions. When a key person approach is working effectively, senior staff can keep closely in touch, through supervision sessions, with the progress of each child and his or her parents' relations with the nursery.

The supervision structure should include all ancillary staff, whose essential part in the effective running of a nursery is sometimes only recognised when one of them is absent. Ancillary staff are often more permanent than the nursery workers, more deeply rooted in the local community and can develop valuable relationships with individual children and families.

> Supervisions mean to me that I can talk about all the positives and concerns I have in my role at the nursery. It definitely makes a difference knowing that there is someone I can talk to every 6 weeks . . . Listening to feedback and using this to improve my performance . . . Talking about new courses and moving my career to the next stage is useful.
>
> (Early Years Practitioner)

Supervision covers three main aspects: (1) Organisational, concerned with setting policy and procedures; (2) Tasks, role and responsibilities – how the practitioner is managing her day-to-day work; and (3) Personal development. How supervision sessions are planned will be different for every setting. However, at a bare minimum, and based on our personal experience, they should:

- Be no less than six-weekly for full-time staff (ideally every month if staffing levels allow);
- Take place in a quiet area, where there will be no interruptions;
- Be planned in, and the date and time respected, with cancellation only in a real emergency;
- Have an agenda at least two days in advance;
- Be based on an agreed contract between the supervisor/supervisee, with paper copies held by each.

A supervision agenda for an early years worker should always include 'Safeguarding' and 'Health and Safety' and may include all or some of the following:

- Monitoring any targets or actions set at the previous meeting (essential);
- Matters of concern relating to individual children and families (it is important for this to be time-limited, as key children should be discussed as part of the room/staff meeting);
- Planning and delivery of children's learning;
- Personal development, appraisal, target-setting, delegation and task management;
- Day-to-day matters not covered in other meetings;
- Holidays/absence/sickness;
- Working relationships – parents, team, community, other agencies.

Depending on the level of responsibility and role of the staff, other areas for discussion at supervision might be resource management, budgets and finance. Where a setting operates a policy of annual appraisal it will need to be made clear if and how supervision links to this. Settings will need to decide if supervision notes are confidential or if they may be used in supporting team and corporate targets.

Staff should be able to talk frankly about what is happening in their room, and about individual children or families. Decisions made about individual children during supervision should be transferred or copied onto the child's records to ensure an audit trail. A supervision policy and contract ensures that both supervisor and supervisee are aware of their responsibility for sharing and acting on shared information. Discussions should be recorded and signed, with both parties keeping a copy of the notes. Agreed action should be specified, with clear target dates for completion.

This is also the time for discussion about performance management (unless something is too important to wait for a supervision session). If a staff member is not performing to the expected standard, or to their job description, or is failing to work within the setting's policies and procedures, this should be flagged up early so that there can be discussion about how the problem has arisen and what extra support might be needed. Annual performance reviews or appraisals should not be the moment when an employee learns for the first time that the organisation or leader is not satisfied with a particular aspect of her work, or that her timekeeping or punctuality is considered unsatisfactory. Regular supervision ensures that both employees and employers have the opportunity to raise their concerns at a stage when consideration of changes and improvements can begin informally. It is, of course, essential that both parties are also aware of the formal policies and procedures to address such issues.

Since implementing a more robust system of staff supervision I have noticed the team are finding them useful and meaningful, as am I. We ensure we have totally uninterrupted time and staff honour and respect this.

Regular supervision sessions ensure everyone is given a fixed time when they know they are able to discuss anything that is worrying them. I enjoy spending one-to-one time with them, and it helps to nip any issues in the bud before they become too big.

I have been able to hold room meetings as soon as I feel there is a common thread, something that needs further discussion and sorting out. It has definitely led to better team communication.

I am currently carrying out supervision every 6 weeks for each member of staff. It has added to my already heavy workload, but I believe that the importance far outweighs this. The staff feel more valued and listened to, which is exactly how it should be! The volunteers are also supervised.

(A childcare manager responsible for two nurseries and an out-of-school setting)

Supervision skills for leaders

Supervision is not always as effective as in the quote from the childcare manager given above. It can be perceived by practitioners as a waste of time unless the supervisor always comes to the session well-prepared and is emotionally attuned to the supervisee. Being able to give constructive feedback is a key skill. Patrick Whitaker points out the importance of non-verbal communication in how feedback is received, either as helpful information or a threat to be resisted. Feedback during supervisions (and other inter-actions) should be:

- Descriptive;
- About the issue, not the person;
- Useful – suggestions with alternatives;
- About the strengths and weaknesses of the practitioner but never destructive;
- Owned by the supervisor – 'This is how *I* see it . . .', '*I* think . . .';
- Well timed at the earliest opportunity, especially if it is in relation to a specific behaviour, which may sometimes mean arranging a supervision session sooner than originally planned.

If the supervision session includes discussions and decisions about individual families and children it is essential to ensure that the discussion is focused and analytical, never judgemental or assumptive. The supervisor needs to use appropriate open-ended questions – questions that help gather the facts, but also elicit how the supervisee is feeling, and their opinions and views on the topic under discussion. Sometimes a supervisee may not want to or be ready to open up or talk about matters that are difficult for them. Giving time and listening carefully may enable the supervisee to share difficult issues – the seemingly unimportant can be the most important. During supervision the supervisor should avoid offering solutions. Effective supervision is about unravelling the supervisee's feelings and thoughts and finding the right questions to ask. Developing reflective practice is a key part of supervision.

Looking after staff

An essential part of the leader's role is to pull together a 'needs analysis' of her team's training and development needs. Continuing Professional Development (CPD) should be a high priority. Despite what was said earlier about workshops, for many practitioners the opportunity to meet people from other settings is an invaluable way of sharing ideas and taking back changes to practice and policy to share with their own team. Ofsted (2012) inspectors look for practice that demonstrates effective and targeted programmes of professional development.

Staff need to understand how expensive it is to send people out for a day or half a day, in terms of staff cover, and the disruption to the youngest children's routines. So it is important that parents and other staff can appreciate the value and necessity of releasing staff for this purpose. A well-planned and focused programme that gives the team opportunities for further development is essential, with discussion at individual supervision sessions as well as part of team meetings. Addressing the question 'What do we need to do to make our setting and our practice better?' brings everyone together with a shared focus, for the benefit of all the children in the setting.

Managing staff absence

Staff absence rates are high in childcare settings, partly due to the difficulty of avoiding the spread of infection when many young children are gathered together. However there is evidence that staff absence can also be linked to lack of well-being and lack of care in the setting.

Events and commitments which involve absence from the setting, the arrangement of shifts, holidays, attendance at training courses or case conferences all call for detailed planning by the leader. Settings will have a range of tools and systems as well as agreed policies related to, for example, leave entitlement and when and how it is taken. Clear systems for requesting and approving leave are needed to allow for arrangement of cover and provision of information to parents.

Absences through staff illness, which are largely unpredictable, can create a major problem. Some local authorities and larger settings have a 'staff bank' of practitioners who are able to respond to the need for cover. This usually works best when the absence is planned rather than for staff sickness. If settings are working over the minimum required ratio of staff to children, then the occasional absence from sickness will be managed by moving staff around and seniors supporting the team at busier times.

When a key person approach is functioning, children will feel the lack of established continuity if a staff member is absent. The staff's own self-care and attitudes to their own health are discussed later, but it has been found that in a number of nurseries the sickness rate in staff is noticeably reduced when they have greater personal satisfaction in their working relationships, both with children and with other staff. Although every-thing should be done to keep unplanned staff absence to a minimum, it does sometimes have the advantage, if the leader steps in, of giving her an opportunity to observe routines and practice at first hand.

Emotional and physical well-being

Far more is required in specific practical ways to reduce what can be called the occu-pational hazards, both physical and emotional, for nursery workers. Unacknowledged stress can lead to conflict within the setting and with parents, and to frequent absences due to sickness, increasing the load on other staff and creating instability. Many of the staff working in childcare settings are young women, which increases the responsibility of the nursery leader to ensure the emotional well-being of these young people. Employees (not necessarily only young ones) may well bring their problems from home to work. They may need support to leave their problems behind when they are working with the youngest children and having to relate to parents who may be dealing with their own worries and concerns. An experienced manager or leader recognises the importance of giving her team five minutes in the morning or before their shift starts to unload any personal issues, before they begin greeting children and parents.

Early years staff may have to deal with feelings related to many new experiences such as leaving their own children in day care, supporting single or separated parents, listening to parents' anxieties about juggling work and home, balancing childcare and employment. Working with children and families living in poverty can be stressful, knowing that for many children home and family life is complex, difficult and sometimes not safe. Staff should get to know the children and parents they are working with and caring for really well, and this is where the key person relationship is so crucial for both child and practitioner. But it can be difficult for staff to ensure that they don't blur the boundaries between professional and personal relationships.

Manning-Morton (2006, p. 42) suggests that early years staff should 'develop a professional approach that combines personal awareness with theoretical knowledge'. She considers that staff need to have a high level of self-awareness, and to be emotionally intelligent in order to deal with what she terms 'the more difficult aspects of children's learning and development . . . and to become experts in themselves, including their own darker side' (Manning-Morton 2006, p. 48). This is an area not often discussed with staff – How do they feel about being rejected by children and criticised by parents? What are their own early memories of being parented? Did they experience early separation? Did they have positive relationships and good attachments with their parents and families? And how might all these things influence the way they work with young children?

Discussions such as these need very careful and sensitive handling and, as Manning-Morton observes, it may not always be appropriate for people to reflect on these personal aspects of their life in a work situation unless they are part of a 'safe' group with established and agreed boundaries. It needs to be clear that the purpose of the group reflection is always about focusing on the impact of personal experience on their work with children, not for it to operate as a counselling session.

Elinor Goldschmied used to ask participants in training sessions on the key person approach to carry out role-plays of simple, but very personal tasks, such as spoon-feeding, and brushing each other's hair. She wanted people to get an understanding of what it felt like to have these quite intimate tasks done in a sensitive manner and also the reverse. What is it like to have such actions carried out by someone not giving you eye contact, talking over you to another member of staff or even pushing something into your mouth that you dislike? Leaders and managers considering opening up this level of reflection and discussion with staff need to prepare very carefully and consider how they might handle any disclosures or difficult situations resulting from what can be very intense interactions.

Caring and loss

One form of emotional strain associated with nursery work which is not sufficiently acknowledged arises from the constant making and breaking of affectional bonds as children move into new groups or leave the nursery. In many European countries with much more generous and comprehensive ECEC provision, children enter a childcare or early childhood education system as a group and move upwards with the same teacher until they start school. In our fragmented system the experience of separation and loss is usually unavoidable. This is where the role of the leader is vital in helping the worker to come to terms with the reality that she has only a temporary role in the child's life, but that the experience of loss, though painful, does not diminish the value of the relationship either for herself or for the child. Staff, parents and the child will welcome preparation and planning for transition to the next room or group in the setting. Parents and the new key person need introducing and time to get to know each other, and careful handing over of important information. Planning will help all involved in the triangle of care and reduce stress for the staff.

Rarely, it may happen that nursery staff have to face the serious illness or the death of a child or parent. The leader will have to recognise and respond to what is needed by her team in these difficult circumstances. It may be necessary to access external professional support. It is important to respond honestly to children's questions but without providing more information than they can understand or process.

Coping with stress

Nursery workers often comment on the stress they experience in their daily work in a number of different situations: in their direct contact with children during the day; when difficult incidents occur with parents; when they come into overt or unexpressed conflict with other staff members; and when a visiting specialist or other outside person makes unplanned demands on their attention.

Children and families often have chaotic and complex lives, which may impact on the nursery – increasing numbers of families are living in poverty; children are in homes or with people who do not keep them safe; children arrive at nursery having not had breakfast or anything to eat since tea the day before. Some kinds of responsibility create high levels of stress for practitioners and affect their emotional well-being. An example would be having to keep careful observations of a child to be shared with a social worker, informing a social worker if a child does not attend nursery, and discussing the reasons with the parent without provoking anger and conflict. Another source of stress is the very long hours that some very young children spend in childcare settings – as much as 50 hours in some cases – and the need for staff shifts to meet this demand.

Group room meetings are a good occasion for staff to examine in detail which are the moments during the day when they experience most stress. When periods of tension have been identified the questions to be asked are: Is this stress inevitable? Can it be modified by better planning? Can it be eliminated? For example, in the early morning a number of children and their parents arrive in a cluster and the worker feels torn between giving attention to parents and supervising the activities of a growing number of children in the room. In the group meeting the problem faced by the staff on the early shift needs to be discussed so that where possible the pressure of numbers can be spread out by negotiating with parents about their time of arrival. When the staff member cannot give full supervision to the children because of the need to listen to parents, one possibility is to provide specific play material to occupy the children that is not offered at other times of the day.

In the period from about 9.30 a.m. to 1 p.m. an effective key person approach can reduce confusion and create greater calm in more intimate contact with each small group of children. Instead of being a time of rush and noise, this part of the day can bring greater satisfaction for both adult and children. Generally, the smaller the group of children for whom a staff member is responsible, the less the strain.

Physical health

Childcare is physically demanding, which was one of the issues raised during the debate about the proposal to increase ratios. The high sickness rate among childcare staff has already been mentioned, and settings need to take active measures to reduce it. One way is to consider working towards achieving the Investors in People 'Health and Well-Being Award' which encourages organisations to work towards better environments for their staff. A simple questionnaire is the starting point for drawing up a plan alongside staff to make changes in the workplace. For some nurseries this might be about offering healthier menus for both children and staff. It might be about removing the biscuits from the staff room and substituting fruit and vegetables and other healthier snacks. Having water freely available for the children in the nursery is now taken as a given and ensuring staff are drinking plenty of water during the day is just as important. Many local authorities and Early Years Teams have their own quality assurance and kite-mark schemes and awards which settings can work towards. Healthy eating and meals for children in nurseries are explored in depth in Chapter 9.

Exercise is, of course, key to good physical health and staff and children should be encouraged to go for a walk at some point during every nursery day, whatever the weather – after all, small children at home would not spend the whole day in one or two rooms. Exploring beyond the nursery garden is also important for young children's holistic development, so a daily walk around the local area is to be encouraged, as described in Chapter 10.

Back trouble is a particular hazard for childcare workers. It is essential that staff have training on lifting, and that they support each other when moving or lifting furniture, and plan to do away with any unnecessary lifting. We have already emphasised in Chapter 3 the importance of organising rooms so as to minimise the need to move furniture. Carrying children who could quite well walk or crawl on their own is another common source of back trouble; the practice of carrying a child on one hip, if done con- sistently through an adult's working life, can create great strain on the alignment of the body. If there is a feeling of rush, it is tempting to try to speed things up by carrying a child to the bathroom or dinner table. Staff can develop each other's awareness of this pattern and agree to try and change it.

Chairs of the right type and height should always be available. As far as possible the caregiver should sit down on an adult-sized chair to cuddle or comfort a child. When seated, the knees and feet take the strain and not the lower back. Upright chairs are essential in the group room for occasions when sitting on a low sofa or on the floor is not the most comfortable or appropriate position for the adult.

As already mentioned, adults who work with young children are vulnerable to infection, especially before they have been in the job long enough to develop some immunity, and this accounts for a high proportion of sick leave. Hand-washing is critical to any reduction of cross-infection in nurseries, and staff should model this good practice by washing children's hands regularly and encouraging the children to take responsibility for their own hand-washing. Good food hygiene practice is also essential and the staff team will have completed the Food Hygiene Standards as required for the level of access or preparation responsibility they have for food. Gloves and protective aprons or tabards should of course always be worn when changing nappies and dealing with any bodily fluids and spills.

Summary

Building a diverse and effective staff team is a crucial part of a leader's role and takes time, effort and energy. New teams need time to settle in, to work together, to 'attune' to each other, just as practitioners need time and space to become tuned in to the children they work with. The leader's role is about nurturing, inspiring, motivating and caring for the staff team, recognising the complexities of their daily work with young children (and their families) and now, more than ever, being part of a wider, multi-agency network. Staff teams may be working with children and families living chaotic and complex lives, and this in turn may impact on nursery life and on the stress levels of staff with little or no experience of these situations. Regular, planned supervision can help to minimise stress in staff and should be carried out by supervisors who have had training in listening techniques, using open-ended questions, and how to give empathetic feedback. Staff training and development should be a regular item on the agenda. Promoting the emotional and physical well-being of staff should have high priority, and will be reflected in enhanced levels of satisfaction among practitioners, parents and children, better performance in official assessments and reduced absence due to sickness or lack of motivation.

13 | Bridging the child's two worlds

The joys of parents are secret, and so are their griefs and fears.
(Francis Bacon)

In this chapter we will consider:

- Working towards inclusion;
- The role of the key person;
- Communication between home and nursery;
- The key person's relationship with the parent;
- Consulting and informing parents;
- Helping with problems;
- Relationship and developmental play.

The way that caregivers and parents talk, behave and feel about each other is inevitably influenced by the reason why the child is attending an out-of-home setting and the function of the nursery or centre. But managers and practitioners have to make a conscious effort to build a bridge between the setting and each child's home and family, over which information can flow freely both ways and people, too, can cross from one side to the other, so that there is as much consistency and continuity as possible for the child. The vital thing to bear in mind in all interactions with parents is that they are by far the most important people in the lives of their children and know more about them than anyone else can do.

Inclusion and diversity

Most of the extensive literature on inclusion in the early years focuses on the 3–5 age group and on children identified as having developmental delay and special educational needs, with less interest in the implications of ethnic and cultural diversity or physical disability (Devarakonda 2013). Early years practitioners usually have a commitment to inclusion but, as Nutbrown (2012a) pointed out, there is a severe shortage of the training and professional development opportunities needed if they are to be properly equipped to support children and their families.

Both government policy as expressed in the EYFS and professional ideology are strongly in favour of including all children in mainstream early years services (Nutbrown and Clough 2013). The Equality Act 2010 recommends that all early childhood settings regularly review practices, policies and procedures to ensure equal opportunities for all children. Three groups of children are at particular risk of exclusion or discrimination: those with special educational needs, those from minority ethnic families, and children in poverty (Booth *et al.* 2006). There are groups of parents who face social barriers to engagement with early childhood services, which may particularly affect those who most need them. These include families living in poverty, black and minority ethnic or mixed families, disabled parents, especially those with learning difficulties, those with limited English language, and fathers in general. Children from these families are much less likely to attend an early childhood education setting than other children unless the parents are positively sought out by an outreach worker and encouraged to enrol their child. Their young children may experience exclusion *from* early childhood care and education altogether or exclusion *within* a setting, being physically present but psychologically absent (European Commission 2012).

The importance of earliest childhood experiences in forming children's views of themselves and others and preparing them to live in a multicultural society has already been discussed in Chapter 8. Here we are more concerned with the parents' experience and how the childcare setting can make a reality of Article 29 of the UN Convention on the Rights of the Child, which states that the child's education should be directed to:

> The development of respect for the child's parents, his or her own cultural identity, language and values, for the national values of the country in which the child is living, the country from which he or she may originate and for civilizations different from his or her own.
>
> (Siraj-Blatchford 2014, p. 173)

This means much more than ensuring that the welcome messages in the foyer include the child's home language, necessary though that is. We have, we hope, reached the point where most professional early childhood workers would not knowingly use racist language or make openly racist remarks, and would challenge colleagues and discourage any child who did so. When the offender is a parent, the situation is more difficult. How do we convey to the parent – without provoking an angry outburst – that not only her language, but her attitude is unacceptable? We have to recognise that discrimination and prejudice are embedded in British history and institutions. That is why settings need a clear policy and equal opportunities training for all staff. Difficult incidents need to be discussed, not swept under the carpet.

When the issue is first raised, nursery workers and teachers often claim to treat all children the same or to provide a neutral environment. This frequently means one in which diversity is not acknowledged or discussed, still less valued. It creates a framework of conformity in which white, often middle-class lifestyles, dress, food, homes, music, art and religions are 'normal' and all others are deviations, and therefore likely to be ignored or seen as inferior. Adopting a passive approach to discrimination on grounds of colour and race is as bad for white children as for African Caribbean or Asian ones. This can be difficult for practitioners to recognise if they have not thought much about these issues before. If all the children in the nursery are white, staff may feel the whole issue is irrelevant to them. Yet if it is not addressed, racist attitudes absorbed from home or the media will go unchallenged.

It is important to distinguish between race (as manifested in skin colour and facial features) and culture. The emphasis on culture sometimes leads to what has been called the 'tourist curriculum', with wall pictures of people in exotic costumes, celebration of festivals and special meals featuring 'ethnic' styles of cooking (though usually eaten in a western manner). These events can be enjoyable and interesting social occasions, but they do tend to stress the foreignness of non-white people, when most parents of black children in nurseries are, and feel, British, and have a lifestyle which is influenced more by social class and the neighbourhood they live in than by the country of origin of their parents or grandparents.

Traveller families[1]

In the past, children from traveller families rarely accessed early years settings, but that has begun to change and it is important that practitioners have some understanding of the cultural differences these children and their families will bring with them. Although they have some legal protection under the Equalities Act 2010, Gypsy Roma families are still recognised to be the most deprived group in Britain in terms of health and education. Justified fear of discrimination and prejudice may mean that these families do not identify themselves. Research in Dorset suggests that the actual number of traveller children may be 50–70 per cent higher than the figures known. This makes it all the more important that settings create a welcoming and positive environment and one in which traveller children's identity is valued.

If travellers are likely to use your setting or Children's Centre due to the proximity of sites or regular stopping-off points it is essential that staff have some understanding of the cultural differences these families may bring with them.

'Traveller' is a term which may include Gypsy Roma, Irish travellers, European Roma, Circus and Showmen and New Age. Chandira Devarakonda (2013) provides a very useful summary of the differences between these diverse groups that it is important for early childhood practitioners to know about. Some areas which are on traditional traveller routes or have designated sites will have specialist teams to work with traveller families and outreach workers who visit regularly. Childcare settings need to make use of their expertise to ensure that they do not violate conventions which may be unfamiliar, such as not discussing women's issues when men are present.

The key person role is even more important with traveller parents who may feel particularly anxious about separating from their children and leaving them with unfamiliar adults. The key person may need to visit them on the site several times before they feel comfortable about doing so, but getting to know one worker well will help them to build relationships with other staff.

When thinking about the learning environment and the child's experiences, interests and skills, staff will need to reflect and consider traveller children's specific development needs and how to engage and promote their learning. It is extremely important that practitioners do not see differences as deficits but are aware of and build on the strengths which the children draw from their family's way of life. For example, traveller children spend a lot of their time with adults in their community, learning skills from being beside their parents. They are used to being outdoors for most of the day and in all weathers. They may find it easier to copy an adult than listen to instruction. They may know much more about animals, birds and plants than other children of their age.

Once staff have got to know the traveller families, they may be a valuable source of objects for Treasure Baskets, heuristic play and the role-play area which reflect their own culture. Examples would be 'Crown Derby style' crockery, satin and lace cloths and bedspreads with gold and silver trim, different coloured bowls and items for 'small world' toy areas such as wooden trucks, trailers, caravans, buses, horses and vardos (waggons), and benders (tents made with hazel sticks).

Becoming bilingual

For some workers it will be a new idea that as much value should be given to children's learning of their home languages as to English. This is a fundamental reversal, which puts the onus on nursery staff to learn as well as the child. For example, the key person can ask parents of children in her small group to teach her some words and phrases in their own language. Can she greet the child and say goodbye, express tenderness, offer comfort, approval and sympathy, understand a few of the child's special words, perhaps sing a favourite song? In turn, she can reassure the parents that the child will learn English without their making special efforts to speak it at home; a second language is learned best when the first language is well established. It is a great help to have some bilingual staff members, even though not all the children's languages can be represented since there may be as many as 50 different ones in some of the larger centres. Perhaps parents can fill some of the gaps and also provide help for new families speaking the same language.

When it is known that a deaf child will be coming to the nursery at least one member of staff, preferably the key person, needs to become proficient in British Sign Language (BSL). That person, and the child's parents, can then teach the rest of the staff group the basics of signing so that there is not only one worker who can communicate with the child.

Disability

How can children be enabled to understand and respond positively to differences of appearance, behaviour, mobility, and sensory and learning capacity? This has been much less discussed than racism and sexism. Awareness of disabilities tends to come later than awareness of gender and race, but by the middle of the third year, children notice and ask questions about physical differences, and may show signs of discomfort which should not be ignored. It is very important for the adults to answer questions clearly and briefly, at the child's level, and not to evade or suppress them.

Children with disabilities are even less likely than black children to see themselves reflected in the world around them, in books, pictures, toys or role models. It will take some ingenuity and inventiveness for nursery workers to tackle this form of discrimination. One possibility is to make use in the nursery of toys and equipment made by people with disabilities and tell the older children about them (see list of organisations). Another is to have at least one picture painted by a foot or mouth artist, along with a photograph of the painter at work. There are small world resources depicting children in wheelchairs, on frames, with visual impairments. Photographs of children with disabilities being active and enjoying activities should be displayed, celebrating difference, potential and achievement.

Some centres have invested in 'persona' dolls, each with its life story, particular family situation and individual characteristics, including in some cases various types of disability (Derman-Sparks and Edwards 2010). They are expensive but well worth the investment. The older children will enjoy making up their own stories about the dolls and their history.

Gender

Girls and boys are treated differently both by fathers and mothers from the moment of birth (B. Jackson 1987). By the time they reach their third year gender identity is usually well established and their play preferences are clearly influenced by perceptions of what is appropriate for boys or girls (Siraj-Blatchford and Clarke 2000).

The question, already discussed in the Introduction, is how far nurseries should accept or challenge conventional images of masculinity and femininity. We have made our own views clear, but just as we cannot necessarily expect our readers to share them, so it is pointless to try to impose non-sexist practice in a nursery unless staff understand and share the values that underpin it and are able to carry parents along with them. This may be difficult if they themselves come from families where traditional gender roles prevailed and if they did their training at a time when the issue was seldom considered. Raising awareness among staff is essential.

The next step is to look critically at the images of girls and boys, women and men, presented to the children in the nursery environment. Publishers of popular children's books are now much more conscious that they should present girls as active and energetic, and show boys, for example, washing up or caring for babies, but older books for children nearly always depict women and men in their conventional roles. Most toys available in high street shops are strongly differentiated, those designed for girls being predominantly domestic or decorative (and very, very pink) and those for boys either mechanical or connected with war and fighting. The greetings cards sold in newsagents' shops illustrate these stereotypes in their crudest form.

Early years practitioners, then, are to some extent rowing against the tide (though with help from the wind of equal opportunities), so to make any headway they have to look for, or make, books and pictures showing women and men engaged in non-typical activities. Perhaps it is as important to combat the idea that all families should be the same, when in reality they are increasingly diversified. Stories and pictures in the setting should reflect the different make-up and identities of families in society today including, for example, those featuring same-sex families. However some parents registering at a setting may be anxious about revealing that they are part of a same-sex partnership, feeling that staff or other parents may disapprove of their relationship. Practitioners need to be conscious of non-verbal cues that might convey this message.

They also need to become aware of their unthinking behaviour that may reinforce gender stereotypes, such as dividing boys and girls into separate groups, or making comments about their play related to their gender rather than the activity. How often do we make a point of encouraging girls to play with construction toys or be physically adventurous? Are boys offered as much chance as girls to bath the dolls? Do we discourage them from dressing up in a tutu? In conversation with children do we assume that they are mainly cared for by their mothers and that all parents are in a heterosexual relationship? What messages do the nursery leaflets and letters home give about how the setting considers gender equality and diversity?

The shortage of men in childcare settings is a difficulty because it conveys the message that only women know how to look after and teach young children, and that only women can be gentle and caring. It can be very hard for a man to work in, or even to enter, the female-dominated atmosphere of a childcare or Children's Centre (Owen 2003) but once there are men on the staff, the chances of drawing in fathers are much increased. Phil Lyons, who ran a men's group in Wexford, found that men greatly welcomed the chance to talk about more intimate feelings and express their sadness at what they experienced as exclusion from the lives of their children (Goldschmied and Jackson 2004). A survey by the Daycare Trust, cited in the previous chapter, found that a large majority of parents were in favour of childcare staff groups including more males, and Children's Centres which run activities specifically for men are meeting with some success.

Of course there are many other forms of discrimination and stereotyping. One which should certainly be given more attention by early years educators is ageism. Involving grandparents as well as parents in centre activities and welcoming them into the nursery or Children's Centre is one of the best ways of dispelling prejudice against older people. But people are also discriminated against for being poor, unemployed, choosing to wear their hair in an unconventional style or living in mobile homes instead of houses. We can often hear echoes of such attitudes in children's spontaneous talk, which will give us the chance to gently challenge them. In this brief discussion we have only been able to indicate some matters for the staff group agenda and suggest sources of further advice and information.

The key person's relationship with parents

The key person has the essential task of setting up an effective channel of communication between the home and the setting. Her relationship with the parents will do much to determine the quality of the child's experience, yet it contains inbuilt tensions that have to be recognised and managed. As discussed in Chapter 1, childcare in the UK was historically regarded as a compensatory or remedial service, and there are still clear signs of that view in many official publications with their increasing emphasis on early intervention for 'disadvantaged' families.

It is important for the setting to be clear exactly what it is offering to the child and parents, and misunderstandings are less likely when this takes the form of a written agreement, as is strongly advised in official guidance and is now standard practice in most settings. Most nurseries and childcare centres have welcome packs, marketing material and curriculum information for parents. There are many different ways in which Children's Centres and childcare settings can support parents and help them to manage their children with less stress and enjoy them more. However, the relationship is not all one-way. Finding opportunities for parents to become effectively involved in the life of the centre can extend staff resources, reveal unexpected skills and talents, and generate energy for new developments. There is evidence that children do better the closer the relationship between their parents and the setting.

Home visits and introduction to the setting

The relationship between centre and parents should be established at the earliest opportunity, preferably by the designated key person making a home visit by appointment before the child starts attending the setting. If staff levels allow, it is good practice for another practitioner to join in the first visit, but with the key person taking the leading part. In some centres we visited, the Deputy accompanied the key person on an initial home visit where the child has a disability or special need, or is subject to a Child in Need or Child Protection Plan. It may be possible for the child's social worker to be present at this point, or at a further meeting in the nursery, partly in order to ensure that the family fully understand the sharing of information between the nursery and social worker and the reasons behind this.

The primary purpose of the first home visit is not to obtain or provide more than basic information, but the practitioner is sure to come away having found out a good deal about the home and family, and it is a good idea to record this immediately afterwards. She will need an early opportunity to share what she has learnt with a colleague or senior and discuss how the setting can best provide a service to the child and parents.

During the visit arrangements will be made for the parents to visit the nursery. First impressions are very important. For example, the key person needs to check that welcoming messages on the noticeboard in the entrance area include the language of the family she is expecting. She also needs to schedule the visit at a time when there will be children present of the relevant age so that the visitor can see play and learning taking place, and observe how the nursery staff relate to the children. Whenever possible, this visit should be made by mother and father together, to establish the expectation that both are equally concerned in the child's well-being and development.

Clearly, it is essential that the parents are warmly greeted when they arrive and that the key person makes herself free to give them her full attention. After showing them round the building and introducing them to a few of the other staff (too many new people at once can be overwhelming) time needs to be made for a full discussion on how parents and nursery can work together to give the child the best possible experience.

Practical arrangements

Much of this discussion will inevitably be taken up with everyday matters: what hours and days the child will attend, who will be bringing and collecting her, how much parents will pay towards fees and/or meals and the precise arrangements for payment. What else they might be asked to provide, such as nappies, formula feeds and spare clothes, needs to be established. Also important are any special dietary requirements (whether for religious or health reasons), daily routines and intimate care, and how the parents respond to unwelcome behaviour (see below).

Working with separated families

Contact numbers for parents (home, work, mobiles) and other relatives need to be carefully recorded. The key person needs to find out who are the other significant people in the child's life – grandparents, step-parents, siblings, aunts and uncles. Where and with whom does she spend her time when she is not in the nursery? Who is authorised to collect the child? When parents are separated or divorced and there are new partners it is essential for the manager/leader and all the staff to be clear who has parental responsibility. This is the only person who is authorised to sign consent forms in an out-of-home setting (Tait 2007). Written consent is necessary if the child is to be collected by someone other than a parent. Sometimes there may be a court order restricting access, but if not, the natural father (assuming the mother has day-to-day care) is also entitled to know about his child's experience in the nursery, and this needs to be managed in consultation with the mother and social worker if there is one. Children's Centres often provide facilities for supervised contact to take place, or fathers to bring their children when they have them for contact. It is important that the setting has a policy, or at least some discussion as a staff team, on how separated families who are still part of the child's life are to be included in the nursery life, with paintings and drawings being shared or invitations to parents' meetings or celebration events. This way difficult conversations and sensitive situations may be avoided or handled more confidently by staff, and everyone knows where they stand.

Building good working relationships

With any family, expectations and obligations on both sides need to be clear and realistic. For instance, if the child will not be attending on a particular day, the parent will inform the setting by nine in the morning. If the reason is illness, the manager needs to know exactly what it is, in case it might be a communicable infection. It should also be clearly set out in writing how parents can make suggestions or complaints, initially to the key person and, if still dissatisfied after discussion, to the head of the unit or the management.

How much time should be allowed for the settling-in period also needs to be agreed. Most parents will want to be sure that the child is happy in the centre before attempting separation, but others may have personal or work reasons for wanting to leave as soon as possible, and this may need tactful negotiation on the part of the key person.

It is important not to offer more than can be delivered. The key person, anxious to be open and available, may say 'Feel free to come and talk to us any time'. This creates a situation in which the practitioner feels obliged to drop whatever she is doing and give priority to a parent who wants to talk to her, when she might be engrossed in an activity with a group of children. Not only does that convey an unfortunate message, that children matter less than adults, but it disrupts the work and probably means that the worker will have only half her attention on what the parent is saying and half on the children. Better to invite the parent to wait in the parents' room or reception area until the nursery worker can make herself free, or book an appointment for another time. Of course, this does not apply when the parent is acutely distressed or there is a real emergency, when the key person will have to ask a colleague to cover for her.

Another essential point is to state rules and boundaries firmly and then operate them with regard to individual circumstances rather than leave parents floundering, trying to guess what is expected of them and what really matters or not. One boundary that needs to be made clear right from the start is collection times. It can be very upsetting to children and cause great inconvenience and irritation to staff when a parent persistently turns up late at the end of the day. When parents have gradually slipped into the habit of collecting children after the official closing time, it is much harder to reinstate the rule.

In the increasing number of settings which have a 'core' day for the majority of children and extended hours for those whose mothers work longer, there can be a particular problem because parents observe that there are staff available after the time when they are supposed to collect their children and do not see why it matters if they leave them for an extra half hour. Of course this can always be negotiated in special circumstances, such as the need to take another brother or sister to a hospital appointment.

Communication between home and nursery

The key person needs to plan how she will know what is going on in the child's home life, keep the parents informed about their child's progress, and sort out any difficulties. Depending on the shift system in the setting, she should always be able to exchange a few words with them on arrival or with whoever comes to fetch the child. It should be standard practice that the person who hands the child over at going home time knows, either directly or from the key person, what the child has been doing that day and can tell the parent. However, we know, both from research and personal experience, that such conversations can be very conventional and convey little information. 'She's been a really good girl and ate all her dinner' may be reassuring but not much else.

The nurseries we visited and many more that we know give each family an attractively bound 'link' book that goes backwards and forwards between home and centre, and this is becoming common practice. Each day the key person makes brief notes of how the child spent the day, describing the occasional incident or achievement at greater length. The family, which can include brothers and sisters or grandparents, usually write about what they did at the weekend, record amusing sayings, or describe aspects of the child's behaviour. Any significant family events can also be recorded. This is different from the child's own personal book or portfolio, which is kept at the nursery (see Chapters 6 and 8).

Regular times need to be planned in over the year for more reflective discussion about the child's progress, to which parents make a full contribution. The link book provides one device for encouraging such exchanges. Photographs, and the child's own paintings and drawings can also stimulate conversation.

Time should be allowed for at least half an hour's uninterrupted discussion; these meetings are usually planned well in advance to enable parents to book time off work. Many of the settings we know offer parents the option of a day or evening meeting. It may sometimes be necessary for the practitioner to raise topics for discussion but she needs to be careful not to fall into the trap of doing all the talking herself. This kind of implicit discounting of the parent's knowledge of their own child is an experience that will be all too familiar for anyone who has attended a school open evening. However it can often be helpful to have a structure to work around, for instance by asking the parents to help complete a developmental assessment schedule. This will be more useful if it is based on systematic observation, both at home and in the setting. (However, Moylett (2013) warns against excessive paperwork and suggests using sticky notes to capture the moment when the child acquires a new skill or says something particularly memorable.)

Meetings like this provide a chance to discuss everyday matters that need a coordinated approach. Toilet training is one example (see Chapter 6). Another, which often causes tension between parents and nursery workers, is sleep. Most nurseries expect under-threes to sleep, or at least rest, after the midday meal, but some children refuse to sleep again until late in the evening if they have an afternoon nap, to the annoyance of their parents. It is of course impossible to keep a child awake when she wants to sleep, but there may be scope for negotiation about the timing and length of the rest.

It sometimes happens that parents have problems in their own lives, such as relationships, debts, housing or welfare rights, and are more interested in talking about those than about the children. They cannot be brushed aside, but the key person has to be clear that she is not a social worker or counsellor. However sympathetic she may be, she has to set limits to the amount of time she can give. She needs to know or find out where the parent(s) can go for help. In multi-agency Children's Centres this may be available from colleagues close at hand.

Parents are generally in favour of the key person approach because they like to feel that their child is especially important to someone in the nursery, and they also find it easier to relate more closely to one staff member than many, but this feeling sometimes has elements of ambivalence in it (Elfer *et al.* 2012). The mother may worry that her child will come to prefer the key person, especially if she is spending long hours in the setting during the week. All practitioners need to be very sensitive on this point. For example if the parent's circumstances make a painful separation unavoidable at times (see Chapter 4), it is not helpful for the key person to tell the mother on her return, 'Oh, she didn't miss you at all after the first few minutes', when what the mother wants to hear is, 'She missed you very much but I was able to comfort her after a while'. One detail which helps the mother not to feel that the key person is taking her place is if the caregiver, when holding the child in the mother's presence, as must occasionally happen, makes a point of having the child's face outwards, towards the mother. It is also better for the nursery worker not to feed or change the child in her mother's presence, unless specifically asked to do so.

Consulting parents

Childcare settings and Children's Centres differ widely in the extent to which they give parents the opportunity to participate in their management and organisation. Children's Centres have advisory boards with parent representatives and parents' forums which feed ideas and proposals into the Board. Voluntary organisations and community nurseries usually have committees made up of staff or trustees of the funding body, local interests, the unit leader and parent representatives. Private childcare centres, especially if they belong to large commercial chains, do not often allow any real influence to parents, as important decisions may be taken centrally. Sometimes there is a separate parents' committee, but too often its functions are restricted to discussion of fundraising activities. This can be useful of course, but it fails to provide the users of the service with any way of expressing their ideas about its policy and operation. Other ways of consulting parents need to be found, such as group room meetings, suggestion boxes, 'ideas' boards, and mini-referendums, offering choices between alternatives, and these are commonly used in Children's Centres to enable parents to contribute to decisions about services and activities.

Direct participation in the work of the setting is usually limited by the time and effort it takes to bring up a young child in our society. Working parents are likely to have very little time to spend in the childcare setting once the child is settled. Practitioners need to understand that the fact that parents are not inclined to linger reflects the reality that they are either rushing not to be late for work or are trying to fit in a bit of shopping before dashing home to prepare the evening meal. It does not mean that they are not interested in talking or hearing about their child.

The parents' room

Some settings are desperate for space and can only find places for parents to get together occasionally for specific purposes, but, especially in centres where a high proportion of families are living in difficult circumstances, a designated parents' room is a valuable asset, a space where they can meet and share experiences informally, as well as somewhere to hold classes and discussion groups. Clearly, there is no point in having such a room unless it is warm, attractively decorated, comfortably furnished, and equipped for tea and coffee making (and preferably washing up). It can also offer facilities that can be useful for some parents, such as a sewing machine, washing machine, and tumble-drier.

It should also be supplied with a large noticeboard on which can be posted information about local events of interest to families with small children (especially free ones), items for sale or wanted, and offers of services on an exchange basis. Even if staffing resources do not allow for organised activities to go on in the room, it can have a useful function as a social meeting place and help to reduce the isolation suffered by so many mothers of young children. It is essential for one member of staff or, better still, a parent volunteer, to take responsibility for seeing that the parents' room is kept in good order and that it does not become a dumping ground for unwanted toys or items for the next jumble sale. If the parents' room is used for other purposes, such as group sessions, cookery classes, work with small groups of children or individual meetings with parents, a booking system will be needed and the information posted on the door, so that parents can see when it is available for social use and do not feel themselves to be intruders.

Figure 13.1 Mothers and babies make friends in an early years group

Helping parents to manage children's behaviour

How far is it a legitimate aspect of an early childhood setting's task to influence the way parents handle their children? This is a question that arouses strong feelings. We are not talking here about the relatively unambiguous situation where attendance of child and parents at the centre is a condition of her being allowed to remain at home as opposed to being placed in foster care. The role of the early years practitioners in that case is discussed in the next chapter. If the setting is primarily offering a service to working parents or offering a better play and learning environment to children living in cramped or unsuitable accommodation, do the practitioners have any right to impose their own ideas about bringing up children on families who may come from a different social class and possibly a different culture from themselves? To some extent this is an unreal question, as most research shows that it is very hard to persuade people to change their childrearing practices (Pugh *et al.* 1994). Generally, practitioners can only hope to lead by example. However there is one aspect of childcare where early years professionals can give a clear lead, and that is in relation to physical punishment.

Hitting people is wrong

In many European countries physical violence against children is forbidden by law (Sweden, Finland, Denmark, Norway and Austria), but in this country it is still both socially and legally accepted. One survey found that almost two out of three mothers admitted smacking a baby under one year old, and nearly all four-year-olds were smacked, often several times a day (Newson and Newson 1963). Successive governments have refused to consider a change in the law, either on the grounds that it would be unenforceable, or that it would be an intrusion in family life. Our tolerance of assault against children is yet another indicator of the low value given to them in our society (Leach 1999; Willow and Hyder 1998).

Some progress is being made. The Singleton Report (DCSF 2010) led to a ban on hitting children in all out-of-home care and education settings, although it stopped short of making it illegal in other situations. The campaigning organisation Children are Unbeatable has been endorsed by more than 350 organisations, and it is less common to see children being hit in public (Lansdown and Lancaster 2001). Obviously it will be made clear that smacking children is not acceptable in the nursery, but practitioners have an important educational role in helping parents to understand the reason for this and to find more effective ways of guiding their children's behaviour. The topic is one which always provokes lively discussion in parents' group meetings, and it can be very satisfying to see attitudes shift, as people come to see in a different light, ways of handling their children that they had previously taken for granted.

Almost all parents feel the need of advice and support at some time, especially in the early stages. They turn for guidance to older relatives, more experienced friends, to books and magazines and the internet. There are many ways in which early years practitioners can be helpful. In particular, they can offer reassurance that a child's behaviour is normal for her stage of development (if it is). They can help parents to enjoy their children in the setting, whatever the stresses of their lives outside. When there is real cause for concern, they can discuss with parents what action might be taken. Some of the ways that nurseries and Children's Centres can help children and families subject to protection plans are described in the next chapter.

Managing difficult behaviour

The handling of young children with difficulties has inspired countless books, articles and television programmes, generally relating to problems which happen within the family. Less has been written to help early years practitioners or childminders who are looking after children away from home. When many children from families with multiple social difficulties were placed in local authority day nurseries, a high proportion had problems of behaviour or development (Bain and Barnett 1980; McGuire and Richman 1986). Melhuish and Moss (1991) pointed to the influence of peer effects, even suggesting that the clustering of severely disadvantaged children in particular settings could turn them into 'training schools in problem behaviour'.

The shift from social services day nurseries to neighbourhood-based and private childcare centres may have reduced that problem, but focusing resources on deprived areas and the increased government emphasis on 'targeting' means that it is unlikely to go away. Research on parenting indicates that over a third of children living in the poorest areas can be classified on standardised tests as 'difficult'. Ghate and Hazel (2002) show how multiple stresses in the physical and social environment contribute to this situation. However, any child can find himself in difficulties, if only temporarily, not only those with obvious problems in the family. We start by considering general principles of managing children in a group care setting and then look at some kinds of behaviour that may cause problems for nursery practitioners.

Difficulties generated by the setting

As adults, we can probably think of situations, such as being squeezed up in an overcrowded train or waiting endlessly in a hospital outpatient department, when we feel oppressed and frustrated and have to exert great self-control not to express our anger. In a childcare setting, equivalent situations are having to sit for a story in a group that is too large, with no room for your legs, or being given a puzzle with two pieces missing or a doll with no clothes on and lacking an arm, or sitting at a table on a chair which is too low and so finding your chin in the plate. When practitioners describe a child's behaviour as difficult, it is essential to ask if the environment we provide may be making matters worse. It is always better to anticipate confrontation with children rather than react negatively once a problem has arisen.

Of course, setting limits is part of the process of socialisation that occurs as the baby, entirely dominated by his physical needs, develops and matures. For his caregivers this means striking a balance between two kinds of interaction with the child: on the one hand, affection, approval, tolerance, sympathy, protection, understanding, reassurance and encouragement; on the other, making requests, forbidding certain behaviour, expressing displeasure. Practitioners need to be sure that they are providing many more communications of the first kind and avoid giving a stream of orders or constantly rebuking a child, which can have a very damaging effect on his self-concept. If there is any doubt on this point, it may be helpful to ask a colleague to carry out a ten-minute observation and share the results.

Reactions to stressful events

When a child who is normally well-adjusted and cooperative suddenly starts behaving in an uncharacteristic way, he is quite likely to be responding to some important event in his family. Where the key person approach is in operation his special adult will be able to give him extra affectionate attention at this time. A typical instance is when a child in his third year experiences the birth of a younger brother or sister. One study found that 93 per cent of firstborn children became less cooperative and more demanding after the arrival of a second child (Dunn 1984), so that a temporary change in behaviour can be regarded as entirely normal. The important thing is for the adults to avoid reacting in a punitive way.

Even though a child has been well prepared and a favourable expectation created, the actual reality of a baby who displaces him and receives everyone's attention can be too hard to bear. He may express his resentment by being thoroughly awkward and screaming for what is thought to be no reason. He may clamour to have a bottle again when he had quite given it up. He has powerful feelings to cope with and, as yet, very limited means of expression. Unless his close adults can help him through this genuine crisis, their exasperation with his behaviour will quickly give him the idea that he is bad and create a downward spiral.

Adults sometimes get very anxious about admitting that jealous feelings exist and a child can be continually hearing how wonderful it will be to have a little brother or sister to play with. When the baby arrives it is not wonderful at all, quite the opposite, and the child, understandably from his point of view, can feel isolated and angry about the denial of the reality he is living at that time.

Other circumstances may also produce a shift in attention away from the child, with similar effects, such as for example the death of a grandparent, a sudden financial crisis or the parents' decision to separate. The situation at home will be known when a key person approach is working well, and the child will gain confidence from feeling that there is an adult in the childcare setting who has a special concern for him. When a young child is going through a period of what he may experience as environmental upheaval, a familiar routine and close contact with a substitute attachment figure have been found the most effective way of reducing distress (Arnold 1990; Whalley 2007).

Overactivity and restlessness

Children sometimes come to a childcare setting labelled as 'hyperactive' or diagnosed with attention deficit disorder. In our view these terms do nothing either to increase our understanding of a child or help to improve what we are able to offer him during a nursery day. It is important for practitioners to know that the whole subject of hyperactivity is extremely controversial. In the United States the phenomenon has been considered largely as a medical problem and is treated with powerful drugs. There is now increasing concern in this country about the numbers of children being given a diagnosis of Attention Deficit Hyperactivity Disorder (ADHD) and the enormous increase in prescription of drugs for the condition, when the causes may lie in their environment, diet and/or interaction with carers (Citizens Commission on Human Rights UK 2012).

Children differ temperamentally in their level of activity, and parents differ in what they are able to tolerate. What one parent will define as normal curiosity and a sign of intelligence, another will consider 'being a nuisance'. Some so-called overactive children may be victims of inappropriate expectations, such as being asked to sit still for long periods, or simply have too little to interest them in their environment. In only a small minority of cases is the behaviour due to neurological impairment.

Once children are provided with more sensitive and responsive care and more stimulating activities the behaviour may disappear; on the other hand, it may have become firmly entrenched as the only way that the child has found of attracting adult attention. It may also be that the nursery programme does not offer enough to engage the child's interest. The key person needs to make a careful assessment, based on systematic observation of the child's abilities and use of available material in constructional and imaginative play, and the quality of his relationships with other children and the other nursery staff (Fawcett 2009). It may emerge from this assessment that the child is capable and energetic but bored and frustrated because he has exhausted the resources that the setting is able to offer him.

More difficult is the child who seems unable to concentrate on any activity, is destructive of play material, and rushes noisily about, disturbing and irritating everyone. By agreement with other staff members, the most effective way of helping a child like this may be to give him very concentrated attention for a certain period of time, taking him on his own into the garden if he seems to need to 'let off steam', or sitting beside him while he plays, trying gradually to increase the length of time he can focus on a particular activity. The attention of his key person gives him emotional anchorage and the control that he needs to gain if he is to join in with the activities of the day.

Elinor Goldschmied was asked to help with Janet, 22 months, who, from the moment when her exhausted mother left, ran frenetically round the rooms and passages of the nursery, creating disturbance and anxiety for everyone. In consultation with staff, an immediate course of action was agreed that enabled them to feel less frustrated. It was decided that Helen, Janet's key person, should make a list of all the things that Janet could do, starting with running. This list turned out to be surprisingly long and, in discussion, the nursery workers were able to move from a total focus on Janet's disruption of the group to consider some of her capabilities.

Starting from her ceaseless running, it was suggested that Helen might use the garden to run round obstacles with Janet, holding her hand. The object of this was to slow the child down and enable her to gain greater skill and control in movement, in close relation to her adult. Another approach was for Helen to hold Janet in her arms until she relaxed and then encourage her to explore the Treasure Basket, picking objects up, mouthing them and putting them down, as if she were a much younger child. Later she would offer receptacles for Janet to put objects in and take them out. Concurrently, the centre leader spent time with Janet's mother, helping her to understand what Helen was trying to do.

Within a few days of this intensive attention, Janet's level of activity began to subside to a level closer to that of a normal, energetic two-year-old. The staff realised that there were many practical steps that they could take to calm her down and engage her in activity, based on their own knowledge of child development. They had no need to wait for an expert diagnosis, which would still leave them to find ways of turning the information into everyday practice.

Non-compliance

Children in their second and third year frequently go through phases of refusing to do what they are asked by an adult as a way of asserting their independence. This is different from the child who habitually ignores adult requests or goes out of his way to do things which have been specifically forbidden. One possibility that needs to be excluded is that the child is suffering from intermittent hearing loss. If the child's hearing is normal, the problem probably lies in the way his parents have handled him. For example, some parents have unrealistic expectations of the child's ability in relation to his age. Others give instructions to their children without either checking that the child has understood what is wanted, or ensuring that the desired behaviour actually happens. The child quickly learns to ignore such communications. Another common situation is where the child gets attention only when he is making a thorough nuisance of himself. Some parents may need help to understand that attention, however negative, is rewarding to a child and will therefore make the undesired behaviour more likely to persist. Together with the parents, nursery workers can analyse the child's behaviour in detail and identify a particular problem to be worked on. Sometimes the difficulty can be eliminated by altering the conditions, as suggested earlier, or by considering whether what is being asked of the child is necessary or reasonable, given his stage of development.

Temper tantrums

Temper tantrums are very common in small children, probably related to their inability to recognise their own wants, the frequent frustrations they experience, and their limited command of language. It is estimated that nearly 20 per cent of two- and three-year-olds have a tantrum at least once a day, and a much higher proportion of children display the occasional tantrum, often unpredictably (Briggs 2011). Although a temper tantrum does not directly affect the other children, it is upsetting to the group because of the noise and confusion it can cause.

Sometimes a tantrum will happen quite suddenly and a child will throw himself on the floor screaming and beating his feet. At moments like this it is clear that words are quite useless; in fact any attempts to check the tantrum generally make things worse. The most helpful thing for the adult to do is to stay near the child, perhaps sitting down, attentive and available but not intervening. It is often noticeable that the other children watch the nursery worker very carefully and are reassured that she stays calm and, once the tantrum has passed, helps the child, with a drink of water and quiet words, to feel all right again.

Some children who have frequent tantrums may have learned that this is the best (or only) way to get what they want. It is of course very important not to reinforce this behaviour, and for the key person to discuss with the parents how to discourage it at home.

Aggression against other children

Aggressive actions which distress, disturb and even injure other children, such as snatching, pushing and pulling, kicking and hitting, pulling hair and throwing play equipment, are particularly testing for practitioners in group settings. Although it is the child who has got hurt to whom we give our immediate attention as we intervene to stop the conflict and comfort the victim, it is important to notice how the aggressor is looking, which is often pretty unhappy. We need to recognise the feeling while making it clear that the action is not acceptable.

Imitation has been shown to be a very influential factor in aggressive behaviour, so that children who often attack others may either be reflecting discord and disharmony in their home, or have been exposed to inappropriate television programmes or video games. Boys in particular have been found to show increased aggression when they have witnessed violence by one parent against another (Arnold 1990) which makes it all the more important for the setting to offer an alternative model.

Most children, when they see that another child has hurt herself, will offer comfort and try to console the other child until they can see that she has recovered. In a few cases we see that the attempt at consolation is cursory, and if the hurt child continues to cry it may provoke an aggressive response rather than a comforting one. Goleman (1996) suggests that this indicates a failure to develop the capacity for empathy and should be a matter for very serious concern, reflecting emotional if not physical abuse in the home background (see Chapter 14).

One of the problems about handling aggressive behaviour in groups is to give the aggressor the attention he or she needs without reinforcing the behaviour. The key person, in consultation with other staff members, can work out a plan to ensure that such children get regular positive attention when they are playing cooperatively with others and that desirable behaviour is rewarded with warm approval.

Conflicts between children

We may recall from our own childhood the way that an adult often arrived on the scene and told us off when they never saw how the quarrel had begun. Often the other child had provoked us in the first place and we felt the injustice of being the only one to be blamed for a conflict for which we were only partly responsible.

When two children have tight hold of the same toy and are screaming 'Mine, mine!' they often turn furious faces to the nursery worker whom they expect to take action. The temptation is to quell the noise by intervening immediately, insisting that one or other child relinquish the toy. However, if the adult can stay quietly beside the contending couple and just wait, the children may come to their own solution when they run out of steam, prevented from injuring each other by the worker's attentive presence.

Conflict over playthings is a good example of the type of behaviour that can easily be increased or reduced by practical arrangements. In a heuristic play session, as described in Chapter 7, where there is a calm atmosphere and an abundance of material, this type of dispute seldom occurs.

Biting

Biting probably arouses more anxiety than any other form of aggression. Being bitten is very painful and when it leaves a mark understandably arouses intensely hostile feelings in parents. One still occasionally hears the suggestion that the adult should 'bite the child back to teach him what it feels like'. Another common but undesirable approach is that the child who bites is pressed immediately to 'make up for it' by kissing the child he has just bitten. This mixes up aggressive and loving gestures and is simply confusing to children.

Biting tends to go in waves when young children are in groups, and practitioners need to know how they will respond when it happens, and have a clear policy to follow. Advice from local authority early years consultants can be sought and training for practitioners from other professionals, such as the educational psychologist, or behaviour support teams can help the setting draw up or improve their policies on behaviour management. The key person is central here because she needs to help the child to control his impulse to bite and convey her affection and concern at the same time as setting limits. One way is to underline the proper use of teeth: 'Let's look at your nice strong teeth in the mirror, let's see how sharp they are – they're for biting food not people.' Sharing an apple or a raw carrot with the child, she can talk about the pleasure of biting a hard, crisp thing, making a clear distinction about what is for biting and what is not. Everyone dealing with the child needs to understand that punishment and isolation will not be effective in bringing about the kind of self-control that is needed.

A review of literature on biting in US day care centres revealed that this is one of the main reasons for children being expelled from day care and can 'sweep through a preschool like measles' (Palmer 2006, p. 178). This was certainly Ruth's experience in a nursery 1–2s group. However, by close working with parents of both the biters and their victims, careful monitoring to record what times of day the biting happened and what was going on in the room at the time, and staff intervening as swiftly as possible, the 'epidemic' played itself out.

If the nursery or the parents feel that extra support is needed with a child's behaviour issues, the advice of other professionals should be sought. Some parents can be helped by a group parenting programme but this does not work for all. It can be useful to find that other families experience similar difficulties, but real commitment is required for a parenting programme and the parents have to be in the right frame of mind to want to effect change. Health visitors may provide support or run programmes. Many local authorities offer evidence-based parenting programmes for babies and three- to six-year olds, such as Incredible Years (also known as Webster Stratton Programmes), often co-facilitated by health professionals or CAMHS staff. There are a range of programmes used in Children's Centres to support parents.

Feeding difficulties

Feeding difficulties can cause staff a good deal of anxiety. They may have their origins in very early relationships or be connected with the way that the child feels about his experiences in the nursery. If the first, then the key person will probably have heard about it during the home visit before admission or during the settling-in period.

Sometimes a child will eat well at home but not in the nursery or vice versa. One of the first things to find out is whether, in spite of eating apparently very little, the child is in fact gaining weight normally and is generally healthy. This can easily be checked by using a growth or centile chart. A child whose weight falls below the third centile would be diagnosed as suffering from 'non-organic failure to thrive' (organic causes for the feeding difficulties having been excluded), which is a very serious condition, certainly requiring expert help (Jenkins and Milla 1988). As with all behaviour termed 'difficult', it is important to see it against the background of the child's experience at home and in the nursery. For example, a child may be used to being fed on someone's knee or moving about while he eats. Inevitably sitting at a table to eat at the nursery will mean a big change for the child, in addition to the different taste and appearance of the food.

Some people are adventurous about sampling unfamiliar food, whereas others react with dismay when offered octopus, blackbird pâté or frogs' legs, so it is not surprising that children are the same. Adults are also allowed to say they just don't feel like eating, and this is understood and accepted. If children are not allowed the same freedom, mealtimes can develop into a battle, which is invariably counterproductive.

When a child is reluctant to eat we can gently offer him a very small amount on his plate and, if he does not eat, take it away, again with gentleness; this is a message of care and concern which is conveyed without words. Taking an uneaten plate of food away can be done in a quiet understanding way or in an exasperated or punitive way and the child's face will tell us exactly how he is feeling about it. As with other behaviour difficulties, all the staff who will be handling a child with feeding problems need to be agreed on their approach.

Comfort and tension-relieving behaviour

Thumb-sucking, head-banging and masturbation are forms of behaviour that may create great concern for adults, but usually become a problem only if unwisely handled. Thumb-sucking, for example, is an activity that is energetically enjoyed by each generation of babies. Some babies are born with a little red mark on one of their thumbs, which indicates that they have been sucking comfortably even before they were born.

Thumb-sucking

'Non-nutritive' sucking seems to satisfy a basic need, but over the years the discussion around 'thumb or dummy' has ebbed and flowed. We confess to a preference for thumbs: dummies are too easy for adults to use as a 'gobstopper', cutting off the communication the child is trying to make and inhibiting vocalisation and early speech development. The advantage of a thumb is that it does not fall on the ground to be picked up and wiped (or not), nor does it get lost in the folds of a blanket, causing frustration and outcry.

Rocking and head-banging

Rocking and head-banging are not uncommon as a form of self-comforting behaviour associated with going to sleep, but in a childcare setting it often indicates that a child has been deprived of stimulation and attention at home. It was very characteristic of children in residential nurseries providing physical care and not much else, and can still be seen, sadly, in childcare institutions, particularly in countries where residential care or that of children with special needs or disabilities is given little importance (Goldschmied and Jackson 2004). Like any other undesired behaviour it is important not to reinforce it by attention, and it tends to disappear quite quickly if the child is given a great deal of loving care and active play with his key person. Meanwhile, of course, it is important to protect him as far as possible from injuring himself.

Masturbation

Young children are full of curiosity about their own bodies and discover very early that they can gain comfort and pleasure from exploring them. This has carried a heavy load of misconception and disapproval in the past, and probably in the childhood experiences of many adults. This means that we need to have accurate information and confidence in our own attitudes (and those of the other staff) in deciding how we respond. Distraction is invariably more effective than prohibition.

Children in many childcare settings will come from a range of cultural and social backgrounds where family attitudes will vary widely. They will have differing degrees of freedom in their families to explore their bodies, to see the differences between men and women and boys and girls, and to know what to call their tummy, breast and navel, penis and vagina. As they grow up they absorb the taboos that belong to their culture and their family relationships. The practitioner needs to find out as much as possible about parents' attitudes and think how to respond when they differ from her own.

When parents are present

The behaviour of children is often specific to particular situations so that a child may present no problem to nursery staff or to his childminder and yet be very difficult for a parent to manage. A child who is perfectly willing to comply with a request from a nursery worker may be irritable and resistant with his mother. This puts the worker in an awkward situation when the mother is in the setting and the child 'plays up'. Usually it is best for the worker to withdraw tactfully for a few moments. If she intervenes, it makes the mother feel incompetent; on the other hand, the parent may be embarrassed by the child's behaviour and react with disproportionate severity. Of course, it has to be made clear that certain forms of control, such as hitting or shouting at a child, are not acceptable, but the practitioner needs to show her understanding that children behave very differently with their own parents, and maintain an uncritical attitude. If the situation looks like getting out of hand it is probably best for the practitioner to lead the child a little way off, allowing the parent to recover his or her dignity and composure, and then suggest some way out of the difficulty. If the incident is symptomatic of general problems in child management, this will need to be tackled separately.

Relationship and developmental play with children and parents

Little children need a great deal of close physical contact with adults who care for them if they are to develop trust and a sense of security. With a strong key person approach the nursery worker is likely to feel an intimacy with her small group of children that makes it natural to engage in the kind of physical play that is usually a normal part of family life. However, sometimes practitioners feel that anything more than an occasional cuddle is inappropriate with children who are not their own. For the majority of children any deficits in the care setting are compensated for at home, but if one or both parents are also inhibited about relaxing physically with their children, the implications are more serious. It would be a pity if our present heightened awareness of the danger of sexual abuse to even very young children were to prevent close bodily contact between children and adults that can be so pleasurable to both.

A few parents, although they say they love their children, find this hard to express physically. They may rationalise their reluctance by saying that the child is 'not cuddly'. Relationship play is particularly valuable to parents who are not physically comfortable with their children, especially if there is concern about the way they care for them. But it also has value in its own right, whether the child is partnered by a nursery worker or by her own mother or father.

Relationship play is a system of physical interaction between two people, in this case an adult and a child, in which power, size, strength and ability become irrelevant. It produces a sense of trust, intimacy and mutual enjoyment between the people concerned, which may be just for the duration of a particular session or part of the process of building or improving a long-term relationship. It also helps a child to develop a sense of her own body, physical agility and confidence. It provides a non-verbal means of communicating with children, but is also an effective way of increasing vocabulary, since words associated with physical experience are more likely to be absorbed and remembered.

The method, based on the theories of Rudolf Laban, was developed by Veronica Sherborne, working with a complete spectrum of children from toddlers to adolescents, including those with special needs. Through Veronica's teaching at Bristol University it came to be used in a wide range of nurseries and family centres. It is unlike anything else we do with parents and has the potential to free even the most tense and over-burdened to be relaxed and loving with their child, at least for a short time.

Many studies have shown that fathers are much more likely than mothers to engage in physical play with their children. Not only do women tend to give up most forms of sport and physical recreation in adolescence, but once they become mothers, they may be so preoccupied with getting through their daily tasks that they come to feel that play for its own sake is not a legitimate way of spending time. Their enjoyment when 'given permission' to play is striking. Elinor Goldschmied, with Rebecca Abrams, ran play workshops for mothers, believing that this could free them to play more uninhibitedly with their children (Abrams 1997).

Relationship play is also a good way of involving parents who may lack confidence to participate in other activities, and in settings where most mothers are working, it can be a fulfilling one-off session, perhaps at the end of the day. With very young children it is essential for each to be paired with an adult. If some parents are unable to be present, this may allow the child to join with a staff member, preferably his or her key person.

One great advantage is that no equipment is needed. Veronica Sherborne herself preferred to work in a large open room with a smooth, uncarpeted floor, but we have seen very enjoyable sessions in relatively small spaces and in carpeted childcare settings. It is important of course to fit the activity to the space as too many adults and children together in a confined area can lead to accidents.

The leader for the session should have a clear plan of the activities to be included in, say, a 40-minute period, and when several people are taking part for the first time, he or she may need to demonstrate first, with a child or another nursery worker, to show that nobody will be asked to do anything difficult or alarming.

Relationship play, as developed by Sherborne, falls into three categories: caring, shared and 'against', the third type only to be introduced when the participants have developed a strong sense of mutual trust and confidence, perhaps after experiencing several sessions. The names of a few of the exercises give a flavour of the activity: cradling, rocking, supporting and rolling, tunnels, rowing the boat, flying, and in the 'against' category, rocks and prisons. This last group involves the child in testing her strength against an older partner, encouraging effort and determination. All these games and exercises were described in more detail in earlier editions of this book (Goldschmied and Jackson 1994, 2004) and for a fuller description and explanation of the underlying developmental theory consult *Developmental Movement for Children* (Sherborne 1990). A similar approach is Jabadao, quite widely used in childcare settings and Children's Centres, though usually with rather older children.

We have seen relationship play used successfully with mothers suffering from depression, with neglectful parents and even some who have harmed their children in the past, and also with inexperienced nursery workers and social workers who need help in communicating with small children. It is one of the most effective forms of direct work with parents who are hard to influence by discussion-based methods, and since there is no right or wrong, no winners or losers, it provides an opportunity for modelling without undermining the confidence of parents.

Summary

In this chapter we have looked at some of the issues which arise when the daily care of a young child is shared between parents and an out-of-home setting, including how to ensure that the setting is as inclusive as possible and that different parental backgrounds and cultures are fully respected. The key person plays a very important role here – lines of communication need to be carefully worked out and expectations clear on both sides. In some settings relations with parents will not go much beyond this. Others have extended their function to involve mothers and fathers in a whole range of activities.

When problems arise in relation to a child's behaviour, it is essential to work closely with mothers and fathers to work out a strategy to overcome them. It may be the environment and not the child that is causing the problem and we need to try to understand what he is trying to say to us. Many behavioural and emotional difficulties in young children can be fairly easily overcome if sensitively handled, and others may diminish or disappear with time as the child achieves more control over his situation. However, there is always a risk that problems ignored at this stage may lead on to more severe difficulties through childhood and sometimes into adulthood. A childcare setting can play an important role in preventing this from happening – by providing affectionate, consistent care and stimulating experiences for the children, by helping parents to understand and look after them more effectively, and, where necessary, by involving other professionals.

Note

1 This section owes much to training delivered by the Dorset County Council EMTAS Team in June 2013 to Children's Centre staff and to the DCC 2013 publication 'Guidance for Early Years Practitioners working with Gypsy Roma Traveller children and families in Dorset'.

14 Safeguarding children

Poverty is a great enemy to human happiness; it certainly destroys liberty and it makes some virtues impracticable and others extremely difficult.

(Boswell's *Life of Johnson*, 1782)

In this chapter we will consider:

- Safeguarding and child protection;
- Childcare as early help for parents under stress;
- Can we change parental behaviour?
- Emotional impact on practitioners;
- Working with other professionals.

Safeguarding and child protection

The terms 'safeguarding' and 'child protection' tend to be used interchangeably, but they have rather different meanings. In many European countries (Spain and Hungary, for example) 'child protection' refers to the child welfare service as a whole, including the care of children away from home in foster families or residential centres, and the aim of the service is to enhance development and social integration (Jackson and Cameron 2014). In the UK, by contrast, 'child protection' usually means investigation and prevention of ill-treatment of children by adults, often their own parents or people in the same household. 'Safeguarding', although it encompasses child protection, has the broader meaning of ensuring that, as far as possible, children's development is not compromised by adverse circumstances, and the active promotion of well-being (DfE 2013; Marmot 2010). In contrast to the emphasis of the traditional child protection service on investigating allegations of abuse or neglect, identifying perpetrators and removing children thought to be at risk of harm, safeguarding takes a more preventive approach, though without ruling out removal when necessary. This approach was epitomised by the *Every Child Matters* (ECM) agenda, introduced by the Labour government in 2004, as described in Chapter 1. Although the Coalition government appears to have sidelined ECM and it is not referred to in the current guidance (DfE 2013), it remains a very helpful framework in thinking about safeguarding.

Despite substantial investment in resources and widespread agreement that early intervention is the best way of preventing harm to children, the number of children with Child Protection Plans increased between 2004/5 and 2010/11 by 63 per cent, and there was a similar sharp rise in the number of referrals to children's social care due to concerns about abuse and neglect (Green 2012). What seems to have happened is that better resources for early intervention (for example through Children's Centres) have led to more identification of need and lower thresholds for referral to social care. In relation to babies and young children there is much greater understanding of the impact of neglect on brain development and how even very small children may be affected by witnessing domestic violence as well as by direct ill-treatment (Allen 2011).

The role of day care in safeguarding

There is curiously little discussion of early years care and education in texts concerned with detection and prevention of child maltreatment, even though very young children are the group at highest risk of death or serious injury as a result of abuse by parents or carers (Cuthbert *et al.* 2011). Since parents are not obliged to send their child to an early years setting, abuse and neglect of young children is most likely to be picked up, if at all, by health professionals. There is an argument for them to take a much more active part in arranging attendance in a good quality early care and education setting for any child where there is cause for concern about risk of harm or inadequate parenting (Platt 2014).

Soon after its election in 2010 the Coalition government commissioned Professor Eileen Munro to undertake a review of child protection in England. The subsequent report (Munro 2011) was mainly concerned with systems and structures and the role of social workers. It made little reference to childcare, although we would argue that, at least in relation to children under three, this is the service which has the potential to make the most effective contribution to protecting the well-being and development of those who may be at risk of neglect or ill-treatment. The most recent government guidance, however, includes only a brief paragraph on childcare (DfE 2013). Munro did introduce the concept of 'early help' for families at risk as a form of prevention. The planned provision of 15 hours a week free early years education and care for 'vulnerable' two-year-olds from September 2013 seems to be mainly aimed at this group of children, but the eligibility conditions are quite stringent. In addition, at the time of writing there are serious doubts if the number of required good quality childcare places can be delivered and if there will be sufficient government funding to cover the cost (DfE 2013). With further changes to the criteria expected at the time of writing, local authorities may be forced to make cuts in other services in order to deliver the number of places required by the government, which are intended to provide for up to 40 per cent of this age group.

The danger of targeted provision

A further problem in childcare settings is that when an extremely disadvantaged group of children is concentrated all together, both they and those who look after them suffer. Caregivers may lose their sense of developmental norms and accept a low level of progress and achievement. They could also become discouraged and overwhelmed by the scale of the problems that these children and families face in their daily lives. The Sure Start initiative (see Chapter 1) recognised that danger by adopting a community-based approach to provision rather than one aimed at individual children or families. Sure Start schemes and, later, Children's Centres were located in districts with about 800 families, with places in neighbourhood nurseries allocated, as in nursery schools, on the basis of residence. This was moving in the direction of a universal, non-stigmatising service and away from the emphasis on the compensatory function of day care. However, because Sure Start projects are mainly concentrated in deprived areas, there are still likely to be a disproportionate number of families in poverty and some with severe problems (Davies and Ward 2012).

Childcare is the service that offers by far the best prospect of identifying young children at risk, relieving parental stress and providing better models of child–adult relationships. Serious case reviews and child death inquiries often comment on the number of visits made by social workers and health professionals to families perceived to have a potential to harm their child, in which the visitors failed to spot what seemed, in retrospect, to be the most obvious signs of abuse (Laming 2009). Social workers have the primary responsibility for investigating allegations of abuse and neglect and for fol-lowing official guidelines for further action but, in contrast to early years practitioners, they may lack the expertise to identify developmental delay associated with maltreat-ment (Munro 2011). Moreover, however often they visit, they will only see the child or children for brief periods. Nursery workers, on the other hand, see children every day and get to know them very well. In the course of providing routine physical care they may see any marks or bruises that cause concern. They are in a much better position to become aware that a child is (or might be) suffering harm, and they then have a duty to take action to safeguard that child.

A common pattern that emerges from analysis of serious case reviews following child deaths is that, before the final catastrophe, a child who has been attending a childcare or nursery setting ceases to do so, referred to by Reder and Duncan (1993) as 'terminal closure'. This may be because the household is in such a chaotic state that nobody gets round to taking the child to nursery, but it is also possible, as in several cases cited by Reder and Duncan and in many more recent ones, that their parents or carers are fearful that professionals will see that the child has been neglected or injured. Either way, a break in attendance should ring alarm bells.

Childcare and child protection

Among the families in difficulties who use childcare and Children's Centres or have subsidised places with childminders, a very small proportion will have admitted to or been convicted of harming their children, but a much larger number may have been referred by health visitors or social workers who believe there is a risk that harm might occur. It is important for early years practitioners to remember that, although child maltreatment is strongly associated with poverty and deprivation, it is not confined to one section of society. Families who are well-off in material terms may also experience relationship difficulties, partner abuse and addiction problems or have misguided ideas about discipline. Children in middle-class families are not immune from physical, sexual and emotional abuse, and all of the issues discussed in this chapter are relevant to private nurseries as well as to community and local authority childcare centres.

Day care is occasionally mentioned as a resource by writers on child protection, but it is obvious that few have more than a passing acquaintance with childcare settings (see, for example, Beckett 2003). Ann Buchanan is exceptional in describing reliable day care as 'central to strategies for breaking cycles of sociopolitical child maltreatment' (Buchanan 1986, p. 172). The most recent official guidance, *Working Together to Safeguard Children* (DfE 2013), endorses the Munro Report concept of 'early help' but includes only a short section on childcare. This is all the more curious since very young children are those most likely to suffer death or serious injury as a result of abuse or neglect (Cuthbert *et al.* 2011; Tickell 2010).

It is very hard to accept that known adults can deliberately hurt a young child, and the impact on childcare providers of this aspect of their work can be devastating. Julia Gilkes (1988) writes of the shock and disbelief that workers experience when they encounter evidence that children as young as two or three have been sexually abused, and the emotional stress this causes. The same applies to physical abuse and neglect. One senior practitioner told us:

> The biggest barrier to disclosure is the existence of emotional blocks in the minds of professionals. These can be so powerful they prevent the recognition of abuse even being considered in quite obvious cases. All who work with children should be warned that their overwhelming impulse on confronting their first case will be to want to cover it up. The most important step in diagnosing any abuse is to force yourself to think it possible in the first place.
>
> (2013, personal communication)

Training and support are essential (see Chapter 12). All childcare workers, not just the head of the centre, need to be familiar with local guidelines and procedures in relation to child protection. This is a requirement under EYFS. Most local authorities provide multi-professional training for childminders and for the Designated Safeguarding Officer (DSO) in each setting. Childcare managers need to be insistent that *all* staff have access to training, not just about procedures or recognition, but to enable them to become familiar with current thinking on the nature of child abuse and approaches to prevention and treatment.

For example, because child abuse was first identified and described within a medical setting there was an emphasis on diagnosis – Was the injury accidental or not? – and on the characteristics of the parents, who were seen as disturbed and abnormal. There is now a much better understanding that child abuse is socially and culturally defined

(Gilbert *et al.* 2011). A theoretical shift has taken place which allows child abuse increasingly to be seen in the context of the wider community and society. Poverty and powerlessness are probably as important determinants of the way people treat their children as are their personal characteristics or family history, and all these factors interact to produce the phenomenon that we call abuse. Beckett (2003) uses a series of vignettes to illustrate how the cumulative stress of living in poverty puts parents at greater risk of maltreating their children.

Owen Gill (1992) wrote a vivid account of family life in a single street on a Bristol housing estate, showing how difficult it is to be a 'good' parent in the circumstances with which these families have to contend. Nearly all the residents were unemployed (no jobs, no day care), had very low incomes from state benefits and lived in flats not designed for families with children. Their immediate environment was rubbish-strewn and dangerous, and they could not afford any relief from care of their children. Gill argues that it is society as a whole that is guilty of abuse, by failing to provide parents with an income adequate to the demands of bringing up children or an environment conducive to their emotional, physical and intellectual development. The idea of a Children's Centre in every local community, along with more generous welfare provision, went some way towards addressing these conditions, but twenty years later the clock is being rapidly turned back and Gill's picture of life for poor families is only too recognisable, as demonstrated by the controversial Channel 4 television programme *Benefits Street* in 2013.

There is a long history of research into the causes of abuse and neglect which shows that risk is highly correlated with social factors, mostly outside the control of the parents (Parton and Berridge 2011). These include:

- Insufficient income to cover everyday needs;
- Parental unemployment;
- Homelessness or inadequate accommodation;
- Low level of parental education;
- Postnatal depression and other mental health problems;
- Living in a disadvantaged community.

Early years practitioners need these wider perspectives if they are to maintain a non-judgemental attitude and not fall into the trap of blaming the victims, who are the parents as much as the children (Andrews and Jacobs 1990). This does not alter their basic responsibility to protect the child, but underlines the importance of looking at the whole life situation of the family rather than focusing exclusively on the parent–child relationship.

The functions of childcare for families under stress

A factor which complicates the task of staff in a childcare setting or Children's Centre with a high proportion of children whose families face severe problems is that the setting serves different functions for the child, the parent(s) and the referring agency.

Some of the dilemmas which arise for practitioners spring from attempting to negotiate the conflicting needs and demands of these three groups.

Looking first at referrers – doctors, health visitors, social workers and other professionals – day care can be the most effective resource on offer, and a first line of defence against the ultimate disaster, the death of a child for which they might be held professionally accountable. For social workers, a day nursery/childminder, or sponsored place in a childcare setting, might occupy a halfway position between leaving a child in a possibly dangerous family and seeking a court order to place her in foster care. The nursery functions that are most important for them are providing appropriate safe care for the child, respite for the parents which may then enable them to cope better, and monitoring the child for signs of abuse or neglect.

For the parents – in practice, mostly mothers, and especially if they are on their own – the nursery can fulfil many different purposes. Overwhelmingly the most important is to provide relief from 24-hour responsibility for childcare. This is true even in settings which insist that parents stay with their children. At least while in the centre they are not responsible for their child on their own. The nursery is also important socially, a place to meet others in the same or similar situations and exchange problems and ideas. The nursery or Children's Centre can also be very useful as the most accessible place to make contact with a knowledgeable professional who is prepared to listen and to offer advice, guidance and support (Andrews and Fowler 2010).

If there is work available in the neighbourhood, a day care place may transform the life of a single parent by making it possible for her (usually her) to go out to work instead of living on social security (Land 2002). Although parents generally welcome the opportunity that the nursery gives their child to play more freely than in cramped home conditions, to run about and shout in the garden without annoying neighbours, the child's experience, provided she is not obviously unhappy, is often a secondary consideration for them. The idea of acquiring parenting skills, an objective beloved of social workers and health visitors, may be rather low on their agenda. Poor parents usually believe (and they may be right) that they could look after their children well enough if their living conditions were not so difficult. So one problem that arises for practitioners is that parents and social workers may have very different ideas about why the child has been offered a place and what her attendance is supposed to achieve.

There is a risk that when the focus is on work with adults, the child's need for an enjoyable and stimulating daily experience may be overlooked (Powell and Uppal 2012). In some nurseries and Children's Centres where staff resources are overstretched, the quality of care and education offered has suffered. It is crucial for nursery workers to remember that their central task is caring for the child. It is the same for the child of a family in difficulties as for any other: to offer affectionate, individualised, responsive care designed to give pleasure and enhance development. Both EYFS and the shift in emphasis after 2004 from child protection to safeguarding were helpful in this regard. Unfortunately the pendulum may be swinging back again. Blyth and Solomon (2012), in a critical account of the Munro Review, point out that the final report does not include the word 'safeguard' or 'safeguarding' once.

The educational function of childcare is even more important for a child who has had a poor start, and this is as true for babies as for four-year-olds. It may require special patience and planned effort. For example, most babies of nine or ten months, even those of a naturally cautious disposition, will start to explore the Treasure Basket within a few minutes of being sat down beside it (see Chapter 5). A child whose instinct to explore has been roughly suppressed may need much gentle encouragement and reassurance before she will feel confident enough to reach out to grasp an object.

Safeguarding children within the setting

It is usually assumed that threats to children's well-being come from outside but the notorious case of the Little Ted's nursery in Plymouth, the first serious case review of a childcare setting, showed that this is not necessarily true (Plymouth Local Safeguarding Children Board 2010). Dame Claire Tickell suggested in her report (Tickell 2010) that CRB (now Disclosure and Barring) checks might give a false sense of security and that practitioners and managers also need to be very alert to signs of neglect or abuse occurring within settings. Examples she gives are adults talking about details of their sex lives in front of children, having sexually explicit conversations or being alone with children in a group setting for unusually long periods of time without good reason. In the Plymouth case, mobile phones were used to take inappropriate photographs, with a result that these are now banned in childcare settings. This case also drew attention to the fact that, although the vast majority of perpetrators of child sexual abuse are men, women can sometimes be involved, either actively or in collusion with a male offender.

Sharing responsibility with parents

Early years practitioners are usually well aware of the danger of 'taking over' from parents and leaving them feeling even less competent and in control of their lives than before. The difficulty is that families under severe stress are often too preoccupied with their problems to keep an overall view of their children's development and undertake tasks essential to their well-being. Most mothers, for example, give high priority to 'keeping children healthy' (Mayall 1986; Robinson 2014) and generally succeed, often against considerable odds, but a few fail to notice that a child needs medical attention or they lack the energy to do anything about it. There are many reasons why parents may be reluctant to take a child to the doctor. These range from a general mistrust of professionals to a specific fear of criticism. The parent may know that the problem has existed for some time and is fearful of being blamed for not having come to the doctor before. A more sinister reason may be the fear that a medical examination will reveal marks and scars caused by injuries inflicted by parents or other adults – Peter Connelly's mother covered his face with chocolate to disguise the scars and bruises inflicted on him (Laming 2009). Confronting a parent in this situation usually provokes great anxiety in practitioners.

In an earlier edition of this book, Sonia describes how she visited a family centre run by a voluntary agency in a very deprived area, headed by a social worker with a strong commitment to 'empowering' parents. The leader took the view that it was the mother's job to take her child to the doctor and that any initiative on the part of the centre workers would undermine the parents' self-esteem. There were children in the centre covered with sores, one with an unrepaired hernia, another in obvious pain from an ear infection. It was unsurprising to learn that the centre had recently suffered a serious outbreak of dysentery (Goldschmied and Jackson 2004).

Although this was an extreme case, it does illustrate the danger of sticking to a theoretical position which flies in the face of common sense. If a parent is unable or unwilling to protect the child's health, this is a form of neglect, and it is the clear responsibility of the nursery to take action. Improving children's healthcare was the primary purpose of day nurseries when they were first set up, but this often got lost in the transfer of management from Health to Social Services in the 1970s. At the time of writing, childhood obesity is a pressing healthcare concern with very serious long-term consequences. Early years practitioners are in a good position to note if a child is putting on too much weight and to help the parents to address the problem before it becomes embedded.

Active work with parents

Children who are the subject of a Child Protection Plan or at risk of removal from their families are often referred to nurseries or Children's Centres by social workers with a stated expectation that the centre will 'work with' the parents, but what this work consists of is not always clearly enough specified. Failure of communication between agencies working with families where abuse or neglect of a child is known or suspected is a key issue highlighted in almost all serious case reviews. When the child has died or has been seriously harmed it is very common for the report to note that professionals in different agencies failed to work together effectively to protect the child, even though individually they had plenty of evidence that the child was in danger (Laming 2009; DfE 2013). There may be a tendency for social workers to reduce their contact with a family once a childcare place has been allocated, leaving the nursery staff to cope on their own. This is understandable, but dangerous. Unless the centre has its own social worker, an agreement to continue to work in close communication, as required by official guidance, is likely to lead to a better outcome for child and family.

Who are the parents?

An important point to establish is, who are the adults whose relationship with or behaviour towards the child the nursery might be attempting to modify or change? In the past it was simply assumed that parent equalled mother, and only recently has this begun to be challenged. From the viewpoint of risk to the child, an approach which focuses exclusively on the mother is clearly inadequate. Although more women than men are implicated in child abuse cases, this is mainly because they spend far more time with their children and are ten times more likely to be bringing them up on their own. Cases of serious injury or death almost invariably involve a man, and, as mentioned above, the preponderance of men among sexual abusers is overwhelming. Despite this, studies of ongoing work following child abuse case conferences show that male adults are rarely involved (Corby 1987). This is not necessarily due to a failure of early years workers to engage with them. In cases where the mother's partner is the perpetrator, he may already be in prison, or the couple may have separated. Among disadvantaged families, living arrangements are often fluid and difficult for practitioners to keep up with. There is the additional difficulty that childcare settings are perceived as women's places, in which men can feel like outsiders. As we saw in Chapter 13, Children's Centres have made much more effort to involve men in recent years, with some success.

The Children Act 1989 greatly extended the categories of adults who are recognised to have a legitimate interest in a child: grandparents, aunts, uncles and family friends, older brothers and sisters. Nurseries are sometimes critical of families when different people turn up to collect a child. Some even go so far as to insist that only the mother or father, or only an adult will do. This is to ignore the varied patterns of caregiving which prevail in different cultures, but also fails to take advantage of the opportunity to meet and make links with members of the child's natural support network. Active work with families implies identifying the significant adults in a child's life and may sometimes mean, in collaboration with a social worker, reviving potentially useful links which have weakened for lack of encouragement and contact. Isolation from extended family resulting in an absence of support networks is a common finding in situations where children suffer harm.

For young children, 'parents' will mean whoever is responsible for their day-to-day care, usually the mother and any other adults who live in the same household. Clearly the most likely 'other' person is the mother's partner, whether or not he is the father of the child. As we pointed out in Chapter 13, the nursery leader and key person play a critical role in determining the man's attitudes to the nursery. There are bound to be ambiguous situations, for example, when the relationship is relatively new or in a fragile state, but it is virtually impossible for a man to remain detached from his partner's young child. The constant need of young children for physical care and protection, and their power to annoy and disturb adults by crying or by innocent but destructive exploration, ensures that any adult in the same household will share the task of parenting either positively or negatively. It is therefore essential that when the child's attendance at a nursery is based on an agreement or contract, which is especially desirable in situations of perceived risk and will certainly happen when the child is subject to a Child Protection Plan, this should explicitly include the father (or father substitute). Any new approach towards the handling of the child needs to be consistent and cannot succeed unless all the adults are in agreement. This can be very difficult since complex and fluctuating relationships are a characteristic of families who are at risk of neglecting or mistreating their children.

Changing behaviour

Childcare practitioners have only limited possibilities of achieving fundamental changes in the way people treat their children. That does not mean that they should make no effort to improve relationships or modify behaviour. There are a number of different approaches directed to the same broad objective: first, to help parents enjoy their children instead of experiencing them as an irritating burden; second, to enable them to learn more about child development and so to find their own children more interesting and have more realistic expectations of them; and third, to build up their self-esteem and awareness of their primary role in the child's life. In practice these aims are inter-linked. For example, modelling is one of the most effective ways that practitioners can expose parents to different ways of behaving. If nursery workers always speak to children in a quiet, affectionate voice, parents who spend any time in the centre will gradually adjust their own style of communication. They will see that other forms of control are more effective than shouting or hitting, which it will have been made clear to them are not permitted in the nursery. The approaches to managing children's behaviour discussed in earlier chapters may need more explanation and demonstration when they are very different from the way the parents have been accustomed to relate to the child. Parenting programmes delivered by organisations or agencies such as Action for Children, Barnardo's or local authorities can be a useful referral for these families. Most Children's Centres deliver (or can signpost to) a range of programmes. Nursery staff, childminders and of course parents can talk to family support/outreach workers for further information or to begin the referral process.

Emotional neglect and abuse

Although physical abuse attracts more attention and is certainly much easier to detect, emotional abuse and neglect can be just as painful and damaging to a child. 'Emotional neglect' is defined as ignoring a child's need to interact, showing no emotion towards her, and denying her the chance to communicate – for instance by persistently refusing to answer questions or engage in conversation. 'Emotional abuse' involves more posi-tive actions, such as telling the child she is worthless or unloved, using an aggressive and bullying tone of voice, making fun of the child, ridiculing or persistently criticising her.

Researchers in a systematic review conducted jointly by Cardiff University and the NSPCC found that emotional neglect in the first two years was strongly associated with later aggression, post-traumatic stress disorder, depression and anti-social behav-iour (NSPCC/Cardiff University 2010). The research identified a warning sign to look out for in children under three as 'lack of attunement' between mother and child – for example, a mother who is unresponsive and uninvolved, ignoring signs that the child needs help. This is also recognised in work undertaken by David and Yvonne Shemmings on disorganised attachment (Shemmings and Shemmings 2011).

A baby or child under 18 months who seems unnaturally quiet or passive and shows no upset at separation from her mother should give rise to concern. Children in their second or third years who are emotionally neglected or abused may, on the other hand, become aggressive and hostile towards other children and angry or avoidant with their mothers. Developmental delay, especially in language, is another possible warning sign and should trigger a formal assessment if there is any reason to suspect maltreatment.

Some parents find it hard to show physical affection to their children, even amounting to a real dislike of touching them except to give the minimum physical care. One technique for overcoming feelings of this kind is the relationship play described in Chapter 13 (Sherborne 1990). Another is to adopt a behavioural approach as illustrated by the following account. This may be considered beyond the scope of most childcare settings or Children's Centres but could still be helpful to the key person in some circumstances (McDaniel and Dillenburger 2014). Darren, aged two, had been admitted to the nursery suffering from serious physical neglect and emotional deprivation. The family social worker had considered placing him with foster carers and was not optimistic about his single mother's ability to look after him. The mother, Susan, insisted that she wanted to keep the child, but Darren's key person noticed that she seemed to shrink from physical contact with him. Susan later confided that she longed for a baby she could cuddle, but Darren had always been 'unloving'. She realised that her reluctance to touch Darren had contributed to the neglect and wanted to change but couldn't see how.

The key person undertook to tackle this problem with Susan while the social worker took practical measures to help Susan improve her home situation and ensure that she received the welfare benefits to which she was entitled. Together, the key person and Susan made a list of all the forms of touching and closeness which might occur between a mother and child, and Susan ranked them in order of difficulty for her. Each week they made a plan for Susan to do the next most difficult thing. If Darren resisted when, for example, Susan took his hand as they walked, she was to let go and try again later. To begin with, progress was slow and the key person had to give much encouragement and think of ways in which contact could occur almost by accident. But gradually Darren began to respond to his mother's changed behaviour, and Susan unexpectedly found this so rewarding that she raced through the later stages of the programme and was quite soon able to respond with a kiss and a cuddle when Darren spontaneously climbed into her lap. She also began to take much more interest in her own and her son's appearance and cleanliness.

Changing perceptions

Some parents, especially those who are very immature and have suffered harsh and inconsistent treatment in their own childhood, have a negative view of their children, seeing normal, childish behaviour as deliberately hostile and designed to annoy them. They avoid interaction whenever possible, thus provoking attention-seeking that they find irritating and to which they respond aggressively. One technique that can help to break into this cycle is the use of video. Through a video camera parents seem to see the child with different eyes, as someone with a separate identity from themselves, an independent person. They may, for the first time since she was a baby, see the child as lovable. They usually greatly enjoy both the filming and watching the playback with their key person. If the video session is repeated several times over two or three months, they have a chance to observe and take pride in the child's developing abilities. It also enables them to see that she can play in an active way without being destructive or disruptive.

Video has proved to be an effective tool in assisting parents to be sensitive to their children's development and to learn how to manage their own and their children's behaviour without resorting to coercive methods (Goldschmied and Jackson 2004). Because of its distancing effect, video seems to be less threatening to parents (who already feel themselves under attack) than more direct methods. It has been widely used in family centres and in child-abuse prevention schemes in Canada (Wolfe 1991). In the Netherlands there is a well-established video home-training programme in which specially trained workers take the video into the homes of families with behaviour management problems (Colton *et al.* 2001; Janssens and Kemper 1996). However, its value is not restricted to situations where safeguarding issues are involved. Both parents and practitioners have much to learn from observing and discussing videoed sequences of children's behaviour, as described by Margy Whalley in her account of practice at Pen Green. Video cameras were used by parents in their homes and practitioners in the nursery, as well as in baby and toddler groups co-led by parents and staff. The project work had shown 'that it was possible for parents who had everything stacked against them in terms of socio-economic status, lack of educational achievement and low levels of family support to become very effective advocates for their children' (Whalley 2007, p. 23).

Group work with parents

Many nurseries and family centres build their parent-involvement programme around groups, but very little has been written about the use of group work in childcare settings with families in difficulties. Discussion groups and parent education classes about alternative approaches to bringing up children and ways of handling problem behaviour are quite common, but here we want to focus on the less usual groups which contain children and parents together. Two rather different types, though with features in common, are 'nurture groups' and 'communication groups'.

Nurture groups

Nurture groups derive from the theory that some mothers are unable to recognise or meet the needs of their children because they have experienced so little love and care in their own lives. The group is designed to provide some of that experience for the mother and child together. One Children's Centre ran a weekly nurture group for ten two-hour sessions in a room apart from the main activity area. Three or four pairs of mothers and children attended with one nursery worker. The room, warm, carpeted and comfortably furnished, was set out in advance with different activities, suited to the ages of the children. Each session began with relationship play, as described in Chapter 13, and ended with relaxation to music. In between, the mother and child played together with each activity in turn (though they could take time out to read a story or just have a cuddle). The mother was encouraged to follow the child's lead and respond to her signals. The session was always followed by a communal meal in which the atmosphere of calm and warmth was maintained by careful preplanning (see Chapter 9). Feedback from mothers who participated in this group was very appreciative. Some felt that they had really enjoyed playing with their children for the first time. They were surprised at how long the children could concentrate with the attentive but unobtrusive presence of an adult beside them, and how much they could find to talk about, even if the child was still at a preverbal stage. They came to trust the group leader and be more receptive to her suggestions, and they also got to know each other well and make friendships that in some cases continued outside the centre and constituted the beginnings of the social network that they so badly needed.

The style of the leader in this group would probably be described as authoritative in that, although her manner was very gentle, she determined the form and content of the sessions, arguing that part of the nurturing consists in setting clear boundaries and relieving mothers temporarily of the need to take decisions.

Communication groups

A different kind of group, set up in a London family centre with a high proportion of children known to have been abused, focused on communication and used a more democratic style of leadership. In this case the centre was committed to inter-professional work and the sessions were co-led by an early years practitioner and a social worker. The value of groups in aiding communication is well documented (Brown 1992; Heap 1985) and inhibition of communication is a typical feature in families who abuse their children (Dale *et al.* 1986). The parents often have difficulty in expressing their feelings and ideas, misinterpret their child's signals and behaviour, and give them confused messages. Dale suggests that in these frustrated and inarticulate families, physical violence and sexual abuse sometimes represent desperate and distorted attempts at communication with children. This issue has not been much discussed in the literature on safeguarding.

The five families who took part in the group all acknowledged communication problems with their children and wanted to work on them. With their key person they each identified personal goals that they hoped to achieve through their participation in the group. At the first meeting they agreed on the aims of the group and how it should be run (the limits of confidentiality was one of the difficult issues, given that all the families were subject to a Child Protection Plan). The sessions included group games involving collaboration between parents and children and between the different families, within-family tasks related to individual goals, observations of children engaged in activities selected and set out by parents, and relaxation, using various techniques and types of music.

Music was also used as a form of non-verbal communication, and parents, especially men, who were reluctant to participate in group games that they saw as childish, happily cooperated to produce a musical performance. The parents who took part in this group made some progress towards achieving their personal goals. They were surprised by the children's participation in the relaxation exercises and by the fact that they kept as quiet as the adults, having previously seen them as always noisy and disruptive. Most of the adults grasped the idea of active listening to their children and felt supported by seeing other parents doing the same thing. Paradoxically, through the group exercises, they became aware of their difficulty in communicating constructively with other adults, which most had not previously recognised as a problem.

The workers felt that running the group was an effective form of intervention and an economical use of their time. It gave the families the opportunity to learn from each other and to use each other's strengths; they felt less pressured and isolated and more hopeful of being able to change. The key elements in its success were very careful pre-planning by the two co-workers and the project leader and a determined effort to include the families at every point – setting the agenda, agreeing objectives, deciding content, evaluating outcomes. This kind of work cannot be done without full management support, allowing time for planning and evaluation and adequate space and equipment, and the current trend is for it to be offered only in specialist centres, which we think is regrettable.

Working with other professionals

Running groups such as those described above requires skills and experience that may not be available within the nursery or Children's Centre team. In-service training in group work should be built into the staff development plan. Another way for nursery workers to acquire group work skills is to work with other professionals. In addition, every child abuse inquiry and serious case review since Maria Colwell (DHSS 1974) has emphasised the need for inter-professional collaboration if children are to be adequately protected. Government guidance on child protection always includes 'Working Together' in the title and current guidelines stress that private and voluntary childcare centres should work closely with their Local Safeguarding Children Board in the same way as organisations in the public sector (DfE 2013).

For very young children, the nursery or childcare centre plays a key role as the agency that has most frequent and regular contact with the child and parents, and may be in the best position to coordinate services in their interests. When there is a Child Protection Plan or a CAF in place, there is a good argument for an early years practitioner to be the lead professional, although this is still unusual. The decision to remove a child into care is not taken lightly and it is unsurprising that attempts at reunification do not have a high success rate (Wade *et al.* 2011). This is especially true for children who have experienced chronic emotional abuse or neglect. The problem is that once the decision has been made to allow a child home there is a reluctance to remove her again even when there is cause for concern. The early childhood practitioner's professional view can be a vital source of support to the social worker in this situation.

The centre needs to establish a clear expectation that social workers do not hand over families to the nursery and then withdraw. Both at individual and group levels the work can be much more effective if tasks are shared. Some children, as a result of having suffered abuse in the past, are acutely disturbed when they come into childcare and very difficult for parents, foster carers or early years workers to handle. A psychologist may be asked to come and observe the child in the nursery and help staff and carers work out a treatment plan. Support may also be available from the local authority School

Improvement Team. Play therapy may help children in the older age group, although most therapists prefer to work with children over four. An increasing number of play therapists are developing special expertise in working with abused children (Cattanach 1992; McMahon 2009), but there are problems in that the timescale tends to be long and behaviour may deteriorate in the early stages, which can be very difficult in a group setting.

When decisive action is needed

Many official inquiries into cases of fatal child abuse have remarked on the risk of collusion between social workers and parents. A notorious instance was the case of Jasmine Beckford (London Borough of Brent 1985) where the report commented that the most favourable interpretation was always put on the parents' behaviour even while the children were suffering horrific cruelty. The same risk exists with the daily contact which occurs between the key person and parent in childcare settings. The parent is likely to see the key person as a friend, and though initially aware that her role is partly one of surveillance, that can quickly be forgotten. On her side, the practitioner may be torn between her sympathy for the parents, with their debts, relationship problems and miserable living conditions, and her awareness of the vulnerability of the child. She is in a good position to see signs of physical abuse in the process of providing normal intimate care, and sexual abuse is frequently revealed through children's play and drawing (Briggs and Hawkins 1997). However, the indications are often ambiguous and there is a great temptation to ignore them or wait for more evidence in order to postpone the need to take action. Especially if a family has been coming to the centre for several months, good relationships have been built up and there is a sense of some achievement, it can seem like a defeat to begin a process that may well result in the child's removal from the family and probably also from the childcare setting.

In this situation it is essential for the key person to share her anxieties with a senior member of staff as soon as possible. She will need to write a careful description of what she has observed – bruises, burns, sexualised play, verbal disclosures – making a precise record of dates, times and names. This will be important if there is a question of placing the child away from home under a care order. In the case of physical ill-treatment or a disclosure of sexual abuse, action must be taken immediately. With emotional abuse and neglect it is more likely that a picture will be built up over time and a decision taken by the centre leader about when to refer to the local Children's Services office. The most appropriate action can then be decided on, in line with procedures laid down by the LSCB and government guidance (DfE 2013).

Acknowledging difficult feelings

The key person may have had to work hard at the time of referral to overcome initial feelings of anger and disgust towards parents known to have hurt or seriously neglected a child. Having come to know them as individuals, and perhaps even to like them, it can be extremely painful to have to give evidence against them in a case conference or in court, and to experience their anger at what they are likely to see as a betrayal.

The staff member in this position needs several kinds of support. The opportunity to discuss feelings of disappointment, inadequacy and sadness in supervision and within the staff group is important, both for herself and for other nursery workers. The leader also needs to remember that any staff group may include one or more people who have themselves experienced abuse. Depending on how the discussion is handled, a disclosure may be liberating or traumatic. Unresolved personal issues may need to be tackled outside the nursery, by encouraging the worker to seek counselling or to join a survivors' group. When there is only one male member of staff, as is not uncommon, he may feel under particular pressure during discussion of sexual abuse. Some social services departments have recognised this by setting up support groups for men working in early years settings, but since there are still so few this may not be feasible outside the main cities. Apart from the emotional stress, there are also problems for practitioners arising from their low status. Of all the people involved with the family they are likely to have the most detailed knowledge of the child and the best understanding of children's needs. They will certainly be the most skilled in communicating with very young children. Yet their expertise is often undervalued by other professionals and their opinions given little weight compared with those of social workers, doctors, psychologists or lawyers – who may have seen the child and family on only one or two occasions (Coombe 2011).

Early years practitioners need training to participate effectively in case conferences and to express their point of view clearly and professionally. Giving evidence in court requires specific preparation and rehearsal for the particular case, as well as familiarity with the relevant law.

The limits of day care in child protection and safeguarding

Potentially, day care is by far the most effective protective resource if the long-term plan is for the child to remain in her own family. However, much more research and thinking needs to go into what actually happens after the child is offered a place. While some settings offer well-thought-out programmes to build parents' self-esteem and competence and help them to make better relationships with their children, others flounder for lack of guidance and support, to say nothing of staffing ratios that take no account of this very demanding and time-consuming aspect of their work. It is essential to accept that the safeguarding role of childcare has limits. Early childhood practitioners cannot undo the effects on adults of a violent childhood, stop parents from misusing drugs and alcohol, give them an adequate income or rehouse them (Davies and Ward 2012). The nursery cannot make a dangerous family safe. Even with a full-time place the child will spend much more time at home than in the care setting. Nevertheless it is important for all childcare practitioners to recognise that they have something valuable to offer the child, irrespective of their success or failure in helping parents. There are many reasons why it is hard for people to change established patterns of behaviour, and even social workers and psychiatrists who are very expert in working with abusive or neglectful parents can struggle to empower families to change (Ward *et al.* 2012). There is a danger that the welcome emphasis on supporting children within their own families, as is their right under the United Nations Convention (UNCRC), could lead to unrealistic expectations of day care. Government guidance warns against being too optimistic. 'Timely and decisive action is critical to ensure that children are not left in neglectful homes' (DfE 2013). Experienced early years workers are in a unique position to assess the quality of the relationship between the child and her close adults. For a few of those children the contribution of the early years professional may be to accept that the best option for this child is a permanent substitute family. For the child, however, a good experience will not be wasted and a secure attachment to their key person in the nursery may provide the foundation for better social and emotional development later.

Summary

In this chapter we discussed the important part played by childcare settings in safeguarding children. They can provide crucial support to families under stress, recognising the need for 'early help', which can be an alternative to separation when mistreatment is known to have occurred or the child is considered to be at risk, and helping the reunification process when children are returned to their families after a care placement. We describe some approaches to changing parental perceptions and influencing behaviour. Staff training is essential, both to identify signs and symptoms of abuse and to know what do when something is wrong. The emotional impact on practitioners cannot be overestimated and adequate support for those affected is vital.

Although we warn against over-reliance on childcare to protect children, both the day-to-day experience of high-quality care and education and the child's attachment to her key person will make a valuable contribution to her future development, even if it is not considered possible for her to remain with her birth family.

15 Elinor Goldschmied 1910–2009

Elinor Goldschmied's life and work spanned almost the whole of the twentieth century. In the course of her long and varied career she introduced new thinking and important innovations to all aspects of early years work, many of them described and discussed in this book. Although she is probably less well known than some of the other pioneers of early childhood care and education, her ideas have had a profound influence on early years practice through her films, her writing and, perhaps most of all, her teaching. The contribution she herself considered most important, the Treasure Basket described in Chapter 5, has now been widely adopted, not only in the UK but in many other countries around the world. It is hard to remember now how long it took for the ground-breaking nature of this apparently simple idea to be recognised. Elinor was far ahead of her time in seeing, before it was scientifically proven, the vital role of sensory experience in forming connections in the rapidly developing brains of the very youngest children. In fact for several years the first edition of this book was the only available text to focus on the group care and education of children under three, that is, below the age at which nursery schooling traditionally started. It was as if learning did not occur until then.

Elinor was never very keen to talk about herself, always wanting to get on with the job in hand, but she did contribute two series of long interviews to the National Life Story Collection at the British Library, from which summaries can be downloaded.[1] This chapter is partly based on information from those interviews as well as the many conversations we had at her house or mine while working on the first edition of this book and during our travels in Italy together.

An Edwardian childhood

Elinor was born on 15 December 1910, in the small village of Lower Tuffley in rural Gloucestershire. She was called Violet after her mother, but much disliked the name and insisted on being called 'Elinor' from an early age. The family name was Sinnott. There were two older brothers and a sister, Carew, with three more sisters to follow. She was always interested in the influence of birth order on children's development, and later reflected on how her own position as the middle child in a large family had shaped her personality. The sisters, like Elinor, all lived to an advanced age, but the younger of her two brothers, Edward, known as 'Ebby', died of peritonitis at the age of eight. She remembered him being driven to hospital in a horse-drawn carriage, but it was too late. He and Elinor had been very close and even at the age of five she felt his loss acutely, especially as his name was never mentioned again, as was the custom at the time.

Elinor remembered her mother as very warm and loving, always finding time to listen and make some affectionate gesture, despite the many demands on her. But more tragedy was to follow, when, soon after her father's return from the First World War, when Elinor was nine years old, her mother fell ill with cancer and died. The children were looked after by a succession of unmarried aunts and cousins and educated at home by governesses.

In some ways it was a very austere Protestant upbringing but the modifying factor for Elinor was her intense relationship with natural things. In the holidays the children had great freedom to roam and make up imaginative games, using everyday materials and whatever came to hand. Looking back, Elinor felt that these experiences and the close contact with nature that she enjoyed during this period of her childhood laid the foundation for much of her later work. It was then, too, that she developed the habit of close observation of detail, which became so important in her practice. For example, she remembered lying on the grass with a magnifying glass to inspect the insects in a small patch of ground.

Distinctions of class

Even as a small child Elinor was aware of the social class divisions that were so strong at that time. Although she used to insist that the family was only professional middle class, not gentry (her father became the county surveyor after leaving the army), they lived in a large house set in twelve acres of land and kept pigs, chickens, bees and horses. Everyone was expected to help with the farm work. The way of life in her childhood home would be familiar to any viewer of television period drama. The servants as well as the children attended daily prayers and church on Sundays. There was no question of the Sinnott girls going to the local school or playing with children from the village. Visitors from the village were expected to come to the side door. The servants called the children 'miss' and 'master' and Elinor noticed that they spoke in a different voice to members of the family from the one they used to each other. Much later, these perceptions fed into the political convictions which she held with such fervour, though never uncritically.

In 1921 her father married Adela Peel, who had set up and run the nursing home where his first wife was looked after in her last illness. She was from an Indian Army family and socially superior to the Sinnotts. Elinor described her stepmother as 'a remarkable, really good woman' whom she greatly admired and loved. Tragically, after only five years, Adela developed a menopausal psychosis, or perhaps what would now be called a bipolar condition. She had occasional periods of remission when she was thought to be recovering, but, unlike her father, Elinor recognised these as the manic phase of the illness, and the last twelve years of Adela's life were spent in a mental hospital. Elinor attributed her later interest in mental health to the painful experience of observing the decline of her stepmother.

School and college

At the age of 12, Elinor was sent with her elder sister to live with their grandfather in Bristol and attend Clifton High School for Girls. Grandfather Sinnott was a benign but remote figure who had little idea about the children's daily lives. Elinor remembered that it was only at the insistence of their stepmother that he provided a one-bar electric fire to heat their room in the depths of winter. However, despite their unconventional early education, Elinor and her sister did well at school and each in succession became head girl.

The career options for girls in those days were strictly limited – teacher, nurse or secretary. Influenced by her teacher, Katie Rintoul, a noted artist in her own right, Elinor's real ambition was to become a choreographer or theatre designer. But her father had a strongly held view, unusual at the time, that girls as much as boys must be able to support themselves and earn a living. Only the youngest sister, Diana, went to university. Elinor had to settle for teaching and thought she had been fortunate to choose the Froebel Institute at Roehampton, then the leading centre for primary education in the country.

Another stroke of luck was that, when she completed her three-year course, her tutor encouraged her to apply for a job at the recently founded 'progressive' school, Dartington Hall, under its famous headmaster, Bill Curry. Elinor's appointment was as a teacher in the Junior School, but she was sceptical about the educational philosophy of the school, informed by the ideas of A.S. Neill, and never enjoyed classroom teaching. As soon as she could, she changed her job to that of housemother in one of the junior houses. This did not mean giving up her educational role, as there was no distinction between the care and teaching staff. As she later observed, 'the beginnings of psychological understanding were beginning to percolate through into education'.

Learning about art and politics

During the 1930s, as the Nazis were tightening their grip on Germany, Dartington became a refuge for artists, writers, musicians, theatrical performers and scientists from all over Europe – including Walter Gropius, the Bauhaus architect. Elinor took every advantage of the arrival of these eminent and gifted refugees to broaden her horizons and learn new skills. She was always proud of having learnt pottery from the world-famous potter, Bernard Leach. During the school holidays she travelled widely, partly to avoid having to go home, which had become a very sad place as a result of her stepmother's illness.

Apart from her instinctive belief in social justice, at that time Elinor was still quite naive about politics. She once told me how much she had enjoyed a six-week trip to

Germany where she spent three weeks in Konigsburg at an Arbeitslager (Nazi youth work camp), quite unaware of the political implications. She did, however, come into contact with Communists at Dartington and in 1934, encouraged by a friend she made there, went on a visit to Moscow, where she hated the food but very much enjoyed the circus and the Bolshoi Ballet. Unlike many British visitors, notably Beatrice and Sidney Webb, she was not impressed by Soviet Communism.

Her political education continued at the London School of Economics where she won a scholarship to the Psychiatric Social Work course in 1938, supplementing her grant by working as an au pair. If Dartington was a Mecca for artists, the LSE at that time was the centre of left-wing political activity as well as a leading institution for the study of psychology and social science. Elinor's teachers included many notable historians and sociologists – including Harold Laski, Karl Mannheim and Eileen Power – and it was there that she met her future husband, Guido Goldschmied, a law lecturer from Trieste in flight from the racist measures introduced by Mussolini.

War, marriage and motherhood

Her practice placements, in a probation service in the East End and with the (very uncharitable) Charitable Organisation Society, gave Elinor her first glimpse of real poverty. But soon afterwards war was declared, and the LSE was evacuated to Cambridge. There she came under the influence of Susan Isaacs and her Malting House nursery school, met John Bowlby, not then as well-known as he later became, and began to develop an interest in early childhood development.

The British authorities at the time were notoriously unable to distinguish between national and political affiliations and Guido, classified as an enemy alien, was deported to Canada, narrowly escaping German torpedoes on the sea voyage. Despite the danger (a high proportion of ships crossing the Atlantic were sunk), he opted to return to England as soon as he had the opportunity, and was recruited to make anti-Fascist propaganda broadcasts to occupied countries. Elinor was able to join him at weekends, and they were married at Kensington Registry Office on 7 November 1941.

After completing her course, Elinor worked for the Advisory Service of the Association for Mental Health. Her son, Marco, was born in May 1944, and when he was only a few months old she was asked to run a residential nursery for 'unbilletable' children in Pewsey, Wiltshire. This was a formative experience for Elinor and clearly, along with her later work in Italy, laid the foundation for the concept of the 'key person'.

Working with child refugees

The nursery in Pewsey provided reasonable physical care but little else. Elinor described the orphaned children, aged between two and four, as 'absolutely wild'. They ran about screaming all the time and were considered uncontrollable. However, the staff ratio was generous. Helped by advice from Anna Freud and Donald Winnicott, Elinor divided them up into groups of four or five in their own rooms with two members of staff and an ample supply of improvised playthings. By her account 'there was no more trouble'. It is noteworthy that one aspect of the regime was that each group was kept apart from the others, using different stairs and corridors in the large house where they were accommodated. The object of this was to prevent the adults from meeting and talking to each other instead of giving their attention to the children. Elinor considered this to be an ever-present danger in early years settings to which she later took a robust approach as an organiser.

Once the job was done, Elinor and Marco returned to London, where she helped to set up a cooperative nursery in Primrose Hill. What is less known is that she also played an important role in collating information for the Curtis Report (1946), the basis for the 1948 Children Act which finally ended unregulated boarding out and the care of children in bleak former workhouses.

The Italian experience

The end of the war led to another major shift in Elinor's life. Guido wanted to return to Trieste and they moved in with his grandfather in the historic family house. The grandfather was described by Elinor as 'a grand old Jewish patriarch', and thanks to her experience with her own father and grandfather, they got on well together despite her lack of Italian at the time. She particularly admired the fact that he had made his fortune by close attention to detail, a consistent theme in her work and writing. However, Guido's position, as an active Communist, became increasingly difficult under the American occupation, and in 1948 they had to move to Milan for him to find work. There, Elinor was recruited to run a playgroup for mothers and babies in the 'Villaggio' for Mother and Child, founded by a charismatic aristocrat, Elda Scarzella, who continued to be an important figure in Elinor's life for many years.

At the time there was no understanding of the importance of play and exploration for children. The youngest ones were either left to roll around in cots or playpens or carried about in nurses' arms. When the family went back to Trieste in 1951 Elinor was employed as an outreach worker from Milan in a state institution for illegitimate children without their mothers, and it was there, in 1954, that she made her first film 'At Least Let Me Play', showing the devastating effect on children of being deprived of stimulation and communication.

The great tragedy of Elinor's life was the premature death of her husband from a rapidly progressing form of cancer in the summer of 1955. Despite this terrible blow she continued to work and made two more films, with support from her sister, also widowed and living in Milan. It was at this time that she began to bring together her psychological training and practical experience to understand and develop the theory underpinning the Treasure Basket and heuristic play.

Returning to England

In 1959 when Marco was 15, Elinor decided to return to England, partly for his education but also because she felt there was no place for her as a woman and single mother in Italian society. With her qualification in social work from the LSE she was able to find work without difficulty, and after a period at the Jewish Board of Guardians Welfare Service and Hammersmith Hospital, she was appointed Inspector of Child Care for the London County Council, working across a variety of services. Her main focus was truancy and school phobia, on which her former colleague in Hammersmith, Lionel Hersov, was the leading authority. In that job she fought against the practice of taking children into care for failure to attend school, which did not improve attendance but often broke up families. That battle was not won until the Children Act 1989 finally did away with non-attendance as grounds for reception into care.

Developing ideas through teaching and consultancy

After the LCC was abolished in 1965, Elinor was transferred to the Inner London Education Authority (ILEA) with a very unclear brief and she virtually had to invent her own job. She continued to work for ILEA as a teacher and consultant until she officially retired. It was at this point that she decided to apply for a Post-qualifying Fellowship at the University of Bristol, under the supervision of Christopher Beedell. By this time she had already written her first book, *Il bambino nel asilo nido* (The young child in the nursery) with help from her Milan-based sister, Vivian, but it had not been translated. Her dissertation was on the Treasure Basket and its potential for use in day nurseries. My first encounter with the Basket was in the training session held in the University audio-visual suite, described in Chapter 5. At the same time, Elinor was working regularly for Hammersmith and Fulham Social Services and it was there that she developed the theory and practice of 'heuristic play with objects', along with Anita Hughes, with whom she later made a film to demonstrate the approach. Another important supporter was Gillian Pugh, then head of the Early Childhood Unit at the National Children's Bureau, where Elinor was a consultant. Peter Elfer and Dorothy Selleck at the NCB were already advocating for personalised care for young children – the key persons system – now incorporated in the Early Years Foundation Stage, but the idea had a long struggle to gain acceptance (Elfer *et al.* 2011).

For several years I invited Elinor annually to teach on the course I ran for managers of day nurseries, particularly those trying to reorganise themselves as family centres. I increasingly came to admire Elinor's style of teaching and her ideas about services for young children and practical ways of making nurseries work for children and staff. By that time she was already in her late seventies and there seemed a terrible risk that all those wonderful ideas and that amazing depth of knowledge would disappear without a record. She was at first apprehensive about writing but eventually, some time in 1990, we agreed to work together on the book which became *People Under Three*.

It was in writing the first edition of this book, discussing and arguing over almost every sentence and paragraph, that I came to know Elinor best. At that time she was still visiting Italy and Barcelona as a teacher and consultant three or four times a year and constantly having new ideas which she would want to incorporate into the chapters, including those I thought already finalised. The new thoughts were always too good to be rejected, but it did mean the book took a long time to come to fruition. We met almost every month when she was in England, either in Bristol or at her beautiful little house, designed by Marco, at the bottom of his garden in Putney, where we were often visited by the two youngest of her five grandchildren, Emma and Daniel. Emma is the baby who gazes solemnly out at the reader on the cover of the first edition of *People Under Three*.

Theory and practice

Politics were very important to Elinor. She sometimes joked that she was the last surviving member of the Communist Party of Great Britain, but she was never dogmatic about her beliefs. Equally, although she spent many years in analysis and psychotherapy and often found it helpful, she had little time for Freudian theory unless it was firmly rooted in real-world experience and a contextualised understanding of human beings and their relationships. Issues of theory and practice were a constant preoccupation for her, thrown into relief by her familiarity with Italian as well as British culture. She could see clearly the weaknesses in both.

Elinor refused to be impressed by fame and reputation. For some reason which I never discovered she always referred to John Bowlby as 'poor Bowlby'. She respected his research but considered that his ideas had been misappropriated and distorted for political reasons, in order to drive women back inside the home after the Second World War. I never heard her mention Montessori, although clearly she was influenced by the approach. I once attended a conference with her in Riccione, near Rimini, which was addressed by the famous psychologist, Loris Malaguzzi. Unlike many early years practitioners in the UK, who were bowled over by the early years service in Reggio Emilia, of which he was the architect, Elinor reserved judgement on the regime, and doubted if many of its features could be successfully translated to the very different environment of Britain or could endure here after the first flush of enthusiasm. However, she usually kept such views to herself, reluctant to dampen the energy of others. Her meeting with Susan Isaacs in Cambridge, on the other hand, played a major part in reigniting her interest in early childhood after her diversion into mental health.

In her later years Elinor had increasing health problems, which she bore stoically, and for a long time did not allow to restrict her activities. Well into her eighties she found it incredible that people would ask her 'Are you still working?' and wrote a memorable poem on the subject. She did not adapt very happily to a move to Battersea, where it was more difficult for friends and colleagues to visit her, and she found it very distressing when she began to feel that she was losing touch with the world of work. Until her last illness she continued to take a keen interest in current affairs, reading books and newspapers and listening to the radio. She had no patience with people, all too common in the early years field, who claimed to have no interest in politics. She understood very well that, however much practitioners want to give the children they work with the best possible experience, they have to operate within the framework set by politicians. That has become increasingly evident at the time of writing, with the enlightened early childhood policies of the 1997–2010 Labour government being thrown into reverse by the Coalition government that succeeded it.

The Elinor Goldschmied Archive project

In 2012 a group of people who had worked closely with Elinor over the years decided, with support from the Froebel Trust, to set up an archive to preserve and commemorate her achievements. This was inaugurated at a conference in October 2013, chaired by Tina Bruce, with contributions from Peter Elfer, Dorothy Selleck, Jacqui Cousins, Barbara Ongari and Sonia Jackson, and a memorable demonstration by Anita Hughes of 100 objects from her Treasure Basket. The DVD, *Discovered Treasure: The Life and Work of Elinor Goldschmied*, was launched on the same occasion. This draws extensively on the rich film material, most of it previously unseen, made by Elinor in Italy and England between 1950 and 1992, and includes an informative illustrated booklet. The final section, filmed at Eastwood Nursery Centre for Children and Families, shows how Elinor's ideas about play and learning continue to be equally relevant in contemporary settings and in particular how heuristic play with objects can be as exciting and stimulating for three- and four-year-olds as for the younger children for whom it was originally designed. The DVD is available for sale and can be viewed by arrangement at the Froebel Institute, Roehampton University (www.froebeltrust.org.uk, (0)20 8878 7546).

Sonia Jackson

Note

1 F883-891 EG interviewed by Rebecca Abrams and F10273-81, F17058 interviewed by Cathy Courtney. Summaries can be downloaded online at http://cadensa.bl.uk or the complete interviews accessed in the British Library.

Acknowledgements

This third edition of *People Under Three* is in many ways a different book from the two previous versions because the field of early childhood studies has changed so much over the past twenty years. However it does build on the first two editions and we want to record our grateful thanks to all those who contributed to them. Above all, of course, to Elinor Goldschmied, whose inspirational practice first gave me the idea of writing a book with her. Elinor and I were indebted to many different sources and people, among them Susan Isaacs, Donald Winnicott, Anna Freud, Jack Tizard and Brian Jackson, Leonard Davis, Kay Carmichael, Thelma Robinson, Katrine Stroh, Anita Hughes, Denise Hevey, Sue Dowling, Miriam David and Michael Duane.

We drew examples of good practice from settings where we worked or acted as consultants, in Britain and overseas. These included nurseries in 35 Italian cities, especially Milan, Arezzo, San Giovanni Valdarno and Cinisello Balsamo. Among others, Mima Noziglia, Mara Mattesini, Anna Mallardi, Luciana Nissim and Elda Scrazella in Italy, Ethel Roberts, Pat Coe and Linda Osborn in England and Irene McIntyre in Scotland, made it possible to try out on the ground ideas which often involved a considerable departure from accepted practice.

Another important source of new ideas, proved in action, was the development projects carried out over nearly ten years by students on the University of Bristol Inter-professional Diploma in Work with Young Children and Families. They showed what could be done with tiny resources, provided they were combined with conviction and enthusiasm. Special thanks are due to Peter Fanshawe, Chris Leaves, Marion Taylor, Sylvia McCollin, Phil Lyons, Judith Chinnery, Fiona Stuart and Val Bean and above all to Annette Holman, the co-leader of the course.

The second edition (2004) was planned at a seminar held in Elinor Goldschmied's apartment overlooking the Thames at Battersea. Surrounded by Treasure Baskets of wonderful abundance and variety, a small group of leading early years researchers revisited the book, chapter by chapter, to consider if it still had a contribution to make. The unanimous view of our advisers was that, although the early years scene had changed dramatically, the book still occupied a unique place in the sparse literature on day care for under-threes. In particular it combined a sound theoretical foundation with everyday practicality in a way attempted by few other texts.

We were especially grateful to those who made time in their extremely busy lives to attend the seminar and give us the benefit of their knowledge and experience: Naomi Eisenstadt, Gillian Pugh, Bernadette Duffy, Peter Elfer, Juliet Hopkins and Dorothy Selleck. We thank the nurseries and childcare centres that allowed us to visit and observe their work, in particular the Thomas Coram Early Childhood Centre.

Others who gave much appreciated help were Margaret Boushel, Wendy Clark, Elaine Farmer, Hayley Hughes, Sarah Long, Tricia Maynard, Peter Moss, Sue Owen, Julie Selwyn, Kay Sargent and Nigel Thomas.

Both previous editions owed a great deal to the unfailing support and encouragement of my late husband, Derek Greenwood, very much missed.

Sonia Jackson
January 2014

Suggestions for further reading

There are now an enormous number of books on early childhood education and care, addressed to parents, students, early years practitioners, policy makers and managers. This is just a small selection of those that the present authors have found particularly useful or inspiring.

Lesley Abbott and Cathy Nutbrown (eds) (2001) *Experiencing Reggio Emilia: Implications for Pre-School Provision*. Buckingham: Open University Press. The northern Italian city of Reggio Emilia is internationally renowned for its provision for young children. The contributors to this book give vivid accounts of its nurseries (*asili nidi*) and pre-schools and the impression they made on visitors from the UK, reinforced by the exhibition 'The Hundred Languages of Children'.

Peter Baldock, Damien Fitzgerald and Janet Kay (2013) *Understanding Early Years Policy* (3rd edn). London: Paul Chapman. What practitioners can offer young children is largely determined by the policy context within which they have to operate. This book brings the story up to the present, disentangling on the way the numerous influences that go to shape early childhood services at any one time. We found the timeline that illustrates this point especially helpful.

Carole Beatty (2011) *Integrated Children's Centres: Overcoming Barriers to Truly Integrated Services*. Abingdon: David Fulton. Children's Centres have been the most important development in ECEC in the past 60 years. Bringing together services with different cultures and histories remains a very challenging task. This book is hopeful but not unrealistic.

Tina Bruce (2011) *Learning Through Play for Babies, Toddlers and Young Children* (2nd edn). London: Hodder Education. Don't be misled by this book; with only 98 pages it might appear an 'easy read', but it has much to offer those studying at undergraduate and postgraduate levels as well as students at earlier stages in ECEC studies. Tina Bruce has a unique ability to translate theoretical principles into easily understood practice, and her assertion that 'play is the highest form of learning in early childhood' is brought to life with illustrative anecdotes and precisely chosen photographs. See also Tina Bruce (2011) *Cultivating Creativity in Babies, Toddlers and Young Children*. London: Hodder Education.

Tina Bruce and Jenny Spratt (2008) *Essentials of Literacy from 0–7*. London: Sage. This is one of the few books that explore literacy with the under-threes in depth, from a theoretical, developmental and historical perspective. It stresses the importance of lullabies, nursery rhymes, finger plays and action songs with babies and very young children as part of the canon of literature in the English language and the foundation for future literacy.

Louise Derman-Sparks and Julie Olsen Edwards (2010) *Anti-Bias Education for Young Children and Ourselves*. Washington DC: National Association for the Education of Young Children. A book about anti-discriminatory practice which combines a clear, jargon-free explanation of the theory with guidelines and suggestions for activities and materials. Unusually, it gives as much attention to disability as to race, colour and gender. It includes some good suggestions about informing parents and involving them in the work. The illustrations and examples are American, but easily transferable to a UK early years setting.

Chandira Devarakonda (2013) *Diversity and Inclusion in Early Childhood: An Introduction*. London: Sage. A wonderfully informative and readable text which gives full attention to the under-threes rather than concentrating on the 3–5 age group. It has a particularly strong chapter on Gypsy, Roma and traveller children.

Bernadette Duffy (1998) *Supporting Creativity and Imagination in the Early Years*. Buckingham: Open University Press. An admirable guide to providing a rich educational environment for young children, with numerous illustrations and anecdotes from the author's experience as Head of the Thomas Coram Early Childhood Centre.

Peter Elfer, Elinor Goldschmied and Dorothy Selleck (2011) *Key Persons in the Early Years: Building Relationships for Quality Provision in Early Years Settings and Primary Schools* (2nd edn). Abingdon: David Fulton. The most comprehensive and authoritative account of the key person approach. Elfer and Selleck worked closely with Elinor Goldschmied.

Shanta Everington (2010) *The Terrible Twos: A Parent's Guide*. London: Need2Know. Although we don't like the title, this is a good book to recommend to parents: easy reading with a sound scientific basis. It recognises that 2–3 can be a difficult stage, when children often assert their independence through defiant, oppositional behaviour. Everington helpfully suggests making a list of ten positive things about life with a two-year-old.

Sue Gerhardt (2004) *Why Love Matters: How Affection Shapes a Baby's Brain*. London: Routledge. A book for parents and practitioners. We now know that relationships are crucial to brain development – this book explains why, and the serious consequences when babies and young children are not able to form secure and trusting attachments to parents and caregivers.

Trisha Maynard and Sacha Powell (eds) (2014) *An Introduction to Early Childhood Studies* (3rd edn). London: Sage. This book is aimed at students on Early Childhood degree courses but will also be useful to update early years practitioners on the latest research and thinking on child development and pre-school policy and services, set in a global context.

Peter Moss and Helen Penn (1996) *Transforming Nursery Education*. London: Paul Chapman. Published before the 1997 watershed, this book provides a useful account of the range of early years services at the time and why there was such an urgent need for reform. Its critique of the standard model of nursery education is probably equally valid today and is counterbalanced by examples of innovative and imaginative practice. The discussion of early years policy is set in a wider social and political context, also drawing on the experience of other European countries.

Janet Moyles (2010) *The Excellence of Play* (3rd edn). Maidenhead: Open University Press. There has never been a time when play has been more in need of defenders and advocates. This book, with a splendidly combative introduction by Wendy Scott, includes chapters by most of the leading UK early years experts. It makes an unanswerable case for the value of free explorative play against the too early introduction of formal learning.

Lynne Murray and Liz Andrews (2000) *The Social Baby: Understanding Babies' Communications from Birth*. Richmond, Surrey: CP Publishing. This lovely book illustrates with sequences of photographs and commentary how even the youngest babies interact with their close adults and can make their feelings known to those who are responsive to their movements and facial expressions. Indispensable for baby room practitioners. See also Clive and Helen Dorman (2002) *The Social Toddler: Promoting Positive Behaviour*. Richmond: CP Publishing.

Linda Pound and Chris Harrison (2003) *Supporting Musical Development in the Early Years*. Buckingham: Open University Press. The authors assert that all children are musical and that music is an integral part of the social development of babies and young children. They give many suggestions for music-related activities for those in the 0–3 age group.

Gillian Pugh and Bernadette Duffy (eds) (2013) *Contemporary Issues in the Early Years: Working Collaboratively for Children* (6th edn). London: Paul Chapman. Gillian Pugh was Chief Executive of England's oldest childcare charity, now called Coram Family. This book, in successive editions, has become a classic of early childhood literature. The introductory chapter provides an excellent overview of current policy and services in the UK.

Jillian Rodd (2006) *Leadership in Early Childhood* (3rd edn). Maidenhead: Open University Press. An essential text for leaders and managers in early years settings.

Veronica Sherborne (1990) *Developmental Movement for Children: Mainstream, Special Needs and Pre-School*. Cambridge: Cambridge University Press. Indispensable for anyone wanting to understand the theory of relationship play. It gives detailed instructions for a planned programme of activities, illustrated with many expressive photographs.

Margot Sunderland (2007) *What Every Parent Needs to Know: The Remarkable Effects of Love, Nurture and Play on Your Child's Development*. London: Dorling Kindersley. First published as *The Science of Parenting*, this book is rooted in the importance of attachment and how love and adult behaviour can affect every element of a baby's development. Although addressed to parents, it is equally relevant to early years practitioners.

Kathy Sylva *et al.* (2010) *Early Childhood Matters: Evidence from the Effective Pre-School and Primary Education Project*. Abingdon: Routledge. The Effective Pre-School and Primary Education (EPPE) project is the largest European study of the impact of early years education and care on children's developmental outcomes. It provides clear evidence of how home learning environments interact with pre-school and primary school experiences to shape children's progress, especially those from disadvantaged backgrounds, and provided the scientific basis for the Labour government's early childhood strategy and Children's Centre programme.

Lin Trodd and Leo Chivers (eds) (2011) *Inter-Professional Working in Practice: Learning and Working Together for Children and Families*. Maidenhead: Open University Press. Inter-professional working has been accepted as desirable for many years: making it work in practice is much more difficult. This book provides helpful guidance from experienced practitioners on how to achieve integrated services in a variety of different settings.

Margy Whalley and the Pen Green Centre Team (2007) *Involving Parents in Their Children's Learning*. London: Paul Chapman. Pen Green, in the former steel town of Corby, led the way in numerous aspects of ECEC, and remains a centre of excellence and inspiration for early years practitioners everywhere. All the ideas in this book are rooted in everyday practice but with a firm theoretical basis.

Jan White (ed.) (2011) *Outdoor Provision in the Early Years*. London: Sage. Lots of ideas, both for new and experienced practitioners, on how to create an outdoor learning environment which provides interest and excitement while also managing risk and ensuring safety. Also by Jan White (2012), one of Ruth's favourites, *Making a Mud Kitchen*. Sheffield: University of Sheffield. The photographs in this alone make you want to get out with the children from your setting and begin creating your own outdoor kitchen.

References

Abbott, L. (2001) 'Perceptions of play – a question of priorities?', pp. 8–20 in L. Abbott and C. Nutbrown (eds) *Experiencing Reggio Emilia*. Buckingham: Open University Press.

Abbott, L. and Langston, A. (2004) *Birth to Three Matters*. Buckingham: Open University Press.

Abbott, L. and Langston, A. (eds) (2006) *Parents Matter: Supporting the Birth to Three Matters Framework*. Maidenhead: Open University Press.

Abbott, L. and Moylett, J. (eds) (1997) *Working with the Under-3s: Responding to Children's Needs*. Buckingham: Open University Press.

Abrams, R. (1997) *The Playful Self: Why Women Need Play in Their Lives*. London: Fourth Estate.

Abrams, R. (2001) *Three Shoes, One Sock and No Hairbrush: Everything You Need to Know About Having Your Second Child*. London: Cassell.

Allen, G. (2011) *Early Intervention: The Next Steps*. London: Department for Work and Pensions.

Andrews, M. and Fowler, K. (2010) 'A healthy child – direction, deficit or diversity?' pp. 83–95 in M. Reed and N. Canning (eds) *Reflective Practice in the Early Years*. London: Sage.

Andrews, K. and Jacobs, J. (1990) *Punishing the Poor: Poverty under Thatcher*. London: Macmillan.

Arnold, L.E. (1980) *Childhood Stress*. New York: Wiley.

Athey, C. (1990) *Extending Thought in Young Children: A Parent Teacher Partnership*. London: Paul Chapman.

BAECE/Early Education (2012) *Development Matters in the Early Years Foundation Stage*. London: DfE.

Bain, A. and Barnett, L. (1980) *The Design of a Day Care System in a Nursery Setting for Children under Five*. London: Tavistock Institute of Human Relations.

Baldock, P., Fitzgerald, D. and Kay, J. (2013) *Understanding Early Years Policy* (3rd edn). London: Paul Chapman.

Beaty, C. (2011) *Integrated Children's Centres: Overcoming Barriers to Truly Integrated Services*. Abingdon: David Fulton.

Beckett, C. (2003) *Child Protection: An Introduction*. London: Sage.

Belsky, J., Vandell, D., Burchinall, M., Clarke Stewart, A., McCartney, K. and Owen, M. (2007) Are there long-term effects of early child care? *Child Development* 78(2): 681–701.

Bercow, J. (2008) *The Bercow Report: A Review of Services for Children and Young People (0–19) with Speech, Language and Communication Needs.* Nottingham: Department for Children, Schools and Families

Bertram, T. and Pascal, C. (2010) 'Introducing child development', pp. 71–86 in T. Bruce (ed.) *Early Childhood: A Guide for Students (2nd edn).* London: Sage.

Bishop, J. (2001) 'Creating places for living and learning', pp. 72–9 in L. Abbott and C. Nutbrown (eds) *Experiencing Reggio Emilia: Implications for Pre-School Provision.* Buckingham: Open University Press.

Blyth, M. and Solomon, E. (2012) *Effective Safeguarding for Children and Young People.* Bristol: Policy Press.

Booth, T., Ainscow, M. and Kingston, D. (2006) *Index for Inclusion: Developing Play, Learning and Participation in Early Years and Childcare.* Bristol: Centre for Studies in Inclusive Education.

Bowlby, J. (1953) *Child Care and the Growth of Love.* London: Penguin.

Briggs, F. (2011) *Smart Parenting for Safer Kids.* Melbourne: JoJo Publishing.

Briggs, F. and Hawkins, R. (1997) *Child Protection: A Guide for Teachers and Child Care Professionals.* Sydney: Allen & Unwin.

Bromley, H. (2010) *Speaking and Listening Outdoors: The Sky is the Limit: Outdoor Learning in the Early Years.* London: Early Education.

Bronson, M. (2000) *Self-regulation in Early Childhood: Nature and Nurture.* New York: Guilford Press.

Brooker, L. (2002) *Starting School: Young Children Learning Cultures.* Buckingham: Open University Press.

Brookson, M. (1999) 'A talk about an educational visit to Reggio Emilia, Italy'. Pen Green MA Programme. Unpublished paper.

Brown, A. (1992) *Groupwork.* Aldershot: Ashgate.

Bruce, T. (1991) *Time to Play in Early Childhood Education.* London: Hodder & Stoughton.

Bruce, T. (2004) *Cultivating Creativity in Babies, Toddlers and Young Children.* London: Hodder & Stoughton.

Bruce, T. (ed.) (2010) *Early Childhood: A Guide for Students.* London: Sage.

Bruce, T. (2011) *Learning Through Play for Babies, Toddlers and Young Children.* 2nd edn. London: Hodder Education.

Bruce, T. and Spratt, J. (2008) *Essentials of Literacy from 0–7.* London: Sage.

Bruner, J. (1977) 'Early social interaction and language acquisition' in H.R. Schaffer (ed.) *Studies of Mother-Infant Interaction.* London: Academic Press.

Buchanan, A. (1986) *Cycles of Child Maltreatment: Facts, Fallacies and Interventions.* Chichester: Wiley.

Cairns, K. (no date) *Five to Thrive: The Things You Do Every Day that Help Your Toddler's Growing Brain.* Dursley: Kate Cairns Associates.

Carruthers, E. (2007) 'Children's outdoor experiences' in J. Moyles (ed.) *Early Years Foundations Meeting the Challenge.* Maidenhead: Open University Press.

Carter, R. (1999) *Mapping the Mind.* London: Seven Dials.

Cattanach, A. (1992) *Play Therapy with Abused Children.* London and Philadelphia: Jessica Kingsley.

Central Advisory Council for England (CAC) (1967) *Children and Their Primary Schools* [The Plowden Report]. London: Stationery Office.

Citizens Commission on Human Rights UK (2012) *Dangers and Consequences of the Misdiagnosis and Prescription of Addictive Drugs to Children for Attention Deficit Hyperactivity Disorder* (White Paper). East Grinstead: CCHR UK.

Clark, A. (2001) *Why and How We Listen to Young Children: Young Children's Voices* (Network First Series). London: National Children's Bureau.

Clark, A. and Moss, P. (2001) *Listening to Young Children: The Mosaic Approach*. London: National Children's Bureau.

Colton, M., Sanders, R. and Williams, M. (2001) *An Introduction to Working with Children: A Guide for Social Workers*. Basingstoke: Palgrave.

Community Playthings (2012) *What Happens in a Baby Room? Supporting Under-2s Practitioners*. Robertsbridge, UK: Community Playthings.

Community Playthings (2013) *A Good Place to be Two: Developing Quality Environments Indoors and Out*. Robertsbridge, UK: Community Playthings.

Coombe, A. (2011) 'Parental mental health, risk and child protection: what does Munro mean to child protection and adult mental health?' pp. 69–90 in M. Blyth and E. Solomon (eds) *Effective Safeguarding for Children and Young People*. Bristol: Policy Press.

Corby, B. (1987) *Working with Child Abuse: Social Work Practice and the Child Abuse System*. Milton Keynes: Open University Press.

Craft, A., McConnon, L. and Matthews, A. (2011) Child-initiated play and professional creativity: enabling four year old possibility thinking. *Journal of Thinking Skills and Creativity* 7: 48–61.

Crawley, H. (2006) *Eating Well for Under-Fives in Childcare*. London: Caroline Walker Trust.

Cuthbert, C., Rayns, G. and Stanley, K. (2011) *All Babies Count: Prevention and Protection for Vulnerable Babies: A Review of the Evidence*. London: NSPCC.

Dale, P., Davis, M., Morrison, T. and Waters, S. (1986) *Dangerous Families: Assessment and Treatment of Child Abuse*. London: Tavistock.

Davies, C. and Ward, H. (2012) *Safeguarding Children across Services: Messages from Research*. London and Philadelphia: Jessica Kingsley.

Daycare Trust (2003) *A Know How Guide: The EYFS Progress Check at Age 2* (www.education.gov.uk/publications/standard/publicationDetail/Page1/NCB–00087–2012, accessed 09.03.13).

Daycare Trust (2013) *Childcare Costs Survey 2013*. London: Daycare Trust/Family and Parenting Institute.

Department for Children, Schools and Families (2008) *The Early Years Foundation Stage: Setting the Standards for Learning*. Revised edn. Nottingham: DCSF Publications.

Department for Children, Schools and Families (2009) *Every Child a Talker: Guidance for Consultants and Early Language Lead Practitioners*. Nottingham: DCSF Publications.

Department for Education and Skills (2002) *Birth to Three Matters: A Framework to Support Children in Their Earliest Years*. London: DfES/Sure Start.

Department for Education (2010) *Childcare and Early Years Survey of Parents*. London: DfE.

Department for Education (2011a) *Childcare and Early Years Providers Survey*. London: DfE.

Department for Education (2011b) *Evaluation of the Graduate Leader Fund – Final Report* (www.education.gov.uk/publications/standard/publicationDetail/Page1/DFE–RR144, accessed 01.03.13).

Department for Education (2012a) *Longitudinal Study of Early Years Professional Status: An Exploration of Progress, Leadership and Impact – Final Report* (www.education.gov.uk/publications/standard/publicationDetail/Page1/DFE–RR239C, accessed 01.03.13).

Department for Education (2012b) *Statutory Framework for the Early Years Foundation Stage: Setting the Standards for Learning, Development and Care for Children from Birth to Five*. DfE: Cheshire (www.education.gov.uk/publications/eOrderingDownload/EYFS%20Statutory%20Framework%20March%202012.pdf, accessed October 2012).

Department for Education (2013) *Working Together to Safeguard Children*. London: DfE.

Department of Health (2011) *Healthy Lives, Healthy People: A Call to Action on Obesity in England*. London: DoH.

Department of Health and Department for Children, Schools and Families (2009) *Healthy Child Programme and the First 5 Years of Life*. London: DoH/DCSF.

Derman-Sparks, L. and Edwards, J.O. (2010) *Anti-Bias Education for Young Children and Ourselves*. Washington DC: National Association for the Education of Young Children.

Devarakonda, C. (2013) *Diversity and Inclusion in Early Childhood*. London: Sage.

DHSS (1974) *Report of the Committee of Inquiry into the Care and Supervision Provided in Relation to Maria Colwell*. London: HMSO.

Dorman, H. and Dorman, C. (2002) *The Social Toddler: Promoting Positive Behaviour*. Richmond: CP Publishing.

Douglas, J. (2002) *Toddler Troubles: Coping with Your Under-5s*. Chichester: Wiley.

Duffy, B. (2010) 'Art in the early years' in J. Moyles (ed.) *The Excellence of Play* (3rd edn). Maidenhead: Open University Press.

Duffy, B. and Marshall, J. (2007) 'Leadership in multi-agency work', in I. Siraj-Blatchford, K. Clarke and M. Needham (eds) *The Team Around the Child: Multi-Agency Working in the Early Years*. Stoke-on-Trent: Trentham Books.

Dunn, J. (1984) *Sisters and Brothers*. London: Fontana.

Early Education (BAECE) (2012) *Development Matters in the Early Years Foundation Stage*. London: Early Education.

Eisenstadt, N. (2011) *Providing a Sure Start: How Government Discovered Early Childhood*. Bristol: Policy Press.

Eisenstadt, N. (2012) 'Providing a Sure Start: Systematizing Early Years in England', paper presented at the March 2012 meeting of the Centre for Social Policy, Dartington Hall, Totnes.

Elfer, P., Goldschmied, E. and Selleck, D. (2003) *Key Persons in the Nursery: Building Relationships for Quality Provision*. London: David Fulton.

Elfer, P., Goldschmied, E. and Selleck, D. (2012) *Key Persons in the Early Years: Building Relationships for Quality Provision in Early Years Settings and Primary Schools*. Abingdon: David Fulton.

Erikson, E. (1955) *Childhood and Society*. Harmondsworth: Penguin.

Everington, S. (2010) *The Terrible Twos: A Parent's Guide*. Peterborough: Need2Know.

European Commission (2012) *Social Inclusion of Youth on the Margins of Society: Review of Research Results*. Brussels: European Commission.

Fawcett, M. (2009) *Learning through Child Observation*. London: Jessica Kingsley.

Fawcett, M. (2012) Innate musicality and very young children: indicators for practice from research. Unpublished paper.

Forbes, R. (2004) *Beginning to Play: Young Children from Birth to Three*. Maidenhead: Open University Press.

Froebel Trust (2013) *Discovered Treasure: The Life and Work of Elinor Goldschmied 1910–2009*. DVD produced and edited by Dorothy Selleck, Anita Hughes and Jacqui Cousins. Roehampton: Froebel Institute.

Frosh, A., Phoenix, A. and Pattman, R. (2001) *Young Masculinities*. Basingstoke: Palgrave.

Fullan, M. (2005) *Leadership and Sustainability: System Thinkers in Action*. Newbury Park, CA: Corwin Press.

Garvey, D. and Lancaster, A. (2010) *Leadership for Quality in Early Years and Playwork: Supporting Your Team to Achieve Better Outcomes for Children and Families*. London: National Children's Bureau.

Ghate, D. and Hazel, N. (2002) *Parenting in Poor Environments: Stress, Support and Coping*. London and Philadelphia: Jessica Kingsley.

Gilbert, N., Parton, N. and Scrivenes, M. (eds) (2011) *Child Protection Systems: International Trends and Orientations*. Oxford: Oxford University Press.

Gilkes, J. (1988) Coming to terms with sexual abuse: a day care perspective. *Children and Society* 3: 261–9.

Gill, O. (1992) *Parenting Under Pressure*. Cardiff: Barnardo's South Wales and South-West.

Goddard Blythe, S. (2009) *Attention, Balance and Co-ordination: The A.B.C. of Learning Success*. Chichester: Wiley-Blackwell.

Goldschmied, E. (1974) 'Creative play with babies' in S. Jennings (ed.) *Creative Therapy*. London: Benbow Press.

Goldschmied, E. (1987, video) *Babies at Work*. London: National Children's Bureau.

Goldschmied, E. and Hughes, A. (1992) *Heuristic Play with Objects. Children of 12–20 Months Exploring Everyday Objects*. VHS Video. London: National Children's Bureau.

Goldschmied, E. and Jackson, S. (1994) *People Under Three: Young Children in Day Care* (1st edn). London: Routledge.

Goldschmied, E. and Jackson, S. (2004) *People Under Three: Young Children in Day Care* (2nd edn). London: Routledge.

Goldschmied, E. and Selleck, D. (1996) *Communication Between Babies in Their First Year*. London: National Children's Bureau.

Goleman, D. (1996) *Emotional Intelligence*. London: Bloomsbury.

Gopnik, A., Meltzoff, A. and Kuhl, P. (1999) *How Babies Think: The Science of Childhood*. London: Weidenfeld & Nicolson.

Green, C. (2012) 'Early intervention', pp. 9–23 in M. Blyth and E. Solomon (eds) *Effective Safeguarding for Children and Young People*. Bristol: Policy Press.

Greenland, P. (2010) 'Physical development' in T. Bruce, *Early Childhood: A Guide for Students* (2nd edn). London: Sage.

Greenman, J. and Stonehouse, A. (1997) *Prime Times: A Handbook for Excellence in Infant and Toddler Programs*. Melbourne: Longman.

Hallden, G. (1991) The child as project and the child as being: parents' ideas as frames of reference. *Children and Society*, 5(4): 334–46.

Heap, K. (1985) *The Practice of Social Work with Groups*. London: Allen & Unwin.

hello (2011) *Universally Speaking: The Ages and Stages of Children's Communication Development from Birth to 5*. London: The Communication Trust/Department for Education.

Holland, R. (1997) 'What's it all about? How introducing heuristic play has affected provision for the under-threes in one day nursery', pp. 116–29 in L. Abbott and H. Moylett (eds) *Working with the Under-3s: Responding to Children's Needs*. Buckingham: Open University Press.

Holman, B. (2013) *Champions for Children: The Lives of Modern Child Care Pioneers*. Bristol: Policy Press.

Holmes, E. (1977) The educational needs of children in care. *Concern*, 26: 22–5.

Holmes, E. (2008) If you go down to the woods today. *Early Years Children and Families*, 2008/9: 6–8.

Hopkins, J. (1998) Facilitating the development of intimacy between nurses and infants in day nurseries. *Early Childhood Development and Care*, 33: 99–111.

House of Commons Education Committee (2013) Foundation Years: Sure Start Children's Centres. Fifth report of session 2013–14 Vols I and II. London: Stationery Office.

Hutt, C. (1979) *Play in the Under-Fives: Form, Development and Function*. New York: Brunner/Mazel.

ICAN (2011) *Understanding Communication Development: Working with the Under 5s*. London: ICAN.

Ipsos MORI (2013) *Childcare and Early Years Survey of Parents 2011*. London: Ipsos MORI.

Jackson, B. (1987) *Fatherhood*. London: Allen & Unwin.

Jackson, B. and Jackson, S. (1979) *Childminder: A Study in Action Research*. London: Routledge & Kegan Paul.

Jackson, S. (1993) 'Under Fives: Thirty years of no progress?' pp. 93–114 in G. Pugh (ed.) *30 Years of Change for Children*. London: National Children's Bureau.

Jackson, S. (2014) 'Early Childhood Policy and Services', pp. 145–58 in T. Maynard and S. Powell (eds) *An Introduction to Early Childhood Studies* (3rd edn). London: Sage.

Jackson, S. and Cameron, C. (2014) *Improving Access to Further and Higher Education for Young People in Care: European Policy and Practice*. London and Philadelphia: Jessica Kingsley.

Jackson, S. and Fawcett, M. (2009) 'Early Childhood Policy and Services' in T. Maynard and N. Thomas (eds) *An Introduction to Early Childhood Studies* (2nd edn). London: Sage.

Jannsens, J. and Kemper, A. (1996) Effects of video home training on parental communication and a child's behavioural problems. *International Journal of Child and Family Welfare* 96(2): 137–48.

Jarman, E. (2009) *Communication Friendly Spaces*. Dorchester: Training for Dorset Early Years Practitioners and Children's Centre Staff.

Jenkins, J. and Milla, P. (1988) 'Feeding problems and failure to thrive', in N. Richman and R. Lansdown (eds) *Problems of Preschool Children*. Chichester: Wiley.

KCH electronic source (2012) 'Babies and tummy time information for parents and carers' (www.kch.nhs.uk/Doc/PL%20–%20469.2%20–%20Babies%20and%20Tummy%20Time.pdf, accessed Nov 2012).

Keohane, N. (2014) Free childcare funding challenge. *Children and Young People Now*, 21 January–3 February.

Krog, D. (2010) Encouraging more outdoor physical activity in Bodo. *Children in Europe*, 19: 6–7.

Laevers, F. (1994) *The Leuven Involvement Scale for Young Children*. Leuven: Centre for Experiential Education.

Laevers, F., Vandenbussche, E., Kog, M. and Depondt, L. (1997) *A Process Orientated Child Monitoring System for Young Children* (Experiential Education Series No. 2). Leuven: Centre for Experiential Education.

Laming, H. (2003) *The Victoria Climbié Inquiry: Report of an Inquiry by Lord Laming*. London: Stationery Office.

Laming, H. (2009) *The Protection of Children in England: A Progress Report*. London: Stationery Office.

Lancaster, Y.P. (ed.) (2003) *Listening to Young Children: Promoting Listening to Young Children: The Reader*. Maidenhead: Open University Press.

Lancaster, Y.P. (2006) 'Listening to Young Children: Respecting the Voice of the Child', in G. Pugh and B. Duffy (eds) *Contemporary Issues in the Early Years* (4th edn). London: Sage.

Lancaster, Y.P. and Broadbent, V. (2003) *Listening to Young Children*. Maidenhead: Open University Press.

Land, H. (2002) *Meeting the Child Poverty Challenge: Why Universal Childcare is Key to Ending Child Poverty*. London: The Daycare Trust.

Lansdown, G. and Lancaster, Y.P. (2001) 'Promoting Children's Welfare by Respecting Their Rights' in G. Pugh (ed.) *Contemporary Issues in the Early Years: Working Collaboratively for Children* (3rd edn). London: Paul Chapman.

Lansdown, G. and Lancaster, Y.P. (2003) *Listening to Young Children*. Maidenhead: Open University Press.

Leach, P. (1999) *The Physical Punishment of Children*. London: NSPCC.

Learning through Landscapes (2007) *Process of Change for New Spaces*, www.ltl.org.uk.

London Borough of Brent (1985) *A Child in Trust: The Report of the Panel of Inquiry into the Circumstances Surrounding the Death of Jasmine Beckford.* London: London Borough of Brent.

McCall, R.M. and Craft, D.H. (2000) *Moving with a Purpose: Developing Programs for Preschoolers of All Abilities.* Bowling Green, OH: Human Kinetics.

McDaniel, B. and Dillenburger, K. (2014) *Child Neglect and Behavioural Parent Education: Research and Practice.* Lyme Regis, Dorset: Russell House Publishing.

McGuire, J. and Richman, N. (1986) The prevalence of behavioural problems in three types of preschool group. *Journal of Child Psychology and Psychiatry* 27: 455–72.

McMahon, L. (2009) *The Handbook of Play Therapy and Therapeutic Play.* New York: Routledge.

McWhirter, J. (2007) *Forest Schools and Practical Risk Education* (www.rospa.com/school andcollegesafety/casestudies/forest–schools.aspx, accessed 12.03.13).

Malaguzzi, L. (2004) *Introduction to the 'Hundred Languages of Children'.* UK Exhibition. ReFocus Sightlines Initiative.

Malloch, S. and Trevarthen, C. (eds) (2009) *Communicative Musicality: Exploring the Basis of Human Companionship.* Oxford: Oxford University Press.

Manning-Morton, J. (2006) The personal is professional: professionalism and the birth to threes practitioner. *Contemporary Issues in Early Childhood,* 7(1): 42–52.

Manning-Morton, J. and Thorp, M. (2001) *Key Times: A Framework for Developing High Quality Provision for Children Under Three Years Old.* Camden, London: Camden Early Years Children's Development Partnership/University of North London.

Manning-Morton, J. and Thorp, M. (2003) *Key Times for Play: The First Three Years.* Maidenhead: Open University Press.

Marmot, M. (2010) *Fair Society, Healthy Lives: A Strategic Review of Health Inequalities in England Post-2010.* London: University College of London.

Marshall, J. (1994) 'Revisiting Organizations by Developing Female Values', in R. Boot, J. Lawrence and J. Morris (eds) *Managing the Unknown by Creating New Futures.* London: McGraw-Hill.

Marshall, T. (1982) Infant care: a day nursery under the microscope. *Social Work Service,* 32: 15–32.

Mathews, J. (2003) *Helping Children Draw and Paint in Early Childhood: Children and Visual Representation.* London: Paul Chapman Publishing.

Mayall, B. (1986) *Keeping Children Healthy: The Role of Mothers and Professionals.* London: Allen & Unwin.

Melhuish, E. and Moss, P. (eds) (1991) *Day Care for Young Children: International Perspectives.* London: Routledge.

Miller, L. and Cameron, C. (2014) *International Perspectives in the Early Years.* London: Sage.

Moog, H. (1976) *The Musical Experiences of Preschool Children.* London: Schott Music.

Morton, K. (2011) Parents Want Men in Nurseries but Male School Leavers "Not Interested" in Childcare. *Nursery World* (www.nurseryworld.co.uk/news/1081860/Parents-want-men-nurseries-male-school-leavers-not-interested-childcare, accessed 1.03.13).

Morton, K. (2012) Nursery Group Chief Exec Warns Child Abuse Cases are Deterring Men from Childcare. *Nursery World* (www.nurseryworld.co.uk/news/1160505/Nursery-group-chief-exec-warns-child-abuse-cases-deterring-men-childcare, accessed 08.03.13).

Morton, K. (2013) Childminder Launches Focus Group over Agency Plans. *Nursery World* (www.nursery world.co.uk/news/1170482, accessed 19.03.13).

Moyles, J. (2006) *Effective Leadership and Management in the Early Years.* Maidenhead: Open University Press.

Moyles, J. (ed.) (2007) *Early Years Foundations: Meeting the Challenges.* Maidenhead: Open University Press.

Moyles, J. (ed.) (2010) *The Excellence of Play* (3rd edn). Maidenhead: Open University Press.

Moylett, H. (2013) *Learning and Teaching in the Early Years: Active Learning*. London: Practical Pre-School Books/MA Education.

Munro, E. (2011) *The Munro Review of Child Protection*. London: Department for Education.

Murray, L. and Andrews, A. (2000) *The Social Baby*. Richmond, Surrey: CP Publishing.

National Audit Office (2012) *An Update on the Government's Approach to Tackling Obesity*. London: NAO/DoH.

National Literacy Trust (2010) Adult-child conversations and their importance to language development (www.literacytrust.org.uk/talk_to_your_baby/policy_research/2333, accessed 17.05.13).

Newson, J. and Newson, E. (1963) *Patterns of Infant Care in an Urban Community*. London: Allen & Unwin.

NSPCC/Cardiff University (2010) *Emotional Neglect and Emotional Abuse in Pre-School Children*. Cardiff: Core Information (www.core-info@cardiff.ac.uk).

Nursery World (2011) (www.nurseryworld.co.uk/news/1086620/Men-childcare-Group-fight-sexist-discrimination, accessed 08.03.13).

Nutbrown, C. (2012a) *Review of Early Education and Childcare Qualifications: Interim Report*. London: DfE.

Nutbrown, C. (2012b) *Foundations for Quality: The Independent Review of Early Education and Childcare Qualifications* (Final Report). London: DfE.

Nutbrown, C. (2013) *Shaking the Foundations of Quality? Why 'Childcare' Policy Must Not Lead to Poor Quality Early Education and Care*. Sheffield: University of Sheffield.

Nutbrown, C. and Abbott, L. (2001) 'Experiencing Reggio Emilia', pp. 1–7 in L. Abbott and C. Nutbrown (eds) *Experiencing Reggio Emilia: Implications for Pre-School Provision*. Buckingham: Open University Press.

Nutbrown, C. and Clough, P. with Atherton, F. (2013) *Inclusion in the Early Years*. London: Sage.

Nutbrown, C. and Page, J. (2008) *Working with Babies and Children from Birth to Three*. London: Sage.

Nutbrown, C., Clough, P. and Selbie, P. (2012) *Early Childhood Education: History, Philosophy and Experience*. London: Sage.

O'Connor, A. and Daly, A. (2009) Learning and Development: Physical Development: Part 2 Tummy Time, *Nursery World*, 15 April.

OECD (2010) *The High Cost of Low Educational Performance: The Long-Run Economic Impact of Improving PISA Outcomes*. Paris: Organization for Economic Co-operation and Development.

Ofsted (2012) *Evaluation Schedule for Inspections of Registered Early Years Provision*. Manchester: Office for Standards in Education.

Opie, P. and Opie, I. (1997) *The Oxford Book of Nursery Rhymes*. Oxford: Oxford University Press.

Ouvry, M. (2000) *Exercising Muscles and Minds*. London: National Early Years Network.

Owen, C. (2003) 'Men in the Nursery', pp. 99–113 in J. Brannen and P. Moss (eds) *Rethinking Children's Care*. Buckingham: Open University Press.

Pagani, L.S., Fitzpatrick, C, Barnett, T.A. and Dubow, E. (2010) Prospective associations between early childhood television exposure and academic, psychosocial, and physical well-being by middle childhood. *Archives of Pediatrics and Adolescent Medicine* 164(5): 425.

Palmer, S. (2006) *Toxic Childhood: How the Modern World is Damaging Our Children and What We Can Do About It*. London: Orion.

Parker, R., Ward, H., Jackson, S., Aldgate, J. and Wedge, P. (eds) (1991) *Looking after Children: Assessing Outcomes in Childcare*. London: HMSO.

Parton, N. and Berridge, D. (2011) 'Child Protection in England', pp. 60–88 in N. Gilbert, N. Parton and M. Skivenes (eds) *Child Protection Systems: International Trends and Orientations*. Oxford: Oxford University Press.

PEAL (2006) *Parents, Early Years and Learning Resource Pack*. London: National Children's Bureau.

Pereira-Gray, D. (2013) 'It's the Relationships Stupid!', 3rd Goodman Lecture, Royal Overseas League, London, 14 March, www.whataboutthechildren.org.uk.

Platt, D. (2014) 'Child Welfare and Protection', pp. 185–96 in T. Maynard and S. Powell (eds) *An Introduction to Early Childhood Studies* (3rd edn). London: Sage.

Plymouth Local Safeguarding Children Board (2010) *Serious Case Review of Little Ted's Nursery*. Plymouth: Plymouth City Council.

Pound, L. (2010) 'Playing music' in J. Moyles (ed.) *The Excellence of Play* (3rd edn). Maidenhead: Open University Press.

Pound, L. and Harrison, C. (2003) *Supporting Musical Development in the Early Years*. Buckingham: Open University Press.

Powell, A. (2001) 'Orchestral Manoeuvres in the Park', *Guardian Weekend*. London: Guardian.

Powell, J. and Uppal, E.L. (2012) *Safeguarding Babies and Young Children: A Guide for Early Years Professionals*. Maidenhead: Open University Press.

Powers, N. and Trevarthen, C. (2009) 'Voices of Shared Emotion and Meaning: Young Infants and Their Mothers in Scotland and Japan' in S. Malloch and C. Trevarthen (eds) *Communicative Musicality*. Oxford: Oxford University Press.

Pugh, G. (ed.) (1993) *30 Years of Change for Children*. London: National Children's Bureau.

Pugh, G. and Duffy, B. (eds) (2013) *Contemporary Issues in the Early Years* (5th edn). London: Sage.

Pugh, G., De'Ath, E. and Smith, C. (1994) *Confident Parents, Confident Children: Policy and Practice in Parent Education and Support*. London: National Children's Bureau.

Purves, L. and Selleck, D. (1999) *Tuning into Children: Understanding a Child's Development from Birth to 5 Years*. London: BBC/National Children's Bureau.

Rapley, G. and Murkett, T. (2008) *Baby-Led Weaning*. London: Ebury Press.

Reder, P. and Duncan, S. (1993) *Beyond Blame: Child Abuse Tragedies Revisited*. London: Routledge.

Richards, C.M. (2010) 'Safeguarding Children: Every Child Matters so Everybody Matters', pp. 69–82 in M. Reed and N. Canning (eds) *Reflective Practice in the Early Years*. London: Sage.

Richardson, R. (2007) Action Points. *Nursery World*, 12 July.

Robinson, S. (2014) 'Children's Health and Wellbeing', pp. 197–219 in T. Maynard and S. Powell (eds) *An Introduction to Early Childhood Studies* (3rd edn). London: Sage.

Rodd, J. (2006) *Leadership in Early Childhood*. Buckingham: Open University Press.

Rodd, J. (2012) *Leadership in Early Childhood: The Pathway to Professionalism*. Sydney: Allen & Unwin.

Rogers, E. (2012) The 2% Club. *Children and Young People Now*, 1–14 May.

ROSPA (2013) *Safety in Schools and Colleges* (www.rospa.com/schoolandcollegesafety/default.aspx, accessed 12.03.13).

Roulstone, S., Law, J., Rush, R., Clegg, J. and Peters, T. (2011) *Investigating the Role of Language in Children's Early Educational Outcomes*. Bristol: University of the West of England.

Rutter, J. and Evans, B. (2011) *Informal Childcare: Choice or Chance? A Literature Review*. London: Daycare Trust.

Schaffer, R. (1977) *Mothering*. London: Fontana.

Schleicher, A. (2006) *The Economics of Knowledge: Why Education is Key for Europe's Success* (the Lisbon Council Policy Brief). Paris: OECD.

School Food Trust (2011) *Laying the Table: Recommendations for Early Years Settings*. National Food and Nutrition Guidance in England (www.schoolfoodtrust.org.uk/laying thetable, accessed 05.11.10).

School Food Trust (2012) *Eat Better, Start Better: Voluntary Food and Drink Guidelines for Early Years Settings in England – a Practical Guide* (www.schoolfoodtrust.org.uk/ eatbetterstartbetter, accessed 05.04.12).

Selleck, D. (1997) 'Baby Art: Art is Me', in BAECE (eds) *Reflections on Early Education and Care Inspired by Visits to Reggio Emilia, Italy*. London: BAECE.

Shemmings, D. and Shemmings, Y. (2011) *Understanding Disorganized Attachment: Theory and Practice for Working with Children and Families*. London and Philadelphia: Jessica Kingsley.

Sherborne, V. (1990) *Developmental Movement for Children: Mainstream, Special Needs and Pre-School*. Cambridge: Cambridge University Press.

Simon, A. and Owen, C. (2006) 'Outcomes for Children in Care: What Do We Know?', pp. 26–43 in E. Chase, A. Simon and S. Jackson (eds) *In Care and After: A Positive Perspective*. London: Routledge.

Siraj-Blatchford, I. (2011) 'How adults can support young children's learning at home and at pre-school'. Presentation, Poole Professional Development Day Dorset.

Siraj-Blatchford, I. (2014) 'Early Childhood Education (ECE)', pp. 172–84 in T. Maynard and S. Powell (eds) *An Introduction to Early Childhood Studies*. London: Sage.

Siraj-Blatchford, I. and Clarke, P. (2000) *Supporting Identity, Diversity and Language in the Early Years*. Buckingham: Open University Press.

Siraj-Blatchford, I., Sylva, K., Muttock, S., Gilden, R. and Bell, D. (2002) *Researching Effective Pedagogy in the Early Years: DFES Research Report 356*. London: Department for Education and Skills.

Siraj-Blatchford, I., Sylva, K., Taggart, B., Sammons, P. and Melhuish, E. (2003) *Case Studies of Practice in the Foundation Stage*. London: Institute of Education.

Stacey, M. (2009) *Teamwork and Collaboration in Early Years Settings*. Exeter: Learning Matters.

Stein, M. (2008) 'Transitions from Care to Adulthood: Messages from Research for Policy and Practice', pp. 289–306 in M. Stein and E. Munro (eds) *Young People's Transitions from Care to Adulthood: International Research and Practice*. London and Philadelphia: Jessica Kingsley.

Sunderland, M. (2007) *What Every Parent Needs to Know: The Remarkable Effects of Love, Nurture and Play on Your Child's Development*. London: Dorling Kindersley.

Sunderland, M. (2013) The Science of Parenting. Presentation. Dorchester: Dorset County Council Children's Services Staff.

Sylva, K., Roy, C. and Painter, M. (1980) *Childwatching in Playgroup and Nursery School*. London: Grant McIntyre.

Sylva, K., Melhuish, E., Sammons, P., Siraj-Blatchford, I. and Taggart, B. (2004) *The Effective Provision of Pre-School Education Project (EPPE): Final Report*. London: Department for Education and Skills/Institute of Education.

Sylva, K., Melhuish, E., Sammons, P. and Siraj-Blatchford, I. (eds) (2010) *Early Childhood Matters: Evidence from the Effective Pre-school and Primary Education Project*. London: Routledge.

Tait, C. (2007) 'Getting to Know Families' in M. Whalley (ed.) *Involving Parents in Their Children's Learning*. London: Paul Chapman.

Thornton, L. and Brunton, P. (2010) Getting the best out of your Early Years Team. *Early Years Update e-bulletin*, 05.11.10.

Tickell, C. (2010) *The Early Years: Foundations for Life, Health and Learning: An Independent Report on the Early Years Foundation Stage to Her Majesty's Government.* London: Department for Children, Schools and Families.

Tizard, B. and Hughes, M. (2008) *Young Children Learning* (2nd edn). London: Wiley-Blackwell.

Tizard, J., Moss, P. and Perry, J. (1976) *All Our Children.* London: Temple Smith.

Townsend, E. and Pitchford, N.J. (2012) Baby Knows Best? The Impact of Weaning Style on Food Preferences and Body Mass Index in Early Childhood in a Case-Controlled Sample (http://bmjopen.bmj.com/content/2/1/e000298, accessed 30.06.13).

Toynbee, P. (2013) 'How do you fit six toddlers into a buggy? Ask Liz Truss'. *Guardian,* 29 January.

Trevarthen, C. (1998) 'The Child's Need to Learn a Culture' in M. Woodhead, D. Faulkner and K. Littleton (eds) *Cultural Worlds of Early Childhood.* London: Routledge.

Trevarthen, C. (2004) *Learning about Ourselves from Children: Why a Growing Human Brain Needs Interesting Companions.* Hokkaido, Japan: Hokkaido University Graduate School of Education (Report No. 26: 9–44).

Turner, R. and Ioannides, A.A. (2009) 'Brain, Music and Musicality: Inferences from Neuro-Imaging', pp. 147–82 in S. Malloch and C. Trevarthen (eds) *Communicative Musicality.* Oxford: Oxford University Press.

Vygotsky, L. (1978) *Mind in Society.* Cambridge, MA: Harvard University Press.

Wade, J., Biehal, N., Farelly, N. and Sinclair, I. (2011) *Caring for Abused and Neglected Children: Making the Right Decisions for Reunification or Long-Term Care.* London and Philadelphia: Jessica Kingsley.

Walsh, P. (ed.) (1988) *Early Childhood Playgrounds: Planning an Outside Learning Environment.* Melbourne: Martin Educational in association with Robert Anderson Associates and Early Childhood Association of Australia.

Ward, L. (2005) 'Hidden Stress of the Nursery Age'. *Guardian,* 19 September.

Ward, H., Brown, R. and Westlake, D. (2012) *Safeguarding Babies and Very Young Children from Abuse and Neglect.* London and Philadelphia: Jessica Kingsley.

Waterbabies (2013) www.waterbabies.co.uk/baby-swimming (accessed 03.03.13).

Wells, C.G. (1985) *Language Development in the Pre-School Years.* Cambridge: Cambridge University Press.

Whalley, M. (2007) *Involving Parents in Their Children's Learning.* London: Paul Chapman.

Whalley, M.E. (ed.) (2011) *Leading Practice in Early Years Settings.* Exeter: Learning Matters.

Wheeler, H. and Connor, J. (2006) *Parents, Early Years and Learning Reader.* London: National Children's Bureau.

Whitaker, P. (2001) Excellence and enterprise: leadership and management in the early years. *Early Childhood Practice,* 3(1): 48–53.

Whitaker, P. and Whalley, M. (2003) 'Developing Leadership Learning and Growing Learning Communities', paper presented at Pen Green Conference. October 2003.

White, J. (2012a) Making the most of outdoor play through the wonderful season of winter. *Early Years Update,* 101: 8–10.

White, J. (2012b) *Making a Mud Kitchen.* Sheffield: University of Sheffield.

Whitebread, D. (2007) 'Developing Independence in Learning', in J. Moyles (ed.) *Early Years Foundations: Meeting the Challenge.* Maidenhead: Open University Press.

Whitebread, D. (2011) *Developmental Psychology and Early Childhood Education.* London: Sage.

Whitebread D. and Basilio, M. (2012) The emergence and early development of self-regulation in young children. *Profesorado* 16(1): 15–33.

Willow, C. and Hyder, T. (1998) *It Hurts You Inside.* London: National Children's Bureau/ Save the Children.

Wolfe, D. (1991) *Preventing Physical and Emotional Abuse of Children*. New York and London: Guilford Press.

Wood, E. and Attfield, J. (2005) *Play, Learning and the Early Childhood Curriculum* (2nd edn). London: Paul Chapman.

Wood, D., Bruner, J. and Ross, G. (1976) The role of tutoring in problem-solving. *Journal of Child Psychiatry and Psychology* 17: 89–100.

Worden, J. (1991) *Grief Counselling and Grief Therapy: A Handbook for the Mental Health Practitioner* (2nd edn). London: Routledge.

Zeedyk, M.S. (2008) *What's Life Like in a Baby Buggy? The Impact of Buggy Orientation on Parent-Infant Interaction and Infant Stress* (www.literacytrust.org.uk/talk_to_your_baby/news/1, accessed 05.05.13).

DVDs and videos

Infants at Work (1987)
Shows a group of babies round the Treasure Basket at play and interacting with each other. Commentary by Elinor Goldschmied suggests items for the basket and discusses questions raised by students, parents and practitioners.
(National Children's Bureau www.ncb.org.uk)

Heuristic Play with Objects (1992)
Directed by Elinor Goldschmied and Anita Hughes. The principles and practical organisation of heuristic play are demonstrated by children in their second year from four London day nurseries.
(National Children's Bureau www.ncb.org.uk)

Babies (2011)
Directed by Thomas Balmes, this is a delightful film following four babies from birth to their first steps. They live in Namibia, Mongolia, Japan and the United States. The film reminds us, entirely through images, how strongly cultural factors determine what we offer to babies and what we expect of them, and also how competent and resourceful they can be in the right circumstances.
(www.studiocanal.com)

Baby It's You: Inside the Baby's World (1994)
Produced by Channel 4 TV. Series consultant Dr A. Karmiloff-Smith. 168 minutes. The complete Channel 4 series showing the world from the point of view of babies and toddlers under three. Sections: In the beginning; First steps; Taking hold; Word of mouth; The thinker; You and me. A book of the series was published in 1994 by Ebury Press.
(Distributed by Beckmann Communications, trade sales: 01624 816 585; mail order sales: 01624 816 777; www.beckmanndirect.com)

Beginning with PEEP: Children's Learning from Birth to School (1998)
This pre-school literacy project, based on estates in Oxford, supports parents as the first educators of their young children at weekly group sessions, and at home. Although *Beginning with PEEP* is not currently available on DVD, a PEEP series called 'Learning Together' including videos on babies, one-, two- and three-year-olds is available.

(Produced by Parents Early Education Partnership, The PEEP Centre, Littlemore, Oxford, OX4 6JZ; 01865 395 145; www.peep.org.uk)

Growing Together at the Pen Green Centre (2001)
Produced by Pen Green Research Development and Training Base. 35 minutes. 'Growing together' groups are held at the Pen Green Centre (Corby, Northants), for parents and their under-threes. Videos were made of several sessions, and include ten sets of parents and toddlers telling their stories. The groups support parents in areas such as child development, attachment relationships and dealing with emotions.

(01536 443 435, www.pengreen.org)

Discovered Treasure: The Life and Work of Elinor Goldschmied 1910–2009 (2013)
This film was created by the Froebel Trust as part of the Elinor Goldschmied Froebel Archive Project during 2011–2013, draws on the rich film material which Elinor made between 1950 and 1992 and shows how her ideas are being carried forward in contemporary childcare settings. In those original films, the Froebel tradition of play, her unique style of teaching alongside practitioners and her reflective conversations with them are clearly seen, along with extracts from her later films about the Treasure Basket and heuristic play. Footage taken at Eastwood Nursery School Centre for Children and Families shows Elinor's continuing influence in current childcare and education practice.

(www.tvroehampton.com www.froebeltrust.org.uk)

Community Playthings
Community Playthings have a collection of DVDs for practitioners, including *What Happens in the Baby Room?* and *A Good Place to be Two*. They have many other DVDs that support the use of their products and examples of excellent environments for very young children. Beautiful, sensitive films.

(www.communityplaythings.co.uk)

Siren Films Ltd
From this beautiful series of DVDs we particularly like *The Wonder Year: First Year Development, Shaping the Brain* and *Attachment and Holistic Development: The First Year*, which is a series of observations of baby Orson. Comes with accompanying notes; can be used with practitioners and parents.

(0191 232 7900 www.sirenfilms.co.uk)

Organisations concerned with young children and families

Association for Improvement of Maternity Services (AIMS)
5 Ann's Court, Grove Road, Surbiton, Surrey KT6 4BE
Helpline: 0300 365 0663
www.aims.org.uk
Publishes information leaflets and provides support and advice on all aspects of maternity care, including parents' rights, choices available, technological interventions, natural childbirth and complaints procedures.

British Association for Early Childhood Education (BAECE)
See Early Education.

Child Accident Prevention Trust
Canterbury Court (1.09), 1–3 Brixton Road, London SW9 6DE
020 7608 3828
www.capt.org.uk
Campaigning and research organisation aiming to increase knowledge and understanding of the causes of child accidents and ways of preventing them.

Childhood Studies at Canterbury Christ Church University
Department of Childhood Studies, Canterbury Christ Church University, Canterbury, Kent CT1 1QU.
01227 782 646
www.canterbury.ac.uk (*search* 'Childhood Studies')
Research, training, practice development and publications relating to children.

Children in Scotland/Clann an Alba
Princes House, 5 Shandwick Place, Edinburgh EH2 4RG
0131 228 8484
www.childreninscotland.org.uk
Promotes and enables the exchange of information on matters relating to Scotland's children and their families between practitioners, policy makers, politicians and the media.

Provides policy advice to Scottish Executive, runs conferences and training events and distributes a range of publications on health, education and children's services.

Children in Wales/Plant yng Nghymru
25 Windsor Place, Cardiff CF1 3BZ
029 2034 2434
www.childreninwales.org.uk/index.html
Umbrella body for all organisations concerned with children living in Wales and their families. Promotes interests of children, young people and their families by sharing information and ideas, identifying issues and campaigning for improved services. Provides advice on policy to the National Assembly and represents Wales in international organisations.

Children's Play Information Centre (*formerly* National Play Information Centre)
See **National Children's Bureau** for address.
020 7843 6303
www.ncb.org.uk/cpis/
Provides information on all aspects of children's play, focusing on school-age children.

Council for Awards in Care, Health and Education (CACHE)
Apex House, 81 Camp Road, St Albans, Hertfordshire AL1 5GB
0845 347 2123
www.cache.org.uk
Official body for training and assessment in childcare and education and play-work. Various awards include CACHE diploma in Nursery Nursing (successor to NNEB).

Daycare Trust – National Childcare Charity
See Family and Childcare Trust (created by merger with Family and Parenting Institute).

Early Childhood Ireland
Hainault House, Belgard Square, Tallaght, Dublin 24
01 4057 100
www.earlychildhoodireland.ie
Enabling the provision of quality early childhood care and education in Ireland, aiming for positive outcomes for children. Publishes magazines and provides information and resources.

Early Childhood Research Centre
Department of Education, Roehampton University, Froebel College, London SW15 5PJ
020 8392 3689
www.roehampton.ac.uk (*Search* 'ECRC')
Research, training courses and publications. Holds Elinor Goldschmied Archive.

Early Education (*formerly* **BAECE**)
136 Cavell Street, London E1 2JA
0207 539 5400
www.early-education.org.uk
Campaigns for provision of nursery schools and day care and provides multidisciplinary network of support and advice for all concerned with care and education of young children. Runs conferences and publishes information. Many local branches.

Early Years (*formerly* **Northern Ireland Pre-School Playgroups Association/NIPPA**)
6c Wildflower Way, Apollo Road, Boucher Road, Belfast BT12 6TA
028 9066 2825
www.early-years.org
Works to promote high-quality childcare for children 0–12 years old in Northern Ireland.

Fair Play for Children
32 Longford Road, Bognor Regis, PO21 1AG
0843 289 2638
www.fairplayforchildren.org
Campaigns for better funding, status and support for play and a stronger legislative framework.

Family and Childcare Trust (*created from merger of the* **Daycare Trust** *and* **Family and Parenting Institute**)
2nd Floor, The Bridge, 81 Southwark Bridge Road, London SE1 0NQ
0845 872 6260 (020 7940 7510)
www.daycaretrust.org.uk
Campaigns for increased day care provision and promotion of equal opportunities. Provides support for parents, carers and professionals through advice, consultancy and publications.

Family Lives
3rd Floor, Culpitt House, 74–78 Town Centre, Hatfield, Hertfordshire AL10 0JW
01707 630 100
www.familylives.org.uk
Confidential freephone helpline (0808 800 2222) offering information and emotional support for anyone in a parenting role. Also runs courses and produces leaflets and publications on a variety of parenting issues.

Foundation Years – from pregnancy to children age 5
www.foundationyears.org.uk
Much useful information and resources on this website, for parents and practitioners.

Gingerbread
520 Highgate Studios, 53–79 Highgate Road, London NW5 1TL
020 7428 5420
Helpline: 0808 802 0925
www.gingerbread.org.uk
Information and referral service. Provides advice and practical support and campaigns for single-parent families.

HighScope GB
HighScope National Training and Demonstration Centre, The Sue Hedley Nursery School, Campbell Park Road, Hebburn, Tyne & Wear NE31 1QY
077 435 04044
www.high-scope.org.uk
Information, publications and training, based on principles developed by successful American early intervention/pre-school learning project.

Home-Start UK
8–10 West Walk, Leicester LE1 7NA
0116 233 9955
www.home-start.org.uk
Offers advice and support to people setting up Home Start schemes (volunteer home-visiting for families with children under five who are experiencing stress).

ICAN – The children's communication charity
0845 225 4071
www.ican.org.uk
A website offering a range of resources and information for practitioners, professionals and parents. Information on the annual Chatterbox Challenge. Split helpfully into three age ranges: 0–5s; 5–11s; 11–16s.

Letterbox Library
Unit 151, Stratford Workshops, Burford Road, Stratford, London E15 2SP
020 7503 4801
www.letterboxlibrary.com
Multicultural and anti-sexist books for children by internet and phone order. Also workshops and publications.

National Childbirth Trust
Alexandra House, Oldham Terrace, Acton, London W4 6WH
Helpline: 0300 330 0700
www.nct.org.uk
Offers information and support in pregnancy, childbirth and early parenthood. Runs antenatal classes and provides information on breastfeeding and local support groups through branches all over the country.

National Children's Bureau
8 Wakley Street, London EC1V 7QE
Main Switchboard: 0207 843 6000
Early Childhood Unit: 0207 843 6064
www.ncb.org.uk
Multidisciplinary organisation promoting interests and well-being of children and young people across every aspect of their lives, emphasising the importance of children's participation. Research, policy development and consultancy, training, dissemination of information to professionals and carers through conferences, seminars and publications. Early Childhood Unit offers similar range of services focusing on young children.

The National College for Teaching and Leadership
www.nationalcollege.org.uk/publications
Publishes a range of materials relevant to leaders and managers of childcare and early education settings.

National Federation of City Farms and Community Gardens
The Green House, Hereford Street, Bristol BS3 4NA
0117 923 1800
www.farmgarden.org.uk
Represents and promotes community-managed farms and gardens to help empower people of all ages and provide an opportunity for urban children to see animals and farming practices.

National Men in Childcare Support Network
0131 664 1202
www.meninchildcare.co.uk
Information, advice, training and consultancy for men working in childcare, based in Scotland.

National Portage Association/NPA
Kings Court, 17 School Road, Birmingham B28 8JG
0121 244 1807
www.portage.org.uk
Home-visiting service for pre-school children with special needs, providing educational activities to help parents enhance their children's development. Provides training and advice and campaigns for better facilities.

PACEY (*formerly* **National Childminding Association**)
PACEY, Royal Court, 81 Tweedy Road, Bromley, Kent BR1 1TG
0845 880 0044
www.pacey.org.uk
info@pacey.org.uk
Cymru-Wales Office, Room 1.4, The Maltings, East Tyndall Street, Cardiff, CF24 5EZ
0845 880 1299

paceycymru@pacey.org.uk
Fax: 0845 880 1277
Promotes the interests of childminders, and works to improve the quality of home-based day care. Also offers training for both new and established childminders.

Parent and Child Empowerment Organisation
82a Gloucester Road, Bishopton, Bristol BS7 8BN
0117 914 7720
www.ecdc.org.uk
Provides designs, resources and training for parent support programmes.

Play England (*formerly* Children's Play Council)
8 Wakley Street, London EC1V 7QE
020 7843 6300
www.playengland.org.uk
Forum for voluntary organisations concerned with promoting and increasing facilities for children's play.

Pre-school Learning Alliance
The Fitzpatrick Building, 188 York Way, London N7 9AD
020 7697 2500
www.pre-school.org.uk
Supports its member pre-schools and playgroups in providing high-quality, parent-involving education and care for children mainly under the age of five.

Priority Area Playgroups
117 Pershore Road, Birmingham B5 7NX
0121 440 1320
www.priorityareaplaygroups.co.uk
Runs several playgroups and day nurseries and provides a home-visiting service in the Birmingham area.

Scottish Pre-school Play Association
21–23 Granville Street, Glasgow G3 7EE
0141 221 4148
www.sppa.org.uk
Coordinating body for playgroups, toddler groups and other facilities for under-fives in Scotland, providing training and advice.

TAIC (*formerly* Comhairle Nan Sgoiltean Araich/Scottish Association of Gaelic Nursery Schools and Playgroups/CNSA)
92 Academy Street, Inverness IV1 1LU
www.gaelicworld.co.uk
Establishes, provides and supports Gaelic-medium pre-school education facilities. Provides full training programmes for pre-school group and field staff.

Thomas Coram Research Unit, Institute of Education
27–28 Woburn Square, London WC1H 0AA
0207 612 6957
www.ioe.ac.uk/research/174.html
Carries out high-quality research on education and care of children with special emphasis on early childhood education and childcare.

Twins and Multiple Births Association (TAMBA)
Hitherbury House, 97 Portsmouth Road, Guildford, Surrey GU2 4YF
01483 304442
www.tamba.org.uk
Supports families with twins, triplets and more, and provides advice and information for professionals involved in their care.

What About The Children?
www.whataboutthechildren.org.uk
A charity working to promote better understanding by parents, professionals and policy makers of the first three years, and the child's need for responsive loving care for optimal brain development.

Working Group Against Racism in Children's Resources
Unit 34 Eurolink Business Centre, 49 Effra Road, London SW2 1BZ
0207 501 9992
www.wgarcr.org.uk
Publishes newsletter and guidelines for evaluation of early years facilities. Runs seminars and training days and gives information on resources and suppliers.

Working on Wheels (*formerly* **National Playbus Association**)
Brunswick Court, Brunswick Square, Bristol BS2 8PE
0117 916 6580
www.workingonwheels.org
Umbrella organisation providing support and expert advice to mobile community projects across the UK.

Yorkshire Children's Centre
Brian Jackson House, New North Parade, Huddersfield HD1 5JP
01484 519988
www.yorkshirechildrenscentre.org.uk
Interdisciplinary collaborative research and action projects, practice development and training. Provides support and facilities for community groups and parents.

Subject index

adult attention 12, 231
adult–child ratio 12
adult education (for Early Years practitioners) 203
adult roles: in group rooms 41–2; in heuristic play 119–21; with treasure basket 84–5
aggression 233–5
allergies and special diets 163
analogies with adult experience 3, 25, 128, 229; depersonalised handling 100; early mobility 69; mealtimes 33; separation 30; unfamiliar food 235
ancillary staff – see support staff
Archimedes and heuristic learning 113
attachment 21–2, 26–8, 31, 34, 256; adult attachment experiences 57, 212, 256; disorganised 249; strengthening 67
attention deficit hyperactivity disorder (ADHD) 231

babies: effects of group care on 57–8; equipment and resources for 73–6; feeding 59–61, 154–6; learning 21; playthings for 75; respecting rhythms of 60
baby-led weaning 60–1
baby massage 67–8
baby room environment 70
baby room practitioners 57
baby walkers 50, 73–4
background noise 104
BAECE (Early Education) 14, 202
'basic trust' 95
bathroom time 99–11, 139
Beckford, Jasmine 253
behaviour problems 228–37; generated by the setting 229–30
behavioural approach 250
bereavement 29

bilingualism 219
'Birth to Three Matters' framework 21
biting 94, 234–5
books 107, 139; for babies 64–5; book corners 137–9; care of 47; choice of 138–9; in second year 107–8
brain development 22–3, 78, 241
breastfeeding 59–60
British Sign Language 219
buggies 73

café-style snack time 158–9
care and maintenance: involving children 45; of outside area 174
case conferences 211, 248, 255
catering staff 152
changing practice 149
CHEW (children eating well) 154
child abuse (see also child protection and safeguarding) 243–4; collusion with parents 254–5; in middle-class families 243; and poverty 243–4; prevention 241; staff attitudes/denial 243; surveillance 242, 254; theories of 240–1
child benefit 8
child development, theories of 14–15
child health 246–7
child protection: within childcare settings 246–7
childcare: choosing 58; educational function of 245–6; for families under stress 244; history 7–8; in other European countries 2, 6; policy 1–3, 9–11; unresolved issues 6; for working parents 10–12, 196
Childcare Act 2006 2, 10
childcare centres: building design 36–45; compensatory function 6–10, 222, 242; educational purpose 245–6; entrance area

Index of names